THE SARAJEVO TRIAL

THE SARAJEVO TRIAL

Narrative by
W. A. Dolph Owings

Translation and editing by
W. A. Dolph Owings, Elizabeth Pribic
and Nikola Pribic

Volume I

DOCUMENTARY PUBLICATIONS
Chapel Hill, NC
U.S.A.
1984

Contents

INTRODUCTION

The morning of Sunday, 28 June 1914, dawned bright and sunny, as if to welcome the Archduke Franz Ferdinand and his wife Sofie Chotek, on their long-planned state visit to the Bosnian provincial capital of Sarajevo (pronounced Sarayevo). The heir to the throne of the once great Austro-Hungarian Empire and his wife rode in an open limousine along a riverside promenade toward the city hall where a formal reception awaited them. The Archduke's automobile moved carefully through the throngs of curious townspeople. Suddenly a sharp crack — sounding like a pistol shot — startled the royal entourage, and their chauffeur glimpsed an object hurtling towards the car. He stepped on the accelerator and the car lunged ahead. His quick reflexes forstalled a disaster. A bomb bounced off the canvas top which was folded down at the back of the car, and exploded in the street behind, wounding two security officers as well as several bystanders.

The royal party, shaken but unharmed, continued hastily toward city hall where, in spite of near tragedy, the mayor began his formal welcoming speech: "Our hearts are full of happiness on the occasion of the most gracious visit with which your Highnesses have deigned to honor the capital of our land . . ."[1] Archduke Franz Ferdinand interrupted him, acidly noting that he did not consider a bomb a suitable token of welcome. An awkward silence was broken only when the Duchess leaned over and whispered something into her husband's ear. The Archduke, apparently calmed by his wife's words, seemed to relax and the welcoming ceremonies were completed as smoothly as possible.

Accounts of the events immediately following the official ceremonies are conflicting. It seems most likely that the provincial governor of Bosnia, General Oskar Potiorek, who was primarily responsible for the safety of the royal family, assured the Archduke that he would be safe in leaving the city, provided that the pre-planned route was changed. Apparently he took it upon himself to alter the motor route by which the Archduke and his wife would leave the capital. The rationale for the new route was a proposed visit by the Archduke to the hospital bed of one of the security officers wounded in the earlier bomb attack. Within moments the official party set out.

Unfortunately the driver had not been informed of the change and unwittingly turned onto the old route. General Potiorek, standing on the running board of the Archduke's vehicle, immediately realized the mistake and angrily ordered the driver to stop. He did so and the car came to an abrupt halt in the midst of a crowd of onlookers. At that moment a slightly-built young man stepped to the front of the crowd, raised a pistol and fired two shots at point-blank range at the occupants of the open automobile.

One bullet each struck Franz Ferdinand and Sofie. Their bodies momentarily remained frozen in their seats; then Sofie's body fell against her husband's. Blood had already appeared on Franz Ferdinand's mouth. He was heard to whisper, "Soferl, Soferl, don't die. Live for my children."[2] The car sped them to the governor's residence nearby, but both were dead by the time they arrived, or very shortly thereafter.

The immediate consequence of the assassination was to

precipitate the greatest military disaster in history: World War I. Hundreds of scholarly volumes have been devoted to the underlying causes of World War I. This book is concerned only with the spark that set off that war, and with the trial of the men who set off that spark.

Austria-Hungary had long viewed with apprehension the growing influence of the minor Balkan state, Serbia. Sarajevo is a provincial capital of Bosnia, a province of Serbia, which was, in turn, a minor yet growing thorn in the side of the decaying Austro-Hungarian Empire. There was a strong element in the Hapsburg court which urged that Serbia be brought to heel while there was still time.

At one time the empire controlled vast regions of Eastern and Central Europe. By 1914 its power and authority were on the decline. Political and military leaders of the empire, however, clung to dreams of past glory, seeking everywhere to forestall any further erosion of the empire's power. Many feared the growing influence of Serbia. A militant faction had been seeking a pretext for bringing this minor Balkan state to heel. The assassination of the Archduke furnished just such a pretext.

No sooner had the assassination at Sarajevo become known in Vienna — the capital of the Austro-Hungarian Empire — than officials there charged the government of Serbia with responsibility for the assassination. Acting upon only the flimsiest evidence, they alleged that the Serbians had either actively participated in the assassination or, at the least, permitted the conditions to exist which encouraged the assassination. The Austro-Hungarian government quickly imposed an ultimatum on Serbia which would have hopelessly compromised her independence and sovereignty. The Serbs rejected some of the points of the ultimatum, as some members of the Imperial court had hoped they would, and the Austro-Hungarian empire took the occasion to declare war on Serbia and begin an invasion.

This called into play the complex network of diplomatic and military alliances that had developed in Europe over several generations. One European nation after the other took sides. France, England and Russia joined the Serbs; Germany and Turkey allied themselves with the Austro-Hungarian Empire. Armies mobilized, diplomats closed embassies and Europe

prepared for battle. By the first of August most of Europe was
aflame with war. The Sarajevo assassination therefore precipitated the cycle of wars which consumed the first half of the
twentieth century, occasioned the deaths of over fifty million
people, and ended only with the crushing defeat of Germany in
1945.

The assassination of an heir apparent is of course a serious
matter, but Franz Ferdinand and Sofie were far from the first
victims of assassination even in the Austro-Hungarian monarchy.
The consequences of the killings were so grossly disproportion-
ate to the provocation that the guns had hardly started firing
before a great debate began over the underlying causes of the
Great War. Here we are concerned with only two related questions: Why did the murderers perform the assassination? and
Why did the imperial authorities knowingly act in such a way
as to precipitate a major war?

The Assassination Plot

The young man who actually shot the Archduke and his
wife was Gavrilo Princip (Printsip), a gymnasium (high school)
student not quite twenty years old — a fact that was to save his
life. He had attended the gymnasium first in Sarajevo and then
in Belgrade, where he learned of the impending visit of the royal
couple to Sarajevo. In Belgrade he had been joined by Trifko
Grabez (Grabezh), a nineteen year old classmate, and Nedeljko
Cabrinovic (Chabrinovich), also nineteen, a would-be intellect-
ual. Cabrinovic, unable financially to attend the gymnasium,
had had to earn a living as a journeyman typographer. These
three had resolved to kill the Archduke, and turned for help in
their plans to members of a Serbian nationalist organization
called the *Narodna odbrana* (National Defense). Some of the
officials of the *Narodna odbrana* were also officials in the Serbian government, and as this trial transcript depicts, able to call
on the assistance of still other government officials to obtain
the contraband bombs and pistols and facilitate their crossing
the border.

The three Bosnians in Belgrade, led by Princip, had therefore resolved on the assassination and taken the initiative to
obtain arms and smuggle them into Bosnia in time for the

Archduke's ceremonial visit. Princip communicated his intentions to a friend in Sarajevo, Danilo Ilic (Ilich), a failed schoolteacher and journalist who at that time was living with his mother.

Ilic recruited a second troika in Sarajevo. That consisted of Cvjetko Popovic (Popovich), a student of eighteen; Vaso Cubrilovic (Chubrilovich), a student of seventeen; and Mehmed Mehmedbasic (Mehmedbashich), aged twenty-six. Neither troika knew of the existence of the other.

How did one go about recruiting accomplices for an assassination? Among the Bosnian students in the spring of 1914, that was easy: simply ask. As this trial transcript reveals, an invitation from one schoolboy to another to join in killing the Archduke was likely to be instantly and unquestionably accepted. Time and again in both Belgrade and Sarajevo the same transaction occurs. One student approaches another and says, "Do you know the Archduke is coming to Sarajevo?" and the ominous reply is "Mi moramo ga ocekati!" ("We must lie in wait for him!")

The translators of this document, Professors Elizabeth Pribic and W.A. (Dolph) Owings, both have grown sons. As we worked our way through the manuscript we tried to imagine our sons at the ages of sixteen to nineteen giving and receiving such an invitation. Finally we came to the questioning of Cvjetko Popovic where he relates how, while strolling in the city park one evening, he instantly agreed to a friend's invitation to join in the killing. Elizabeth and I leaned back in our chairs and stared at each other in disbelief. Returning to the manuscript, we discovered that the court was equally incredulous. The chief judge asked Popovic: "Do you mean that one had only to invite you to the assassination, and you would agree?" to which Popovic replied, "Yes."

The judge at the trial did not ask Popovic for an explanation, but sixty years later I was able to do so. Popovic and Vaso Cubrilovic were still alive in 1976.

I interviewed both of them at that time. Cubrilovic, although he became one of the most distinguished Yugoslav historians of his day, refused on principle ever to discuss the assassination. He felt that a cause, holy to him, had been degraded to the level of a "kriminalisticki roman," a mere adventure story, by an irresponsible press. Popovic, who became a distinguished ethnologist, freely discussed the affair and published two books of memoirs of the event (unfortunately, only as late as 1969 when his memory had been flawed by the passage of time).

I met Popovic in the coffee-shop, the *kafana*, of the Hotel Central in Sarajevo. (Yugoslavs live in their *kafanas*). He was a rather heavy-set man of medium height, still sprightly in spite of his eighty years, alert and forceful in his speech, punctuating his statements with rapid glances from his penetrating blue eyes. He himself reminded me of the transaction with the judge at his hearing.

"Yes," he said, "they asked me and I instantly agreed. Look, you have to realize what it was like to live under foreigners. There we were, in our own country, and these fellows were telling us what to do. We students led the demonstrations against the Austrians. I had been in jail already for agitation (the Pjanic-Ljubibratic affair). Right down the street here in front of the cathedral we had burned the Hungarian flag. We were steeped in the literature of the Russian Social Revolutionaries (who practiced assassination). When we met, when we walked in the evenings in the park, we would ask each other, 'Have you read this or that book?', and if our *kolege* (buddy) hadn't, we would pass the book from hand to hand. We didn't have to spell things out. We knew instantly what each other had in mind."

"Look," he said, "there is no way of telling you what it is like to live under foreigners. You have to have experienced it yourself. We hated them with a burning hatred. Our ideal was Yugoslavia. Yes, I agreed instantly, and under the same circumstances I would do it again!" The passage of more than sixty years had done nothing to dull the intensity of his convictions. The gleam in his eye convinced me that there was still a man willing to kill and be killed for his ideal, a free Yugoslavia.

What of the leader of the affair, Gavrilo Princip? It was he who had formed the Belgrade troika, saw to it that weapons were obtained and smuggled into Bosnia, and arranged the connection with Ilic. His determination alone was unwavering.

When he arrived in Sarajevo to await the fatal day, he roomed with Ilic. On the eve of the assassination Ilic got cold feet and wanted to call the affair off. It was Princip who steeled his resolution. What kind of youth was he?

Princip does not do much to help us understand him. He was a very closed person, who left almost nothing behind to reveal the person behind the events. He came from a family of considerable local reputation in the hill country of Hercegovina, one of the most impoverished parts of the mountain province. Like many others of his generation, he made his way to the gymnasium in Sarajevo and then Belgrade, hoping to improve his position through education. Such students often had to live in grinding poverty, sometimes literally on the edge of starvation.

Ill-health was the natural consequence of such poverty. At the time of the Balkan wars (1912, when he was eighteen) he tried to enlist for service in the guerrilla bands fighting the Turks, but was rejected for physical reasons. Cocktail-party psychoanalysts may speculate that the rejection, by questioning his manhood, might have made him feel the need to prove himself. Yet his committment to a free Yugoslavia was uncompromising. Later, while in prison in 1913, Princip was interviewed by a psychiatrist, Dr. Martin Pappenheim of the University of Vienna.[3] He reiterated his determination to achieve a free Yugoslavia at any cost to himself.

To Pappenheim, and in his letters that have been published, Princip revealed almost nothing of himself. He cuts off the interviews whenever they begin to touch on sensitive matters. The published text of the intervews suggests that they lasted at most some three or four hours, certainly not long enough for any kind of insight to appear if the subject were resistant. As to unpublished documents, there is in the possession of the estate of Professor Bogicevic a file of letters to a sweetheart. That was a wholly platonic romance, light-years removed from the direct sexuality of our day, couched in the tender romanticism of first love, flowers pressed between the pages. These letters tell us only that a Victorian romantic lived behind the facade of the assassin. Perhaps it was another manifestation of this romanticism that made Princip willing to sacrifice himself in the cause of freedom for his people.

But why the assassination became the occasion for starting such a disastrous war remains to be explained.

The Ideal of a Free Yugoslavia

The reaction of the Imperial authorities is of course rooted in the historical circumstances leading up to the assassination, and those circumstances involved the tangled question of Balkan nationalism. The Balkan peninsula throughout the nineteenth century had been a theater of conflict among the great European powers, principally the Ottoman empire, the Austro-Hungarian empire, and the Russian empire. The Balkans had been overrun by the Ottoman Turks in the fifteenth century. In 1458-61 they conquered the mountain district of Bosnia and Herzegovina, where they had established a military headquarters, a *seraj* (literally a military encampment), whence "Sarajevo." At the peak of their power the Turks twice laid siege to Vienna itself (1529 and 1683). Toward the end of the seventeenth century the Ottoman empire began to recede, and during the eighteenth century the Hapsburg empire established a military frontier along the Sava and Danube rivers.

The district immediately to the south of the confluence of the Sava and Danube rivers, with the ancient fortress city of Belgrade as its capital, was inhabited by an ethnic group known as the Serbs. Serbia had enjoyed a brief period of power as a medieval kingdom before being overwhelmed by the Turks (1389), and the Serbs had never forgotten their days of glory. They were always restless subjects, and the Turkish administration was always more or less subject to harrassment by Serbian equivalents of Robin Hood, who were "bandits" to the governing Turks but who were heroes to the subject Serbian peoples. The exploits of the *hajduks* (pronounced "highduk") gave rise to one of the world's great body of folk epics, and the Serbs saw them as bearing the burden of resistance to foreign oppressors. This tradition is so deeply embedded in the consciousness of the Serbs and the other South Slav peoples that to this day their automatic response to any suggestion of foreign invasion is that "We will fight!" completely without regard to political ideology. That tradition has had a good deal to do with the acceptance of the Tito regime in our own time, Tito being able to present himself (after 1948) as the leader of the liberation from Nazi and Fascist tyranny and of a successful resistance to an attempt at domination by the Soviet Union under the Stalin regime.

As the Ottoman empire weakened during the course of the nineteenth century, particularly in connection with the Napoleonic wars, the local Serbian leaders were able to raise the first successful resistance movement against the Ottoman empire, establishing an autonomous principality of Serbia by 1817. The two principal leaders were successively George Petrovic (Petrovich), known as "Black" (Kara) George, and Milos Obrenovic (Milosh Obrenovich). Bitter personal enemies, they were the founders of rival dynasties which contended for power in Serbia throughout the nineteenth century. During that time Serbia was preoccupied with two principal problems: the dynastic struggle, and the fact that most of the ethnic Serbs still lived outside the boundaries of the principality (from 1882, the kingdom) of Serbia. Fanatical nationalism was part of the heritage of the French revolution and Napoleonic period. As the power of nationalism increased, it became increasingly intolerable that fellow Serbs should be subject to the rule of others. Then as now, nationalistic drives could unify the Serbian people even when they bitterly opposed each other domestically because of dynastic or class rivalries. Likewise, ethnic Serbs who still lived under foreign domination longed for union with their brothers in Serbia. Irredentism, the drive to unify ethnic groups which live under alien regimes, became a primary political force.

The two principal groups of Serbs under foreign domination that concern us in the context of the Sarajevo assassination comprised the Serbs living across the Danube river from Belgrade in Hapsburg territory, and the ethnic Serbs living in the adjoining mountain region of Bosnia, still under Turkish domination. The Bosnian Serbs were particularly restless. Their rulers belonged to an alien religion, Islam, and in the Balkans, religion had come to be equated with nationalism. The Turkish conquerors had in the fifteenth century established a feudal system with themselves as lords and the Serbs as serfs, initiating a social conflict. Many Serb landowners had converted to Islam. These converted Serbian Moslems were likely to be the staunchest

oppressors of the predominantly Serbian serfs. Under these
conditions, revolution became endemic. There were numerous
major rebellions in Bosnia in the early 1800's, and by mid-
century the decaying Ottoman empire had acquired the reputation of being the "sick man of Europe." Russia and the Austro-
Hungarian empire both wanted to take possession of, or at least
exercise hegemony over, the Balkan lands where Turkish power
was weakening. Britain and France also wanted to protect their
interests in the Near East. The great powers had already fought
a major war in the Crimea (1854-6) over Near Eastern affairs.
Any further serious weakening of the Ottoman empire in the
Balkans therefore presented serious likelihood of engaging the
great powers in another major war.

In 1875 another rebellion broke out in Bosnia, which
drew support from Serbia and by 1877 drew Russia into a war
with Turkey. The crisis was ended by the Congress of Berlin
which settled Near Eastern affairs to the satisfaction of the
great powers, but without consulting the Balkan peoples directly involved. The ambassadors of the great powers in Berlin did
not even extend the courtesy of a hearing to the Serbian delega-
tion. The settlement provided that the Austro-Hungarian empire be given the right to administer Bosnia and Herzegovina, although the suzerainty of the Sultan was to be respected — a
hybrid arrangement which was to be important to the trial of
the Sarajevo assassins. The Bosnians, placed under Hapsburg
rule, had no more use for the Austrian empire than the Turkish
one. The Austrian army had to impose order by force in 1878,
and again in 1881. Thereafter the people of Bosnia settled
down more or less passively to an acceptance of Austrian
imperium.

By 1881 the Austrians had also imposed a *de facto* control
over Serbian affairs, so that from 1881 to 1903 the Balkans
were relatively quiet so far as Austria was concerned. In 1903,
however, the increasingly restless natives began to reassert themselves. The initial sign was a palace coup in which the king of
Serbia, Alexander Obrenovic (Obrenovich), and his queen, were
murdered by a group of army officers. The officers installed on
the throne the pretender from the rival dynasty, Petar Karadjeordjevic (Karageorgevich). King Petar was a cultivated Euro-

pean who had participated as an ordinary citizen in the Bosnian insurrection of 1875. His main claim to fame before 1903 had been to translate J.S. Mill's *Essay on Liberty* into the Serbian language. He was aided by a gifted minister, Nikola Pasic (Pashich). One of their primary concerns for the next decade was to diminish the influence of the cabal of officers which had brought King Petar to power.

One of those officers was Major Dmitrije Dmitrijevic (Dmitrijevich), a giant of a man, known to his school companions as "Apis" because of a supposed resemblance to the Egyptian god. He had been deeply implicated in the plot to kill Alexander Obrenovich, and there were suspicions that he might resort to regicide again if he feared that his influence with the Karageorgevich dynasty was waning. During the Balkan wars (1912) Apis, as a military intelligence officer, was involved with raising and deploying in Turkish territory bands of guerrilla warriors who played a significant role in the struggles with the Turks. Many Bosnian Serbs volunteered for the bands. By 1914 Dmitrijevic-Apis, by then a colonel, was chief of Serbian military intelligence and a leading figure in an underground organization known as *Ujedinjenje ili smrt* (uyedinyenye ili smrt), "Unification or Death," commonly known as the Black Hand. The purpose of the organization was the unification of all ethnic Serbs under Serbian rule, and uncompromising hostility to all, whether foreign or Serb, who would stand in the way of unification.

While the first world war was in progress Apis was accused of plotting the assassination of the Serbian Prince Regent (later king) Alexander. He was tried by court-martial at the Serbian army headquarters in Salonika, convicted, and shot. The Salonika trial remains one of the most mysterious episodes in Balkan history. It was easy, however, to suppose that a man like Apis, who had plotted and helped to carry out the assassination of one king and allegedly plotted the assassination of another, might also have plotted the assassination of the Archduke Franz Ferdinand. The trial of the Sarajevo assassins was intended in large part to expose and prove the complicity of agents of the Serbian government such as Apis in the killing of the royal couple.

The Austrian government confused the roles of the *Narodna odbrana* and the Black Hand, and at the Sarajevo trial tried to make a case for the proposition that it was the *Narodna odbrana* that had plotted the killing. In fact, the *Narodna odbrana* was an overt, legitimate organization primarily engaged in "cultural" activities. "Cultural" activities in the context of the national liberation struggles of the Balkan peoples at that time largely involved national consciousness-raising through propaganda. It is now nearly certain that the *Narodna odbrana* as such had nothing to do with the assassination, but it is equally certain that some of the individuals in it supplied the arms and aid that the Belgrade troika required. Direct complicity of the Black Hand even to that extent had never been proved, but some of the members of the *Narodna odbrana* who helped the boys were also members of the Black Hand. After all, Serbia was a small country, and people engaged in similar activities were likely to know each other.

By 1903 the Bosnian Serbs were stirring again. Although pathetically impoverished and backward by the standards of the rest of Europe, education and culture had begun to develop, beginning with the establishment of the rudiments of a system of education. Gymnasia, schools whose graduates had about the equivalent of a junior-college education, had been established in Sarajevo and elsewhere. The formal curriculum was similar to that in the other schools of the Austro-Hungarian empire, but besides the formal curriculum, the students in the schools were also deeply steeped in the ideals of nationalism and national liberation. These students became the cutting edge of the revolutionary nationalism that developed after 1903. As we have seen, revolutionary nationalism was nothing new for the Bosnians. What was novel was that the standard-bearers of revolution were the youth rather than established leaders of the community.

These youth were deeply steeped in the revolutionary literature of the Russian Social Revolutionaries, or "SR's," from which the Bosnian youth coined the word "eseri." The SR's were the heirs of the tradition of the Russian student revolutionaries of the 1870s and 1880s who had carried out a number of assassinations, including that of Tsar Alexander II in

1881. The goal of the revolutionary youth was national liberation; their chosen tactic, assassination; their teachers, the
"eseri."

The practice of assassination began as early as 1910, when
one Bogdan Zerajic (Zherayich) unsuccessfully attempted to kill
the then-governor of Bosnia and Hercegovina. Zerajic committed suicide on the spot. He was considered a hero by the
radical Bosnian youth. His grave became an object of pilgrim-
age, and his example an inspiration to others. Some of the
youth acquired practical experience in the Balkan wars, joining
the guerrilla bands raised by the Serbian government and par-
ticipating in the wars against the Turks. One of those was Vladimir Gacinovic (Gatsinovich) who, although not directly involved in the plot for the Sarajevo assassination, was to a great
extent considered by the radical youth to be their spiritual
leader. Zerajic was twenty-four when he killed himself in 1910,
and Gacinovic was twenty-four in 1914. We might speculate
that their age enabled them to stand in the relation of elder
brothers to the students still in the gymnasium in 1914 and
therefore serve as models whom the boys would hold in esteem.

The nationalistic radicalism of the Bosnian youth was of a
distinctive type. They said of themselves that they did not
merely seek a unification of Bosnian Serbs with their ethnic
brothers in Serbia. That would not suit conditions in Bosnia.
Bosnia may once have been primarily Serbian, but that was before the Turkish invasion (1458-61). Since then many Turks
had settled in Bosnia and had made their home there. Many
more ethnic Serbs had converted to Islam, and, while of the
Moslem faith, had roots as old as any Serb. Furthermore,
Bosnia contained many Croats. Croats are also Slavs, and speak
a language which is for all practical purposes the same as the
Serbian. The common language is called Serbo-Croatian, and
the dialectical differences are no greater (although of a different
kind) than between British English and American English. The
principal cultural difference is that the Croats are Roman Catholic in religion, while the Serbs are Eastern Orthodox (and, in
the case of Bosnia, sometimes Moslem). These peoples are in-
extricably intermingled. It is often the case in Bosnia that a
village contains both a Christian church and a mosque, their

steeples and minarets respectively dominating the village. Whatever Bosnian Serbs might gain by union with Serbia would certainly be lost by their Moslem and Catholic neighbors. The Bosnian youth were sensible enough to recognize that. Furthermore, they were well aware of the nature of the Serbian government, and saw it as being badly in need of reform as any. Rather than seek a simple union with Serbia, the most idealistic element of the Bosnian youth adhered to the ideal of "Yugoslavism."

Yugoslavism was an outgrowth of the peculiar conditions of the Austro-Hungarian empire. The Hapsburgs in medieval times had patched the empire together out of a grab-bag of peoples, mainly using the device of dynastic marriage to cement the medieval states into a personal union with the Hapsburg crown. Joseph II (1780-1790) attempted to create a unified, culturally Germanic state, but failed. The principal result of his attempt was to strengthen the national consciousness of the non-Germanic peoples of the empire. The problem was that no single ethnic group was in the majority. The two most numerous groups were the Austro-Germans and the Magyars (Hungarians). The attempt to Germanize the Magyars merely made them fanatically nationalistic Magyars. The result was rebellion in 1848, which was repressed; but by 1867 the Magyars forced the division of the Empire into Austrian and Hungarian kingdoms, theoretically joined only in personal loyalty to the Hapsburg monarch.

That, however, merely whetted the appetite for autonomy of the third major element of the Empire, the Slavs. The Slavs were neither geographically nor culturally homogenous. In the north of the Empire were the Czechs and Slovaks; in the southern part, the Slovenes, Croats, and considerable numbers of ethnic Serbs. What they really wanted was impossible to determine, since almost up to the outbreak of the first world war the press was under censorship, and nationalistic agitators were subject to trial and punishment for high treason. The demand most frequently heard was for "Trialism," that is, a division of the Empire into three parts, one of them Slav. Geography would at best have made that an awkward arrangement. From about 1890, particularly in Slovenia, and later among the Bosnian

students, an adherence to the idea of Yugoslavism, the creation
of an autonomous state for the South Slavs (Slovenes, Croats,
and Serbs) developed. By 1914 the ideal of Yugoslavism had
become almost a crusade among the most idealistic of the youth.

The position of Serbia in a "Yugoslavia" was of course a
problem. The Serbs of Serbia were also South Slavs, but Serbia would most certainly not consent to entering the Austro-
Hungarian empire. What was much more serious for the Hapsburg monarchy was the possibility of the alternative solution —
a "Yugoslavia" built about Serbia as the core, but including the
Slavic peoples and lands of the southern part of the Empire, a
"Greater Serbia." Should such a "Yugoslavia" evolve it would
mean the dissolution of the Hapsburg empire.

This consideration was the crux of the political crisis that
came from the Sarajevo assassination. The youthful assassins
were committed to the ideal of Yugoslavism, seeking the forma-
tion of a state comprised of South Slavs, which would inevitably
have to be carved largely out of the Hapsburg empire, which in
turn meant the dissolution of the Empire. The existence of
Yugoslavism in general, and of Serbia as the magnet drawing the
other South Slavs into a common state, therefore represented a
clear and present danger to the existence of the Hapsburg empire. Not because Serbia could ever hope to destroy the Empire
by direct attack — no one ever dreamed of that in the predict-
able future, but because by presenting the ever-present example
of one South Slav people freely managing its own affairs, it encouraged the others to make demands which, if granted, would
dissolve the empire.

This situation had led the Hapsburg monarchy to take control of Bosnia in 1878. In 1903, when the Empire lost control
of Serbia in the aftermath of the assassination of Alexander
Obrenovich the Empire began to fear the corrosive effect of the
mere existence of Serbia on her southern frontiers. The danger
had increased so much that by 1908 the Empire risked general
European war by formally annexing Bosnia, thereby hoping to
put an end to the aspiration of the Bosnians for unification with
the other South Slavs. Some elements of the Hapsburg court,
notably the military chief of staff, Conrad von Hötzendorff,
urged still stronger action — a preemptive war on Serbia which

would end the menace of dissolution of the Empire once and
for all. With the successes of the Serbian army in the war with
Turkey in 1912, her corresponding growth in prestige, and the
evident sympathy with Serbia on the part of many of the Bosnians, a preemptive move against Serbia grew even more attrac-
tive. Hence the harsh reaction of the imperial government to
the assassination of the heir apparent in Sarajevo. To those who
favored dealing with Serbia while there was still time, the assassination was a welcome event. To them it was clear that the
Serbian government had at least permitted, if not planned, the
assassination. A government which harbored a regicide such as
Colonel Dmitrijevic-Apis and continued him in such an important post as chief of military intelligence was indeed vulnerable
to such charges.

In fact, the degree of complicity of the Serbian government, if any, has never been determined. There is no question
that some of the officials of the Serbian government helped the
high-school boys to obtain and transport arms from Belgrade to
Sarajevo in order to carry out the assassination. This trial transcript affords proof of that. It is also known that Colonel Dmitrijevic-Apis knew of the boys' intentions, and at least permitted their activities to progress, and that he sent an agent to Sarajevo who made a feeble attempt to stop the assassination before
it was carried out. It would, however, have been an act of the
greatest folly for the Serbian government (the crown and ministry) to have planned such an assassination. A Serbia small in
size and exhausted by the Balkan wars was in no position to
provoke her powerful neighbor, and her prime minister, Nikola
Pasic was one of the ablest statesmen of his day. Unless some
convincing evidence to the contrary is someday discovered, the
idea that the Serbian government planned the killing of the
Archduke Franz Ferdinand can safely be dismissed.

That did not mean that the Austro-Hungarian government,
having decided to engage in war with Serbia, would not try to
prove that the killing was Serbia's fault. A good way to begin
was to conduct a show trial of the killers (five of whom were in
the hands of the Austrian police) and their accomplices.

The Accused
A total of twenty-five persons were placed on trial in

Sarajevo. Of the six who had lain in wait for the Archduke, one, Mehmed Mehmedbasic (Mehmedbashich), escaped to Montenegro. Nedeljko Cabrinovic and Gavrilo Princip were seized immediately after they made their attempts. The remaining three students made no, or only feeble, attempts to escape and were arrested within twenty-four hours. As a result of police investigation, a total of twenty others were arrested as accomplices. All were placed on trial in the military garrison of the city of Sarajevo from 12 to 23 October, 1914. Of the twenty-five, sixteen were Serbian Orthodox in religion, the religion of four was not determined, and four declared themselves Roman Catholic. Of the four Catholics, three were acquitted of complicity in the killing. Thus the persons implicated in the Sarajevo assassination appear on the face of the proceedings to have been overwhelmingly Serbian in nationality. This conclusion is compromised, however, by the fact that the trial was in large part intended to implicate the Serbian government.

In order to have a criminal trial there must first be a charge. Here a curious fact appears in the closing statement of the prosecution and the reply of the defense counsels thereto — the insistence that the accused must be charged and found guilty of the crime of high treason. As the prosecution states, its task was to prove three things: that a crime had been committed, that it had been committed by the accused, and that the crime committed had been high treason, and specifically not murder. Since the Archduke was just as dead as if he had been murdered, why the insistence on qualifying the crime as high treason?

The need arose partly from the need to implicate the Serbian government. But there was also a technicality of Austrian law that made it necessary to qualify the crime as high treason. An archduke had been killed; someone had to hang. Those convicted of the crimes of either murder or high treason were liable to the death penalty — provided they were over 20 years of age when the crime was committed. But five principals were all under 20 years of age at the time of the killing (Princip's case doubtful, but resolved in his favor); therefore they could not hang. But no one else could be convicted as principals to the crime of murder, and accessories to the crime of murder were not liable to the death penalty. Accessories to the crime of

high treason were. Therefore, if anyone was hanged, it had to
be as accessories to the crime of high treason.

The result was a heated debate as to whether a Bosnian
could commit the crime of high treason at all. The Bosnians,
after all, had never been consulted as to whether they had accepted Austrian rule. The Congress of Berlin in 1878 settled
Bosnian affairs to the satisfaction of the great powers without
consulting Bosnian representatives. At that time and until 1910,
there was no recognized constitutional device such as an assembly through which the Bosnians might have been able to express
their desires. "Public opinion," such as it was, could only be
expressed by extra-legal means, by conflict, which in 1878 and
again in 1881 took the form of deadly quarrels between certain
Bosnians and the Austrian military occupation. Thus Austria
could at no time claim to have the sanction of the Bosnians for
their occupation, which until 1908 retained the legal status of a
military occupation. Social contract political theory therefore
would hold that no Bosnian could be charged with high treason,
since no Bosnian was a party to the contract. It is difficult to
see on what grounds the Monarchy could claim the loyalty of
its Bosnian subjects, or why there should have been any particular surprise when the quarrel began to stir again in 1896.

Of course the question is not as clear-cut as that. The
monarchy based the legitimacy of its rule of Bosnia on historic
rights rather than natural law. The Monarchy did have the sanction of the great powers for its occupation, which in international law at that time gave her the right and responsibility to
maintain order. The terms of the Treaty of Berlin, however,
provided that the nominal suzerainty of the Sultan not be compromised. The proviso was a legal fiction, of course, but politics functions largely on the basis of fictions. The annexation
of Bosnia in 1908 was a unilateral action not even sanctioned
by the international community until it had caused a crisis that
almost precipitated general war. Consequently, it could be
argued that the Sultan was the Bosnians' suzerain, and therefore
that it was impossible for a Bosnian to commit high treason
against the Monarchy.

Two of the defense counsels arrived at the same conclusion by an interpretation of the laws of the Monarchy itself.

This question had been already raised in connection with the Zagreb High Treason Trial, and had been the subject of study by Austrian legal scholars, of whom one Dr. Finger was cited by the defense counsels. Dr. Rudolf Zistler gave the lengthiest summing-up of Finger's opinion. He made two principal points. First was the provision of the Treaty of Berlin reserving suzerainty to the Sultan. Second, the act of October 1908 by which Bosnia and Hercegovina were annexed to the Monarchy provided that the provinces could not be incorporated into the Dual Monarchy without the consent of both parts. At the time of the trial the necessary consent had not been obtained from Hungary. Therefore, the defense counsels concluded that the relation of Bosnia-Hercegovina to the Monarchy was that of a separate state, and as such no act of high treason could be committed by a Bosnian against the Monarchy. At that point Zistler had gone too far: The prosecutor vigorously objected, and as Zistler pressed his arguments the president cut him off and eventually reprimanded him. The only reply the prosecutor made to Zistler's argument was simply that it was not true, without citing grounds for his conclusion. The court naturally allowed the charge of high treason to stand. It was upon the conviction of this crime that the hanging of three persons, none of whom were in the assassination squads, were justified by Austrian law.

The Trial Transcript
As a public document, one would expect the transcript of the trial to be readily available to scholars. Such is far from the case. On the contrary, while the first world war was in progress the Austrian government had much more pressing things to consider. The official transcript, known later as "the official 1914 copy," together with its many supporting documents, was forwarded from Sarajevo to Vienna in 1915; returned to Belgrade in 1919; and reshipped to Vienna in 1941-45. An official copy was forwarded to Belgrade and then to Sarajevo after the second world war. However, in the course of these moves, the "official 1914 copy" disappeared, together with its supporting documents. The copy that arrived in Sarajevo, held in the custody of the archives of the People's Republic of Bosnia and

Hercegovina (whose director was Vojislav Bogicevic), was a copy referred to as "the Belgrade copy of 1925." That copy was authenticated in 1939 by the then chief archivist of the main archives of the Yugoslav government, Vojislav M. Jovanovic (Yovanovich). During the second world war a group of scholars in Vienna known as "Research Group 1941-45" examined and authenticated both the "official 1914 copy" and "the Belgrade copy of 1925" and certified the 1925 copy to be faithful to the original. It is this 1925 copy which the then-director of the archives of the People's Republic of Bosnia-Hercegovina, Vojislav Bogicevic (Voyislav Bogitsevich), edited and had published in the Serbo-Croatian language in 1954.

Considerable editing was required for two reasons. First was the problem of the original manuscript. Only two court reporters were used. These recorded the proceedings in shorthand. They worked in relays: The one who recorded in the morning transcribed his notes in the afternoon, and vice versa. Ordinarily in a trial of this importance teams of three stenographers would have been used. Inevitably, therefore, there were gaps in the recording, and in places the proceedings were condensed by the reporters. When interviewed, both Cubrilovic and Popovic emphasized that those deficiencies reflect no discredit on either the stenographers or the editor. The deficiencies were simply the inevitable consequences of the conditions under which the trial was recorded.

Contrary to the usual practice, both stenographers kept their personal notes, expecting them to be valuable in time. One died in the course of World War I. About 1921 or 1922, the other tried to reconstruct the transcript from the two sets of shorthand notes. Because of the passage of time, unfamiliarity with his colleague's shorthand, and the fading of the pencilled notes, it proved difficult to reconstruct a version of the transcript. Furthermore, the postwar Yugoslav government abruptly stopped the stenographer from completing his work. Apparently the Yugoslav government was not eager to have the transcript published, for fear of reopening the question of the Salonika trial. The result of the attempt to reconstruct an unofficial transcript of the trial was that Bogicevic had a partial, unofficial transcript made from the shorthand notes of the court reporters against which he was able to check the authenticity of parts of the "Belgrade copy of 1925."

The second need for considerable editing stemmed from the existence of earlier translations of the trial proceedings, in all cases inaccurate to some degree and in some cases deliberately shortened and falsified. Of these purported transcripts, only two are of significance. The first was *Der Prozess gegen die attentäter von Sarajevo. Nach amtlichen Stenogrammen des Gerichtsverfahrens aktenmässig dargestellt von Prof. Pharos* (Berlin, 1918). This version was only 165 pages long, about one-fifth or one-sixth of the full text. "Prof. Pharos" turned out to be Father Anton Puntigam, a Jesuit professor at a Catholic gymnasium in Travnik in Bosnia, who is frequently though inaccurately referred to as the confessor to the Archduke. Well-known as a supporter of the Austrian imperium in Bosnia, he had once had an audience with the Archduke, and was one of the few private persons allowed to attend the trial. His severely-shortened version of the trial transcript was intended to implicate the Serbian government in the assassination plot, and apparently the Freemasons as well. "Pharos" had evidently used notes made by a journalist of a local (Sarajevo) newspaper as his source.

A considerably improved translation of the transcript was published in 1930 by a French journalist (and Freemason) named Alfred Mousset under the title of *Un drame historique de l'attentat de Sarajevo. Documents inedits et texte integral de stenogrammes du proces* (Paris: Payot, 1930). Upon comparison, Bogicevic found that Mousset had evidently had "the Belgrade copy of 1925" as his basic text; but that where it had suited him, Mousset had also supplemented and amended the text from the same (inaccurate) source as "Pharos" had used. In his annotation Bogicevic notes most, although not all, of the inaccuracies in the Mousset version. Furthermore, the translators of this transcript into English (Pribic and Owings) found that Mousset had not translated literally some of the difficult passages. Particularly in the closing arguments of the prosecution and defense, the text is difficult to follow, partly because of the difficulty of transcription by the court reporters, but apparently also because the counsel were evidently thinking in

German although speaking Serbo-Croatian. Pribic and Owings found it necessary first to translate the text from Serbo-Croatian into German, and then into English. Only then was it possible to compare the English translation with the original and make sense of it. At those places Mousset often condensed or paraphrased. To put it bluntly, he skipped the difficult parts. The Mousset text, therefore, while it is the only previous translation from the Serbo-Croatian that has much claim to accuracy, leaves much to be desired as a translation to be used for scholarly purposes.

In his introduction to the edited trial transcript in the Serbo-Croatian language (1954) Professor Bogicevic devotes most of the introduction and about two-thirds of the annotation to pointing out the deficiencies in the "Pharos" and Mousset versions of the trial transcript. The translators have assumed that scholars who wish to check the validity of Bogicevic's work will use the originals, and so have omitted those parts. We have retained the notes in which he explained the text for the benefit of his Yugolsav readers, and have added to those such additional explanations as we think a non-Yugoslav reader might need. In each case we have denoted the source of each note as either Bogicevic's (B.) or ours (Ed.). In those explanatory notes, where Bogicevic has referred to a Yugoslav source we have again assumed that any scholar who wishes to use the reference will use the original, and therefore left the reference in the Yugoslav form.

The primary concern of the translators has been to render a literal translation suitable for scholarly purposes rather than a smooth-reading literary work. At best, therefore, there are some awkwardly-worded passages. Where the peasants testify we have attempted to render the peasant dialect into an equivalent American farmer dialect, but without much success. The original has a good deal more of a "country" flavor than the translation. The peasants attempt to use the formal third-person form of address, but slip readily into the more-familiar second person. At times the court officials respond to them in the second person. Occasionally the translators sense that the court officials might have been using the second person in a familiar or contemptuous sense. At those points the translators have so indicated in notes. In all cases, meticulous accuracy in translation has been the primary goal, with a smooth-reading text the secondary, although still important, objective.

W.A. Owings
Little Rock, Arkansas
June, 1982

Photographs

Official death portraits of Archduke Franz Ferdinand and his wife Sofia.

General Oskar Potiorek, provincial governor of Bosnia, who was riding with the Archduke when he was shot.

Vladimir Gavinovic (on left), spiritual leader of the Bosnian youth movement. In uniform of a Serbian soldier while on service during the 1912 Balkan War.

A cult hero, Bogdan Zerajic, who tried to assassinate an Austrian official in 1910. Shown here in real life and after committing suicide. Zerajic was mentioned during the trial as a hero to the conspirators.

*Colonel Gragutin Dimitrijevic-Apis and Major Vojislav Tankosic,
two of the leaders of the secret Bosnian terrorist organization,
the Black Hand.*

Nedjeljko Cabrinovic

Gavrilo Princip

Trifun (Trifko) Grabez

Parents of Gavrilo Princip

Misko Jovanovic

Danilo Ilic

Veljko Cubrilovic

Nedjeljko Cabrinovic   Gavrilo Princip   Trifun Grabez

Mihailo (Misko) Jovanovic   Danilo Ilic   Veljko Cubrilovic

CONSPIRATORS

Vaso Cubrilovic

Cvjetko Popovic

Muhamed Mehmedbasic
Later photograph, 1940-1941

Popovic, Cvjetko

Dukic, Lazar

Cubrilovic, Vaso

Kranjcevic, Ivo

Zagorac, Branko

Kalember, Dragan

Forkapic, Nikola

Kerovic, Nedjo

Stjepanovic, Cvijan

CONSPIRATORS

Trifko Grabez (left), Gavrilo Princip (right) and friend in city park in Belgrade in May 1914. The friend, Djuro Sarac (center) played a role in the conspiracy in Belgrade.

Franz Ferdinand and his wife Sophia leaving the Town Hall.

A few seconds before Princip fired the fatal shots.

Princip stood on the corner in front of the house to the right of the bridge when he fired at Franz Ferdinand.

The corner where Princip stood when he fired the fatal shots.

Princip is apprehended.

The military barracks in Sarajevo in which the trial was conducted.

Princip on the way to the courtroom.

A scene from the courtroom. The principals are on the front row; Princip, third from left.

Dr. Rudolf Zistler, defender of four of the accused, the defense counsel who put up the most vigorous defense.

The cell in Therezienstadt prison (now in Czechoslovakia) where Princip was confined until his death in October, 1918.

The First Day

MAIN HEARING

TRIAL OF
GAVRILO PRINCIP AND HIS 24 ACCOMPLICES

SARAJEVO
12 OCTOBER 1914
BEGINNING AT 8:10 A.M.

Court Officials Present (Senate):[1]

President:	Senior Councillor Alois pl. Kurinaldi
Jury:	Councillors Naumowicz & Dr. Majer Hoffman
Alternates:	Councillors Emanuel Fialka & Anton Pitha
Court Clerk & Court Assistant (Assessor):	Nikola Rasic
Public Prosecutor:	Franjo Svara
Assistant Public Prosecutor:	Sark
Defense:	Dr. Premuzic, Dr. Perisic, Dr. Cistler, Strupl, Malek & Feldbauer
Stenographers:	Professor Kestercanek & Lawyer Prpic

ARRAIGNMENT

The court clerk Nikola Rasic announces the opening of the main hearing in the criminal case against Gavrilo Princip and accomplices charged with the crime of high treason.

Therefore **The President** summons the accused in turn.

President: — Gavrilo Princip.

Accused: — Here.

Pr.: — Age?

Acc.: — I was nineteen at the time of the assassination.

Pr.: — When were you born?

Acc.: — 13 July 1894.

Pr.: — We will speak of that later.[2] Where were you born?

Acc.: — In Grahovo, in the village of Oblijaj.

Pr.: — Where did you go to school?

Acc.: — At the gymnasium in Belgrade, the eighth class.

Pr.: — Religion?

Acc.: — Serbian Orthodox.

Pr.: — Married?

Acc.: — No.

Pr.: — Have you any prior convictions?

Acc.: — No.

Pr.: — Nedeljko Cabrinovic.

Acc.: — Here.

Pr.: — Age?

Acc.: — Nineteen.

Pr.: — Date of birth?

Acc.: — 20 January 1895 by the old calendar.

Pr.: — Father's name?

Acc.: — Vaso.

Pr.: — Where are you from?

Acc.: — From Sarajevo.

Pr.: — Where is your legal residence?

Acc.: — In Trebinje.

Pr.: — Religion?

Acc.: — Orthodox.

Pr.: — Not married?

Acc.: — Yes.

Pr.: — Occupation?

Acc.: — Typographer.
Pr.: — Have you any prior convictions?
Acc.: — No.
Pr.: — Trifko Grabez.
Acc.: — Here.
Pr.: — Father's name?
Acc.: — Djordje.
Pr.: — From where?
Acc.: — Pale.
Pr.: — Age?
Acc.: — Eighteen.
Pr.: — Date of birth?
Acc.: — 28 June 1895.
Pr.: — Religion?
Acc.: — Serbian orthodox.
Pr.: — Single?
Acc.: — Yes.
Pr.: — Where did you go to school?
Acc.: — To the gymnasium, the eighth class in Belgrade.
Pr.: — Have you any prior convictions?
Acc.: — Yes, I got fourteen days in jail for slapping Professor Truhelka.[3]
Pr.: — Vaso Cubrilovic.
Acc.: — Here.
Pr.: — Age?
Acc.: — Seventeen.
Pr.: — Date of birth?
Acc.: — 1 January 1897 by the old calendar.
Pr.: — Where are you from?
Acc.: — From Bosanska Gradiska.
Pr.: — Where did you live last?
Acc.: — In Sarajevo.
Pr.: — Where did you go to school?
Acc.: — Sixth class of the gymnasium.
Pr.: — Have you any prior convictions?
Acc.: — No.
Pr.: — Cvjetko Popovic.
Acc.: — Here.
Pr.: — Father's name?

Acc.: — Djuro.
Pr.: — Where are you from?
Acc.: — From Prnjavor.[4]
Pr.: — Where did you live last?
Acc.: — In Sarajevo.
Pr.: — What did you do there?
Acc.: — I was a candidate teacher in the third year.
Pr.: — When were you born?
Acc.: — 13 March 1896.
Pr.: — Your birth certificate says 4 March 1896.
Acc.: — Yes.
Pr.: — Have you any prior convictions?
Acc.: — No.
Pr.: — Danilo Ilic.
Acc.: — Here.
Pr.: — Father's name?
Acc.: — The late Ilija.
Pr.: — Age?
Acc.: — Twenty-four.
Pr.: — Date of birth?
Acc.: — 20 July 1890.
Pr.: — Religion?
Acc.: — Serbian orthodox.
Pr.: — Occupation?
Acc.: — At first I was a teacher, and most recently an associate editor of *Zvono* (The Bell)[5] in Sarajevo.
Pr.: — Married?
Acc.: — No.
Pr.: — Have you any prior convictions?
Acc.: — No.
Pr.: — Ivo Kranjcevic.
Acc.: — Here.
Pr.: — Father's name?
Acc.: — Djuro.
Pr.: — Age?
Acc.: — Nineteen.
Pr.: — Date of birth?
Acc.: — 20 May 1895.
Pr.: — Religion?

Acc.: — Roman Catholic.
Pr.: — Married?
Acc.: — No.
Pr.: — Are you a student?
Acc.: — Yes, I am in the second class of the Business
School.
Pr.: — Have you any prior convictions?
Acc.: — No.
Pr.: — Lazar Djukic.
Acc.: — Here.
Pr.: — Father's name?
Acc.: — Stevan.
Pr.: — Where are you from?
Acc.: — From Kljuc.
Pr.: — Where did you live last?
Acc.: — In Sarajevo.
Pr.: — Are you a student?
Acc.: — Yes, in the fourth class of the Teacher's School.
Pr.: — Age?
Acc.: — Eighteen.
Pr.: — Date of birth?
Acc.: — 12 March 1896.
Pr.: — Religion?
Acc.: — Serbian Orthodox.
Pr.: — Have you any prior convictions?
Acc.: — No.
Pr.: — Single?
Acc.: — Yes.
Pr.: — Veljko Cubrilovic.
Acc.: — Here.
Pr.: — Father's name?
Acc.: — Jovo.
Pr.: — Is he still alive?
Acc.: — No.
Pr.: — Where are you from?
Acc.: — From Bosanska Gradiska.
Pr.: — Where do you live?
Acc.: — In Priboj, the district of Zvornik.
Pr.: — Occupation?

Acc.: — I am a teacher in a confessional school.[6]
Pr.: — Age?
Acc.: — Twenty-eight.
Pr.: — Married?
Acc.: — Yes.
Pr.: — How many children?
Acc.: — One.
Pr.: — Have you any prior convictions?
Acc.: — Yes, because of an incident I was fined 20 crowns.
Pr.: — Mitar Kerovic.
Acc.: — Here.
Pr.: — Father's name?
Acc.: — Ilija.
Pr.: — Where are you from?
Acc.: — From Tobut, the district of Zvornik.
Pr.: — Age?
Acc.: — Sixty-five.
Pr.: — Religion?
Acc.: — Serbian.[7]
Pr.: — Orthodox?
Acc.: — Yes.
Pr.: — Married?
Acc.: — Yes.
Pr.: — How many children?
Acc.: — Four, one a girl.
Pr.: — How old is the youngest one?
Acc.: — I know the name, but I don't know the age.
Pr.: — What is the name of the youngest?
Acc.: — Nedjo.
Pr.: — How old is he?
Acc.: — I can't rightly tell you.
Pr.: — Are all of your children grown?
Acc.: — Yes, they are.
Pr.: — Are you a peasant?
Acc.: — Yes.
Pr.: — Do you have some property?
Acc.: — I have about 100 *dunuma*[8] of land, four oxen,
two cows and two horses.
Pr.: — Are you the head of the household?[9]

Acc.: — I am.

Pr.: — But in the records it says that Blagoje is the head of household. Have you any prior convictions?

Acc.: — None.

Pr.: — Jovo Kerovic.

Acc.: — Here.

Pr.: — Father's name?

Acc.: — Mitar.

Pr.: — Where are you from?

Acc.: — From Tobut.

Pr.: — Age?

Acc.: — I don't know, but father knows.

Pr.: — Religion?

Acc.: — Serbian Orthodox.

Pr.: — Married?

Acc.: — Yes.

Pr.: — Do you have children?

Acc.: — Yes.

Pr.: — How many?

Acc.: — Five.

Pr.: — How old are they?

Acc.: — One is seven, and the youngest is six months.

Pr.: — Have you any prior convictions?

Acc.: — Yes, two days.

Pr.: — Do you know how to write?

Acc.: — Only my name. I didn't go to school.

Pr.: — Nedjo Kerovic.

Acc.: — Here.

Pr.: — Father's name?

Acc.: — Mitar.

Pr.: — Where are you from?

Acc.: — From Tobut.

Pr.: — Age?

Acc.: — Twenty-eight.

Pr.: — Are you married?

Acc.: — Yes.

Pr.: — How many children?

Acc.: — Two.

Pr.: — How old are they?

Acc.: — One is three, and the other eighteen months.
Pr.: — Occupation?
Acc.: — Peasant.
Pr.: — Have you any prior convictions?
Acc.: — No.
Pr.: — Do you know how to write?
Acc.: — Yes.
Pr.: — Glagoje Kerovic.
Acc.: — Here.
Pr.: — Father's name?
Acc.: — Mitar.
Pr.: — Age?
Acc.: — I think thirty-four.
Pr.: — Religion?
Acc.: — Serbian Orthodox.
Pr.: — Married?
Acc.: — Yes.
Pr.: — How many children do you have?
Acc.: — Three.
Pr.: — How old is the oldest, and how old is the youngest?
Acc.: — I think the oldest is eight, and the youngest is not yet one year old.
Pr.: — Occupation?
Acc.: — Peasant.
Pr.: — Have you any prior convictions?
Acc.: — No.
Pr.: — Do you know how to write and read?
Acc.: — Yes.
Pr.: — Nedjo, Jovo and Blagoje, do you have your own property?
Acc.: — We have.
Pr.: — How much?
Acc.: — 35 *dunuma*.
Pr.: — How did you get it?
Acc.: — My wife's dowry was in money. I began to work and make a profit with this money, and wherever land was sold, and wherever there were no houses to be bought, I bought the land and registered it in my name, and not in the names of my brothers or my wife.

Pr.: — Jovo has no property?

Acc. Jovo: — I have, together with my brothers.

Pr.: — Nedjo and Jovo have their own property, what is its value?

Acc.: — I don't know.

Pr.: — Cvijan Stjepanovic.

Acc.: — Here.

Pr.: — Father's name?

Acc.: — Ilija.

Pr.: — Where are you from?

Acc.: — From Tobut.

Pr.: — Age?

Acc.: — I think thirty-seven.

Pr.: — Religion?

Acc.: — Serbian Orthodox.

Pr.: — Married?

Acc.: — Yes.

Pr.: — How many children?

Acc.: — Three.

Pr.: — How old are they?

Acc.: — The oldest is just over eight, and the youngest past one.

Pr.: — Do you have property?

Acc.: — No.

Pr.: — How do you live?

Acc.: — Various ways. I have two oxen and three cows. They belong to my wife, but I also have debts.

Pr.: — Have you any prior convictions?

Acc.: — No.

Pr.: — Do you know how to write?

Acc.: — Yes.

Pr.: — Mihajlo Jovanovic.

Acc.: — Here.

Pr.: — Father's name?

Acc.: — Pero.

Pr.: — Where are you from?

Acc.: — From Tuzla.

Pr.: — Age?

Acc.: — Thirty-six.

Pr.: — Religion?

Acc.: — Serbian Orthodox.

Pr.: — Married?

Acc.: — Yes.

Pr.: — Have you any children?

Acc.: — One child.

Pr.: — Occupation?

Acc.: — Recently I had a cinema. My father gave it to me to work and earn a living from it.

Pr.: — Do you have some property?

Acc.: — One meadow of 100 *klafters*.[10]

Pr.: — Do you know how to read and write?

Acc.: — Yes.

Pr.: — How much schooling did you complete?

Acc.: — The Serbian elementary school in Tuzla, then two classes at the Business School in Tuzla, and two classes of the private German *real* school in Tuzla.

Pr.: — Have you any prior convictions?

Acc.: — No.

Pr.: — Branko Zagorac.

Acc.: — Here.

Pr.: — Father's name?

Acc.: — Pero.

Pr.: — Where are you from?

Acc.: — From Kadina Voda, district of Banja Luka.

Pr.: — Where do you live?

Acc.: — In Sarajevo.

Pr.: — What do you do?

Acc.: — I am a student in the first class of the Business School.

Pr.: — How old are you?

Acc.: — Eighteen.

Pr.: — Date of birth?

Acc.: — 21 October 1896.

Pr.: — Have you any prior convictions?

Acc.: — No.

Pr.: — Marko Perin.

Acc.: — Here.

Pr.: — Father's name?

Acc.: — Jakov.
Pr.: — Where are you from?
Acc.: — From Nevesinje.
Pr.: — Where do you live?
Acc.: — In Sarajevo.
Pr.: — What school do you attend?
Acc.: — The sixth class of the gymnasium.
Pr.: — Age?
Acc.: — Seventeen.
Pr.: — Date of birth?
Acc.: — 13 August 1897.
Pr.: — It says here August 24th.
Acc.: — By the new calendar the 26th.
Pr.: — Have you any prior convictions?
Acc.: — No.
Pr.: — Nikola Forkapic.
Acc.: — Here.
Pr.: — Father's name?
Acc.: — Luka.
Pr.: — From where?
Acc.: — From Trebinje.
Pr.: — Where did you attend school?
Acc.: — In Sarajevo, the fourth class of the Teacher's School.
Pr.: — Age?
Acc.: — Nineteen.
Pr.: — Date of birth?
Acc.: — 7 December 1894.
Pr.: — It says here 25 October 1894.
Acc.: — That is a mistake. You can tell that from the documents.
Pr.: — Religion?
Acc.: — Serbian Orthodox.
Pr.: — Have you any prior convictions?
Acc.: — Never.
Pr.: — Dragan Kalember.
Acc.: — Here.
Pr.: — Father's name?
Acc.: — Radoslav.

Pr.: — From where?
Acc.: — From Korenica in Croatia.
Pr.: — Where were you born?
Acc.: — In Reljevo.
Pr.: — Where do you live?
Acc.: — In Sarajevo.
Pr.: — Are you a student?
Acc.: — A student in the sixth class of the gymnasium.
Pr.: — Age?
Acc.: — Sixteen.
Pr.: — Date of brith?
Acc.: — 30 April 1898.
Pr.: — Religion?
Acc.: — Serbian Orthodox.
Pr.: — Have you any prior convictions?
Acc.: — No.
Pr.: — Mico Micic.
Acc.: — Here.
Pr.: — Father's name?
Acc.: — The late Djoko.
Pr.: — From where?
Acc.: — Where? From Janja, district Bijeljina.
Pr.: — Age?
Acc.: — Twenty-six.
Pr.: — Religion?
Acc.: — Serbian Orthodox.
Pr.: — Single?
Acc.: — Yes.
Pr.: — Occupation?
Acc.: — A baker, but recently I worked on the land.
Pr.: — Do you have your own land?
Acc.: — A little bit.
Pr.: — How much is it worth?
Acc.: — 5000 forints with my mother's part.
Pr.: — And your own?
Acc.: — Two to three thousand forints.
Pr.: — Did you rent the bakery to someone else?
Acc.: — Yes.
Pr.: — Have you any prior convictions?

Acc.: — I got twenty-one days because I hit a man with a bottle.

Pr.: — Jakov Milovic.

Acc.: — Here.

Pr.: — Father's name?

Acc.: — The late Vasilije.

Pr.: — From where?

Acc.: — From Bodrniste, district of Gacko.

Pr.: — Where do you live?

Acc.: — In Obrijezje.

Pr.: — Age?

Acc.: — Forty-three.

Pr.: — Religion?

Acc.: — Orthodox.

Pr.: — Married?

Acc.: — Yes, but my wife is dead.

Pr.: — How many children?

Acc.: — The oldest is 13, the second 11, one is 7 and one 8.

Pr.: — Do you have mobile property?

Acc.: — A little.

Pr.: — What do you do?

Acc.: — Agricultural worker.

Pr.: — Do you know how to write?

Acc.: — No.

Pr.: — Have you any prior convictions?

Acc.: — No.

Pr.: — Obren Milosevic.

Acc.: — Here.

Pr.: — Father's name?

Acc.: — Milos.

Pr.: — From where?

Acc.: — From Trnovo, district Zvornik.

Pr.: — Age?

Acc.: — Thirty-eight.

Pr.: — Religion?

Acc.: — Orthodox.

Pr.: — Married?

Acc.: — Yes.

Pr.: — How many children?

Acc.: — Four.
Pr.: — Of what ages?
Acc.: — From twelve down to one and a half.
Pr.: — Are you a farm worker?
Acc.: — Yes.
Pr.: — Do you have property?
Acc.: — No.
Pr.: — Do you know how to write?
Acc.: — No.
Pr.: — Have you any prior convictions?
Acc.: — Never.
Pr.: — Ivan Momcinovic.
Acc.: — Here.
Pr.: — Father's name?
Acc.: — Antun.
Pr.: — From where?
Acc.: — From Kresevo, and now I am in Sarajevo.
Pr.: — Age?
Acc.: — Sixty-seven.
Pr.: — Religion?
Acc.: — Croatian Catholic.
Pr.: — Married?
Acc.: — I am. My wife died.
Pr.: — How many children have you?
Acc.: — One married daughter, one married son, and one mentally-retarded daughter.
Pr.: — How do you live?
Acc.: — From rents.
Pr.: — Do you have property?
Acc.: — I have a house in Skenderija, worth 8000 forints.
Pr.: — Have you any prior convictions?
Acc.: — No.
Pr.: — Franjo Sadilo.
Acc.: — Here.
Pr.: — Father's name?
Acc.: — Josip.
Pr.: — From where?
Acc.: — From Pozega.
Pr.: — Where do you live?

Acc.: — In Sarajevo.
Pr.: — Religion?
Acc.: — Roman Catholic.
Pr.: — Age?
Acc.: — Forty.
Pr.: — Married?
Acc.: — Yes.
Pr.: — Do you have children?
Acc.: — One little girl.
Pr.: — Age?
Acc.: — Five.
Pr.: — What do you do?
Acc.: — I am a cabinet-maker.
Pr.: — Do you have property?
Acc.: — I don't.
Pr.: — Have you any prior convictions?
Acc.: — Not ever.
Pr.: — Angela Sadilo.
Acc.: — Here.
Pr.: — Father's name?
Acc.: — Ivan Momcinovic.
Pr.: — From where?
Acc.: — Sarajevo.
Pr.: — Age?
Acc.: — Thirty-one.
Pr.: — Religion?
Acc.: — Catholic.
Pr.: — Is Franjo Sadilo your husband?
Acc.: — Yes.
Pr.: — What do you do?
Acc.: — I am a housewife.
Pr.: — Do you know how to write?
Acc.: — Yes.
Pr.: — Do you have any prior convictions?
Acc.: — No.

After that **The President** called the witnesses and announced that two witnesses are in jail and two did not appear.

He further announced that the persons who had been injured, were invited and had permission to listen to the hearing, but were not required to attend.

The President informed the witnesses that they were required to tell the absolute truth before the court, and arranged them into groups: those who were to attend the court on Saturday, and those on Monday.

Then the court proceeded to the reading of the charges.

After the reading of the charges the president announced the names of the defense counsels and their clients.

After that he ordered that all of the accused except Nedeljko Cabrinovic be returned to jail, and recessed the court for five minutes.

After the recess

THE HEARING OF NEDELJKO CABRINOVIC
12 OCTOBER 1914

Pr.: — Nedeljko Cabrinovic, do you feel yourself guilty?

Acc.: — Yes.

Pr.: — Of what crime?

Acc.: — Guilty of the killing of the Archduke Franz Ferdinand.

Pr.: — How did that come about? Tell everything from the beginning. Where you were and where you worked as a typographer. How you came to Belgrade.

Acc.: — I finished two classes of the Business School, and did not continue because my father would not permit it. I studied the second year in Trebinje, and at the end of the year my father called me to Sarajevo. That was in the eighth or ninth month of the school. I was sick. The curriculum was not the same and I failed in many subjects. My father was angry, hated me and mistreated me, and I ran away from home. I tried to learn a trade. I was all on my own. First I tried to become a locksmith, then a sheet-metal worker, and finally I worked in a printing plant.

Pr.: — How old were you when you took up a craft?

Acc.: — Fourteen. I worked with the Serbian press in Sarajevo for two years, but I left there because an older worker slapped me. I did not feel myself guilty. I went to Zagreb and stayed with a friend of my father for a month and then I went back. On one occasion when I was at home my father threw me in jail for a month because I did not apologize to the maid. He jailed me for three days in a police jail. Afterward I went to learn a trade at Kajon's. I was there for half a year until the strike began. At that he fired all the workers, and he told me to come back to work the next day. I came. Meanwhile at night a policeman came to my house and wanted to take me to jail. When I went to the police the next day, I stopped at Kajon's and told him that I could not come. I mentioned that, because I was called before the district court several times under suspicion that I wanted to burn Kajon's printing plant.

Pr.: — Were you a member of the typographer's union?

Acc.: — Yes, but only later, when I freed myself. When I left Kajon's I went to Novi Sad. There the former journeyman Vukicevic found me a job with the Serbian press in Karlovci. Because I did not have documents as a typesetter, I was not able to go on working, and so I went to Sid to the socialist press. I left there of my own will, and went to Serbia and worked in Belgrade in Dacic's press. There before I became a journeyman I became ill, and so I could not remain in Belgrade.

Pr.: — When was that?

Acc.: — A year and a half ago. The anarchist newspaper *Komuna* (The Commune) was published by that press in Serbia.

Pr.: — In what city was that?

Acc.: — In Belgrade. I set the type for that newspaper and its journalists came and debated with us. I was a socialist worker and I refuted their theories as best I could. One day I was no longer able to resist because I myself felt the same anarchistic ideas as they. They gave me their own newspapers and books and invited me to come to their lectures which were held every evening, beginning generally between eight and nine o'clock and lasting until one or two and sometimes even until three in the morning. When I became ill I went to Sarajevo. They gave me plenty of newspapers, books, and brochures. One of the most prominent representatives of the anarchists in the Balkans was Krsta Cicvaric[11] who published *Novo Vrijeme* (The New Time) which was printed in the same printing plant as *Komuna*. I

became acquainted with him, and he gave me a lot of books, all
his own works. I took those books to Sarajevo. My mother
found several books and burned them, and the rest I read and
gave to my most intimate friends to read. I was also a member of the youth organization and for some time I was its
president.

Pr.: — Where was that?

Acc.: — In Sarajevo when I was sick. First I went home
and I did not work for two months. After I recovered, I went
to work at the press *Narod* (The People).[12] I was there until
the typographers' strike of 1912, and then I left. My father was
not satisfied with that and drove me from the house. Then I
went to Stevo Obilic's. He had the same ideas as I. The two of
us divided the tactics of the typographers in two directions. We
held to the anarchistic direction. I was his assistant in all enterprises, I retained the workers and received those who came from
Serbia. Meanwhile because of that there were false accusations,
as the informed themselves conceded, and the court condemned
me to five years' exile. I went to Belgrade. There I did not
work permanently anywhere. I helped out here and there as a
day worker. Then one day I received a telegram telling me that
I would be permitted to return. My father appealed to the
government to permit my return,[13] and some typographers'
representatives did the same. When I received the telegram, I
wished to go, but I did not have the money. Then a guest in the
cafe which I visited said that I could go with him.

Pr.: — You frequented the cafe *Zirovni Vijenac* (The Green
Acorn)?

Acc.: — Yes. All the Bosnians went there.

Pr.: — Who went there?

Acc.: — Only Bosnians; students and workers.

Pr.: — How long were you in Belgrade at that time?

Acc.: — One month.

Pr.: — Were you acquainted with others?

Acc.: — Yes.

Pr.: — Are any of them among the defendants?

Acc.: — At that time Gavro Princip was already there. I
got acquainted with him here in Sarajevo.

Pr.: — What about his ideas? Did you agree?

Acc.: — No. He felt himself a radical nationalist, and I am an anarchistic socialist. But still those conceptions were not clearly determined. That guest in the cafe, I don't know his name, took me to an association where I could get money, but he told me that I had to pay him a half-litre of native brandy. He took me to the *Narodna odbrana* (National Defense).[14] That was in August on the eve of Emperor's Day.[15] One of my friends and I went there and we were introduced to the late Major Milan Vasic, secretary of the *Narodna odbrana*. He asked me who I was and what I was doing.

Pr.: — What were your intentions in going to him?

Acc.: — To get money.

Pr.: — For what purpose?

Acc.: — I didn't have money for the trip.

Pr.: — What did he ask you?

Acc.: — Who I was, what I was doing, and why was I there? When I told him, he said, "Good." and told me to come back that afternoon, I came and got 15 dinars.

Pr.: — Did you tell him your ideas?

Acc.: — I didn't.

Pr.: — Did he ask about them?

Acc.: — No. In my pocket I had a book by Guy de Maupassant. He took it out of my pocket and asked, "What is it?" When he saw the title, he said that such reading was not for me and gave me a copy of *Narodna odbrana: Statut Narodne Obrane and Narodne junacke pjesme* (National Defense: Statutes of the *Narodna odbrana* and Popular Heroic Songs). He gave that to me and my friend who was with me. Besides those books I received money. "I don't know how to thank you for your kindness," I said to him, and he told me always to remain a good Serb. Now the nationalists no longer seemed to me to be chauvinists, but were friends. This late Milan Vasic was an agreeable person, and any one who talked with him could not think badly of him. With the money which I got I bought myself some books.

Pr.: — What kind of books?

Acc.: — The best-known socialist writers: Zola, Tolstoy, Krapotkin. Most of them translated from Russian literature. About then I unexpectedly received travel money from my father, and besides that I got twenty crowns from the typographers' union. With all of that I bought books, filled a suitcase, took it over to Zumun and mailed it to Sarajevo, and I went on foot myself. When I arrived in Sarajevo I went to work at the printing plant *Narod*.

Pr.: — For the second time?

Acc.: — Yes, for the second time. I stayed there until I became a journeyman. Just before I became a journeyman, that was in December of 1912, in the union some of my friends and I, to some extent of the same ideas, wrote a note and I took it to the editors of *Srpska Rijec* (Serbian Word).[16] That note was directed against the people around the *Glas Sloboda* (Voice of Freedom),[17] because those people considered me a spy and an untrustworthy person, an agent of the Serbian government, and I wanted to prove to them that I was not so bad. I wrote the note under the impact of that impression and took it to *Srpska Rijec*. A campaign evolved from that. Several others and I wrote, and *Glas Sloboda* wrote against us. They had the newspaper in their hands and therefore they won. They referred to me as a spy, and I was offended and did not want to stay.

Pr.: — Did they throw you out of the organization?

Acc.: — From the party. I couldn't stay. That would have been shameful for me. I felt that I might do something bad and in the month of March I left on a trip to Germany. I went to Trieste and there I took private lessons and stayed with *Edinost* (Unity)[18] for half a year until September. While I was working there, the Bulgarian war began.[19] Already at the time of the Serbo-Turkish war — the first Balkan war — I felt a great sympathy for all the warring states, and especially for Serbia. All the more for her, because they wanted to take the fruits of her work from her. I hated what the Austrian press said, that there would be war with Serbia. While all the Serbs were at Kumanovo, Serbia would be empty and then they could invade her with 100,000 men.[20] That angered me and I didn't like it. I felt that I had nationalism in me. When that Balkan war began there developed in me a great desire to go to Serbia. At first I wanted most of all to be in the war. However, the war was almost over when I arrived in Serbia. There was a great economic crisis after the war and I could not get a job right away.

Pr.: — In what month did you arrive in Belgrade?

Acc.: — In October of last year. One day on the Kalimeg-dan I saw an acquaintance whom I knew from the staff of *Srpska Rijec*.[21]   He recommended me to Zivojin Dacic,[22] director of that state press in Belgrade.

Pr.: — Who is that Zivojin Dacic?

Acc.: — He is a member of the Executive Committee of the *Narodna odbrana*, a professor and journalist.   I worked there with a beginning pay of 90 dinars.   I suffered there.   It was frightful.   I did not want to write home, because I was not on good terms with my father, who even forbade my sisters to write to me.   I became desperate.   Later they gave me a little raise, but my need was great.   I wrote home, but no one wrote back.   It was as if to them I was not alive.   I am pretty senti-mental.   Every day I was caught up in more desperate thoughts. In the cafe *Zirovni Vijenac* and *Zlatna Moruna* (Golden Stur-geon) I talked in revolutionary terms with people with whom I met at that time.

Pr.: — Did you meet with students and typographers?

Acc.: — Mostly with the guerrillas.[23]

Pr.: — What did you talk about?

Acc.: — Polemicized.

Pr.: — Did you talk about socialism, anarchism, and politics?

Acc.: — About the politics of Austria.   We judged them from our point of view.

Pr.: — What is your point of view?

Acc.: — My point of view is anarchistic.

Pr.: — Have you ever been a nationalist?

Acc.: — Yes, but what remained were anarchistic ideas.

Pr.: — Were the others the same?

Acc.: — The others were radical nationalists.

Pr.: — What does radical nationalism mean?

Acc.: — Unification of all Serbs under one crown.   The re-vival of the old empire of the Tsar Dusan.[24]

Pr.: — Under Austria?

Acc.: — No.

Pr.: — By what means would you realize that?

Acc.: — War against Austria to strip away Bosnia and Hercegovina, Srijem, and the Banat.

Pr.: — And you agreed with those views?

Acc.: — My ideal was one South Slav republic, in a general Slavic republic.

Pr.: — How did you think that you might realize that?

Acc.: — That is impossible in a legal way.

Pr.: — How could that be? In Serbia there is a dynasty. Is it beloved?

Acc.: — Yes, it is.

Pr.: — How did you imagine that?

Acc.: — I think that it would be possible to achieve it by means of an organization such as Mazzini used in Italy. But because the Serbians and all those among whom I moved have as an ideal the separation of Bosnia from Austria and its annexation to Serbia, we could agree on that point. We disagreed only in that they were adherents to the dynasty under the crown of the Karadjeordjevices, while to the end I remained faithful to anarchistic ideas. I could change only insofar as I could permit some compromise, that that dynasty or if it were possible only King Petar, while he lived, remain king, but after his death it should become a Yugoslav republic.

Pr.: — You were an adherent of the idea that Serbia declare war and take Bosnia and Hercegovina from Austria?

Acc.: — I would prefer if possible that there not be war, for I am a cosmopolitan and I do not wish to shed blood.

Pr.: — You communicated with these students, listened to their ideas and developed your ideas. How long did you stay in Belgrade?

Acc.: — I left Belgrade about a month before the assassination.

Pr.: — You came to Bosnia because of the assassination?

Acc.: — Yes.

Pr.: — When did the idea of the assassination come to your mind?

Acc.: — The idea of the assassination did not come directly to me. I received an anonymous communication, a clipping from a newspaper, evidently from *Pokret* (Movement) because it is printed in the breadth that *Pokret* uses.

Pr.: — From what region?[25]

Acc.: — I don't know. It wasn't legible, but the stamp had

the picture of Franz Josef.

Pr.: — What was in that clipping?

Acc.: — "From Sarajevo it is announced, that the Archduke Heir Apparent with his wife will come to Sarajevo and partici- pate in the maneuvers." Nothing more.

Pr.: — In which month and day was that?

Acc.: — I don't know, March or April.

Pr.: — In any case before Easter?[26]

Acc.: — Yes.

Pr.: — When did you read that?

Acc.: — During the working day I didn't have time to think about it. I read it, put it in my pocket and forgot it while I was working at my job.

Pr.: — Was there anything written on the clipping which you received?

Acc.: — The word "Greeting."

Pr.: — In Latin or Cyrillic script?[27]

Acc.: — I don't remember. About noon I went to dinner to the *Zeleni Vijenac* (Green Wreath) and I dined alone. After that I went to the cafe *Zirovni Vijenac*. There I ordered coffee and read the newspaper. Next to me Princip danced with a cou- ple of Bosnians. One was called Mane, and the other Branko. They were from somewhere in the Krajina. After the dance I remembered the clipping and showed it to Princip. He read it and said nothing to me. I attached no importance to that com- munication, although I thought of an assassination. I did not think that communication would play such a significant role in my life. I put it in my pocket and went out for a walk. In the evening I went out to supper to the *Zeleni Vijenac* and when I was finished with supper Princip came. He said to me, "Let's go out and talk about that report." I realized at once that Princip was thinking of an assassination.

Pr.: — Had you ever before talked with the students about assassinating the Heir Apparent?

Acc.: — Yes, we had.

Pr.: — What did they say?

Acc.: — All of those people were inspired with terroristic ideas.

Pr.: — Was the carrying out of an assassination presented

also as a means of unification?

Acc.: — That was considered as a step toward the goal, as fostering national consciousness and culture. For example, in December, before the opening of the *Sabor* (Assembly)[28] I said that it would be necessary to go also to Sarajevo and carry out an assassination in the *Sabor*. Assassination was often discussed.

Pr.: — As soon as you received the note, did you know right away what it concerned?

Acc.: — I knew at once, but I did not grasp its importance. When I left with Princip we went into the park at Obilic's and there Princip suggested that we two carry out an assassination of the Heir Apparent.

Pr.: — And of his wife?

Acc.: — We said that we would make every effort to spare her. We condemned Lukeni's[29] assassination and considered that a common crime.

Pr.: — In what words did he tell you that?

Acc.: — He suggested to me that we two go and carry out the assassination. To me that assassination was not as important, as big a thing as it really was. I thought than an assassination in the *Sabor* would be more important if it were carried out against an Assembly bootlicker.[30] After a short hesitation I agreed to the assassination.

Pr.: — I cannot believe that you agreed as soon as you spoke to him! Surely you talked about the purposes which the assassination served?

Acc.: — There in the indictment it says that we carried out the assassination for the purpose of annexation.

Pr.: — Forget the indictment. You mustn't criticize it. Why did you do it?

Acc.: — The assassination would serve to spread nationalism in the people, national consciousness and revenge.

Pr.: — Why did you choose the Heir Apparent? Might you have chosen someone else?

Acc.: — When the "exceptional measures"[31] were declared I think that I was then in Sarajevo in order to carry out an assassination of Pitiorek. On that day Djoko Bajic was in the *Zeleni Vijenac*. He was suspected of being an Austrian spy. I debated

with him, but again I was cautious. I read in the newspapers the
news that Nastic[32] had come from Belgium where he studied
some sort of polytechnical trade and that in Vienna he became
a clerk in the Ministry for Foreign Affairs. Someone added,
"Some day Nastic might come to Belgrade as consul." If an
assassination were to be carried out at all, I most of all wished it
be of Nastic, because I considered him a traitor. Bajic said to
me, "When you think of assassination, it is better that you kill
Franz Ferdinand." I hesitated and was afraid, but nevertheless
I took out the notice: "Just today I got this communication."
Later, when Princip came, we broke off the conversation.

Pr.: — Had you previously spoken of the assassination of
Franz Ferdinand?

Acc.: — He[33] did not talk to me about it as much as to
Princip. Princip said to me, "Watch out. He often speaks about
assassination. Maybe he is paid to spread the idea." Because he
(Princip) suggested the assassination, after a short deliberation I
agreed, and we two decided to carry it out. We gave each other
our word of honor, shook hands, and left. Before that we had
deliberated as to how we would obtain the means. In Belgrade
there were people who would contribute to that end. We did
not know anyone. We thought that we might go to the *Narodna
odbrana*. Princip complained that he was at the *Narodna odbrana*, that he had asked for a stipendium, but Pribicevic had
refused him. Because of that, Princip was angry with him. We
did not mention Dacic at all, because Dacic was my director,
and I hated him. Both of them were on a trip at that time, so
the *Narodna odbrana* was out of the question. We parted, and
Princip took it on himself to find the means. We met every day,
but there was no more news until one day I met with Milan
Ciganovic.

Pr.: — Did you know him before?

Acc.: — Yes.

Pr.: — Did he know about the assassination?

Acc.: — No.

Pr.: — Who is Ciganovic?

Acc.: — He is a clerk on the railroad, a low-ranking clerk.

Pr.: — From where?

Acc.: — From Bosnia.

Pr.: — Was he a guerrilla?

Acc.: — He was a prominent guerrilla and because of that, everybody liked him.

Pr.: — Did he talk with you about nationalistic ideas?

Acc.: — Yes.

Pr.: — Was he an adherent of that movement?

Acc.: — He was the sort of political person of whom it would not be easy to say what was in his mind.

Pr.: — How did you meet with Ciganovic?

Acc.: — He was in the cafe reading the newspaper. After the usual greetings I asked how things were and how he was and I showed him that news of the arrival of Franz Ferdinand in Sarajevo.

Pr.: — Was that the same day or later?

Acc.: — Later.

Pr.: — You carried that clipping with you for two days?

Acc.: — For several days. When my pocket was full, I put it in an envelope. It was in my pocket that day by accident and I showed it to him, and he said to me that was fine only if there were people. I replied that there were people but not the means. To that he replied that we would get the means. I said that two or three more of my friends and I had decided on the assassination, and he said that he would get the means.

Pr.: — How could you say two or three of your friends, when you had only talked with Princip about it?

Acc.: — Princip counted on Ilic whom he had written.

Pr.: — And Grabez had not yet joined you?

Acc.: — The four of us decided to do it ourselves. Princip did not follow our agreement in everything. I did not know that he had written to Ilic to find others. I knew nothing about that.

Pr.: — Did you tell Princip about that meeting with Ciganovic?

Acc.: — Yes. After a long time, I think a month. We met: "Hello." "Hello." "Anything new?" "Nothing." In that way we knew there were no means. He said that he would look in every way. I did not know what was involved. I thought: Nothing is going to come of it. I worked a lot at that time. I worked overtime from seven in the morning to ten in the evening, in order to pay off debts, and I wished first of all to go to Kossovo on St. Vitus' Day[34] and then to travel through the liberated districts and return to Sarajevo. I had just bought clothes, paid my debts, when I found Ciganovic in the *Zirovni Vijenac*. He said: *Sabaile* (a Turkish expression).

Pr.: — What does that mean?

Acc.: — "Early in the morning." He showed me a package of cartridges. He had previously given Grabez and Princip cartridges and a revolver and they had practiced shooting at Topcider (a park near Belgrade).

Pr.: — And you?

Acc.: — Nobody taught me to shoot. Princip and I went to a camp to see which of us was the better shot. I also fired on the firing range of the Belgrade Gun Club. When I got the means for the assassination, they already had them. I got a Browning and six boxes of cartridges and two bombs. Then I went to the typographers' union and took my typographers' book[35] and the day after the following I left.

(The President shows the accused a Browning and one bomb.)

Pr.: — Where did you meet with Princip and Grabez?

Acc.: — In front of the cafe. We sat there because it was a beautiful day. We came to terms.

Pr.: — Were you all of that idea?

Acc.: — We were all sympathetic to the idea of the assasination. We were all hostile toward Austria, and we all wanted Bosnia and Hercegovina to be annexed to Serbia. I wanted a Yugoslav republic.

Pr.: — Of what opinion were Grabez and Princip?

Acc.: — They liked King Petar and wanted to be under his scepter.

Pr.: — Did Grabez say immediately at the first meeting that he would participate in the assassination?

Acc.: — I don't know.

Pr.: — And when did you learn that he would participate?

Acc.: — Princip told me on the occasion of a meeting.

Pr.: — Where did Ciganovic get the Browning and bombs?

Acc.: — Tankosic gave the money for the Browning.

Pr.: — Who bought it?

Acc.: — I think Ciganovic.

Pr.: — Why do you think so?

Acc.: — According to what Ciganovic said.

Pr.: — Had you previously met with Tankosic?

Acc.: — Never.

Pr.: — Did anyone else meet with him?

Acc.: — Grabez.

Pr.: — Why did Grabez go to see him?

Acc.: — One day we sat in front of the cafe and it was decided that one of us go to see him. At first I wanted to go, but because I laugh at the most serious moments and don't have strong features, Princip suggested that Grabez go because he looks solemn.

Pr.: — Did he go alone or with Ciganovic?

Acc.: — When he was at Tankosic's, there were several officers there. Tankosic took him out. Cigo Ciganovic asked him if everything were ready, and when he answered that it was, then he asked about us, about his friends: whether he could rely on us? He said that he trusted everyone as himself. I don't know what Tankosic said to Cigo. That was that visit.

Pr.: — It is astonishing that you decided on the assassination without precise goals.

Acc.: — I figured that the assassination of the Archduke would not have great consequences, that I would be the only one punished.

Pr.: — What was said about Franz Ferdinand in your circles?

Acc.: — That he was a capable man; that he gets results. Somewhere I read that he was involved in the idea of an Austrian federation, and that the Monarchy should annex Serbia and Montenegro. Grabez and Princip wanted all Yogoslavs to be united in one state. I read somewhere that the writer Nenadovic at the time of the Serbo-Trukish war sought help and didn't find it, and he said: "Be damned to any Serb who would believe a Kraut." Schwab, here derogatory: "I am not an adherent of the monarchy. It gravels me when at the head of the monarchy there stands a man who is paid 60,000 daily."

Pr.: — If you had the idea to carry out an assassination on just anyone, you could have done that in Belgrade, and you would not have had to seek the means.

Acc.: — We decided on the assassination of Franz Ferdinand.

Pr.: — I would like to know what you said about that.

Acc.: — We read that he would conduct maneuvers at the beginning of this year in the vicinity of Vienna. Those maneuvers were intended to see how a war which might break out between Russia and Austria might turn out. Then 200 staff officers were demoted and retired, because he found out that they weren't good officers. Subsequently maneuvers in Bosnia were forbidden and we saw that that fellow was working hard.

Pr.: — At what?

Acc.: — To prepare for war with Serbia and Russia.

Pr.: — Did you talk about what might happen in Austria in case of war?

Acc.: — We did not know that there was an organization in Bosnia. But there had to be an organization which would organize a substantial number of Bosnian Serbs everywhere. It would be necessary to supply bombs and dynamite in case of war — before the beginning of war — to raise a revolt, and Serbia would come to Bosnia to restore order.

Pr.: — How did you think that you would take those lands away from Austria?

Acc.: — By war.

Pr.: — Austria is a great empire, it has enough troops to fight Serbia.

Acc.: — Serbia is not as small as you think. You underestimate her.

Pr.: — In the pre-trial hearing you said that Austria was rotten?

Acc.: — An empire which is not national, which suppresses others, cannot be considered as a unit; within it there is no cohesion, there is only discipline. There is only the power of the bayonets.

Pr.: — Is that what you and the other students in the cafes said? What did the Serbs throughout Serbia think?

Acc.: — I haven't been in all of Serbia.

Pr.: — And how can you know that everyone talks like that in Serbia?

Acc.: — By the press, and everyone I met asked about

Bosnia; how we are, and why we are not liberating ourselves. They mocked us. People who knew said that every day 50 military deserters passed into Serbia.

Pr.: — You said that you decided on the assassination for terroristic reasons, and in the pre-trial hearing you said explicitly that you had decided on it because you knew that if he did not exist, Serbia would take over Bosnia more easily.

Acc.: — Anyway I thought: easier without him than with him.

Pr.: — Do any of the honorable judges have anything to ask?

Hoffman: — Did the Crown Prince Aleksandar come to the printing plant?

Acc.: — That was on the 27th of November. He came to see the printing plant at nine o'clock in the evening. Zivojin Dacic showed it to him. The Crown Prince talked with everyone and asked each whether he had been in the war. When he came to me, Dacic said, "That's a Bosnian."

Hoffman: — What did he say to you?

Acc.: — I said that I am a Serb from Bosnia. "From where?" "From Sarajevo." When my turn came, he asked me whether I wanted to stay. I said, "I think not." Nothing more, and he left. It was a conversation of only a few words.

Naumowicz: — Did you know when you talked in the cafe, when it was said: "That is a man," that it meant that he is a good man.

Acc.: — I didn't know that.

Naum.: — When the assassination was planned was there in Belgrade any talk about Misko Jovanovic and Veljko Cubrilovic?

Acc.: — I had never heard of Veljko Cubrilovic.

Premuzic: — Tell me: Did Tankosic in the cafe show you a picture of the late lamented Archduke Franz Ferdinand? Did he say anything?

Acc.: — I can't remember.

Prem.: — Did you read his books about Freemasonry?

Acc.: — As a typesetter I had set the type.

Prem.: — Did you read the book by Cicvaric as to how Serbia would defeat Austria?

Acc.: — Yes.

Prem.: — What sort of faith have you? Are you a deist or
an atheist?

Acc.: — Atheist.

Prem.: — You maintain that there is no God? Are you a
Freemason?

Acc.: — Why do you ask that? I can't tell you.

Pr.: — If you don't say, that means that you are.

Prem.: — Have you heard that Austria is reproached most
because it is Catholic?

Acc.: — Yes.

Prem.: — Would that be true of your circle?

Acc.: — Yes, that the Jesuits have the final word.

Prem.: — Was that taken as a reason that Austria must be
destroyed?

Pr.: — That is a suggestive question.

Prem.: — I wished to complement your question, which
was the true reason for the assassination.

Pr.: — Did you know that Franz Ferdinand was a pious
man?

Acc.: — Yes.

Pr.: — Is that the reason you hated him?

Acc.: — Yes. I knew that his counselor was Father Puntigam
who is present.

Pr.: — That is still not a reason to hate him.

Acc.: — That is proof that he swam in Catholic water, that
he was a chauvinist from head to foot. Because of that he was
not appealing to me.

Pr.: — Some men are not appealing to me either, but nevertheless I will not kill them. Was the fact that he was an en-
thusiastic Catholic incidental or decisive in your decision?

Acc.: — That was incidental. That wasn't the main thing.

Prem.: — Do you know anything about Djoko Bajic's past?
Do you know where he had been before he came to Belgrade?

Acc.: — He travelled several times in Austria, and then he
was in Sarajevo.

Prem.: — Was Vojo Tankosic a Freemason?

Acc.: — Why do you ask about the Freemasons?

Prem.: — An adherent of the Christian doctrine does not
engage in assassination.

Acc.: — He was.

Pres.: — How do you know?

Acc.: — I know positively from the account of Cigo. He is also a Freemason.

Prem.: — How can you positively assert that Cigo and Tankosic were Freemasons?

Acc.: — Tankosic wrote an article against the Serbian government in which he spoke of the assassination.

Prem.: — Was that article signed?

Acc.: — No.

Prem.: — And from whom did you know that Tankosic wrote it?

Acc.: — Cigo told me.

Prem.: — From which it follows that you are also a Freemason?

Acc.: — I did not confirm that. I request that that be passed over. I can't talk about that.

Pres.: — The court will recess until 2:45 this afternoon.

Concluded at 12 o'clock.

CONTINUATION OF THE MAIN HEARING
12 OCTOBER 1914
In the afternoon
THE HEARING OF NEDELJKO CABRINOVIC

Pres.: — We had come to the point when you received the weapons from Ciganovic.

Cabrinovic: — I must supplement the morning's statement with the motives which guided me. I spoke only of the future, and I left out the past. In the first place I was guided by feelings of revenge for all of the injustices which the Serbian people in Bosnia and Hercegovina had suffered, which were imposed on them, such as the "exceptional measures," etc. I was driven by personal motives of revenge. I began to deliberate about the assassination for the first time when I was driven from Sarajevo. I did not like it, that a foreigner who came into our land, could drive me from my home. When I was expelled I was ordered to

go to the lieutenant-governor, Rohony.[36]   I thought that he
would pardon me for the offense for which I had been convicted, but he didn't.   Instead, his secretary read me a moral sermon
on life from his point of view and gave orders to show me the
door.   I was sorry that I didn't have weapons then, I would have
blasted him with all six shots.   Then I began to think about
Zerajic and all the others.   When the "exceptional measures"
were declared I thought even more about an assassination.   I
was sorry in general that such things could happen with the Serbian people in Bosnia.   I considered that revenge was man's
moral duty and thought of sacrificing myself.
     Pr.: — That doesn't conform with your opinion as an anar-
chist? You said that you have no feeling of nationalism.
     Acc.: — I said personal motives.   An anarchist does not
recognize any sort of laws but considers himself chosen for revenge.   I knew from readings and debates that there is a clique
at the Ballplatz which is called the war party, that the chief of
that party was the late Ferdinand, and that it had aspirations to
conquer Serbia and the other Slavic lands.   I thought: having
taken revenge on him, I would also have taken vengeance on all
the others.
     Pr.: — Now you have somewhat shifted the point of view
of the inquiry, because you said that the Serbs had aspirations
toward Bosnia and Hercegovina and you knew that you could
make that easier, and today you say that you wanted to prevent
the conquest of Serbia.
     Acc.: — This refers to the late Ferdinand.   I knew that the
Emperor Franz was at one time a good friend of the Serbian
people under Prince Mihailo, and also the late Rudolf.   In Serbia
I had heard laudatory things about them.
     Pr.: — You decided to carry out the assassination from
your own motives, but official circles in Serbia did help you.
How is that possible?   Ciganovic, Tankosic, Popovic, that other
captain in Loznica, the teacher and others.   All gave you a hand
so that you could transport the arms.
     Acc.: — I didn't know them.
     Pr.: — How is it possible that they placed at your disposi-
tion the means to execute the plan, when you intended to carry
out the assassination for your personal reasons?

Acc.: — I knew neither Tankosic nor Popovic. I had never heard anything about Cubrilovic and Jokovljevic. I had a letter addressed to someone else. I think his name was Sunja,[37] and if he were not there, then for Jakovljevic. I didn't even know those people.

Pr.: — Do you have anything to add concerning the motives?

Acc.: — Ever since I read newspapers, all the injustices which I read about in our newspapers accumulated in me and on St. Vitus' Day all that burst out.

Pr.: — But you decided before St. Vitus' Day.

Acc.: — Yes.

Pr.: — Let's finish the question which the honorable defender put before noon. Did you know before the assassination that Tankosic and Ciganovic were Freemasons? Before you made your decision?

Acc.: — That was after.

Pr.: — Did the fact that they were Freemasons, that is, that you were, play a part in your decision to kill the Heir Apparent?

Acc.: — Yes, that also played a role.

Pr.: — In what sense? Why? Explain this to us. Did you just receive an order from the Freemasons to carry out an assassination?

Acc.: — I didn't receive any kind of order.

Pr.: — Why then did the Freemasons Tankosic and Ciganovic play a role in the assassination?

Acc.: — I did not bring the Freemasons into any kind of connection with the assassination, but confirmed that they were Freemasons.

Pr.: — I ask whether the circumstances that they were Freemasons played a part in the assassination?

Acc.: — Insofar as we are adherents to the Freemasons' ideas.

Pr.: — Does that idea also suggest that one carry out assassinations on authorities, insofar as you know?

Acc.: — It suggests it. Ciganovic himself told me that the late Ferdinand was condemned to death by the Freemasons. He told me that after I made my decision.

Pr.: — Where?

Acc.: — I don't know where.

Pr.: — But nevertheless, did you know that before you decided on the assassination?

Acc.: — Not before, but after.

Pr.: — Did he tell you that at once or several days later when you conveyed to him your wish to carry out an assassination?

Acc.: — We had previously spoken about these things, but he didn't tell me until I had decided to carry out the assassination.

State Prosecutor: — If you permit me the question, in Belgrade did you know the association *Crna ruka* (Black Hand)?[38]

Acc.: — Yes.

Pros.: — What is it?

Acc.: — I don't know for sure. I know only from reading the newspapers that the "Black Hand" exists in officers' circles.

Pros.: — What is its goal?

Acc.: — I don't know.

Pros.: — Do you know that it is a subcommittee of the *Narodna odbrana*?

Acc.: — No.

Pros.: — Do you know a student association in Belgrade of revolutionary character which incites war against Austria?

Acc.: — Mainly there was *Mladost* (Youth), a club in which there were only students.

Pr.: — Do you know the *Narodna odbrana*?

Acc.: — Yes.

Pr.: — What are its goals? Were you a member?

Acc.: — No.

Pr.: — What did you know about the society and its goals?

Acc.: — It is a cultural society which has the task of promoting culture and humanitarianism in the Serbian people. It has also a political character, insofar as it has as a goal the political unification of the Serbian people.

Pr.: — In the opinion of *Narodna odbrana*, how should that unification be promoted?

Acc.: — In a revolutionary manner.

Pr.: — How do you know this? Did one talk about it?

Acc.: — Yes, from talk.

Pr.: — Did you know members of the *Narodna odbrana*?

Acc.: — I don't know whether there is an active membership

as in all other associations. I knew many guerrillas, but I don't know whether they were members, or only adherents.

Pr.: — Is Ciganovic a member?

Acc.: — I don't know about him.

Pr.: — And Tankosic?

Acc.: — He was some kind of functionary.

Pros.: — I will add that he says that he received brochures from the late Major Milan Vasic. Did you read them or not?

Acc.: — Not all. He gave me several, and I read some, but not all.

Pros.: — This is one brochure.

Acc.: — He gave me more of them.

Pros.: — You said this morning that Vasic gave you one brochure from the *Narodna odbrana*, and now you want to say something else, that he gave you more?

Acc.: — Yes.

Pr.: — After you got arms you met with Princip and Grabez and you agreed as to how you would travel. Did you meet with Ciganovic later?

Acc.: — Ciganovic told us how we would travel.

Pr.: — Did he give you some kind of letter?

Acc.: — He gave us a small calling card in a sealed envelope addressed to Captain Rade Popovic in Sabac.

Pr.: — What was written there?

Acc.: — I don't know.

Pr.: — Grabez and Princip say that there was nothing written.

Acc.: — I don't know. Maybe it was some kind of code.

Pr.: — Princip says that there were two letters.

Acc.: — I don't know because it was sealed. Then we departed by steamboat and paid for the tickets. When we got to Sabac we looked for Captain 1st Class Popovic.

Pr.: — Is he in the army, or is he a revenue officer, or a district administrator?

Acc.: — He is in the border guards. We looked for him and found him in a cafe. Then he took us from the cafe to headquarters.

Pr.: — Did you introduce yourselves?

Acc.: — Yes.

Pr.: — What did you tell him?

Acc.: — That we came from Belgrade. We gave him the note. He rose from the table where he was playing cards.

Pr.: — Did you tell him your purpose in coming?

Acc.: — No.

Pr.: — And that you had weapons?

Acc.: — No. Then he bought us railway tickets and we got half-fare tickets for the railway. That was a private railroad. On a state railway they are free.

Pr.: — How could the captain give you half-fare tickets when you didn't say who you were?

Acc.: — He had a calling card.

Pr.: — You say that there was nothing written?

Acc.: — I don't know. It was sealed. Maybe there was some kind of code from which he knew.

Pr.: — Ciganovic was a low-ranking railway clerk. He couldn't give orders for important matters. How then was it that Popovic took you?

Acc.: — I don't know about that. Maybe that was organized in advance, that trip of ours, although I don't know anything about it.

Pr.: — Then you conclude that your passage into Bosnia was organized?

Acc.: — Maybe they agreed, because the day before that the captain was in Belgrade. He told us that. Maybe they told him that we would come. Maybe the code was enough.

Pr.: — Then Popovic gave you a letter for the captain in Loznica. What was his name?

Acc.: — Prvanovic.[39]

Pr.: — Then you three arrived in Loznica. How did Prvanovic receive you?

Acc.: — We brought him the letter.

Pr.: — What was in that letter?

Acc.: — It wasn't open. I know that there were printed letters.

Pr.: — Did he ask you for what purpose you had come?

Acc.: — No. He called some of his sergeants at the neighboring watchtowers. He tried to get a connection, and because he couldn't, he said that we should return tomorrow. When we came the next day, three sergeants also came whom he had summoned, and he asked which of them had the safest passage. The securest was at Grbic's post.[40] Meanwhile, before that I had quarrelled with Princip and Grabez. We were on Koviljaca and I wrote five or six cards, and on one card I wrote a stanza

> Drino vodo plemenita medjo
> Izmedj' Bosne i izmedj' Srbije.
> Naskoro ce i to vrijeme doci,
> Kada cu ja i tebeka preci
> i cestitu Bosnu polaziti.

(Drina water, noble border/Between Bosnia and Serbia./Very soon will that time come/When I will cross thee/And set out to dear Bosnia.)

That is a stanza of Karadjeordje.[41] When Princip read that, he became angry because of my irresponsibility, and we didn't speak again for the entire trip. Then they decided between themselves to push me aside and to take my weapons.

Pr.: — Who first set out from Loznica?

Acc.: — They went first.

Pr.: — Where to?

Acc.: — To Ljesnica. I went to Koviljaca and to Mali Zvornik. First I looked for the revenue director. It seems to me his name is Suna. When he was not there, I went to Jakovljevic and gave him the letter.

Pr.: — Was it open?

Acc.: — It was closed.

Pr.: — Did the captain tell you if you didn't find Suna to go to Jakovljevic?

Acc.: — It was written on the note: Suna or Jakovljevic.

Pr.: — Did you read that letter?

Acc.: — No.

Pr.: — Among the documents which were found at Jakovljevic's, there was found also a letter in which the officer in charge in Loznica says that one should lend a hand to our reliable persons who pass through Mali Zvornik. Is this that letter?

Acc.: — I think that it is. He took me to the watchtower and gave my passport to a soldier to record.

Pr.: — There is exhibited letter X R. 1474/dn. br. 2.

Acc.: — Then we went to a cafe and Jakovljevic treated me to coffee. After we drank coffee, we went back and I took my passport. Then he called a little Moslem child who took us to Veliki Zvornik.

Pr.: — You came to Veliki Zvornik with Jakovljevic. Whom did you find there?

Acc.: — First I went to the guard post and there they took my passport and recorded my arrival in a book. I talked briefly with the gendarme.

Pr.: — Did you introduce yourself?

Acc.: — As Trifko Grabez. At that time Jakovljevic came and we went out. Outside we happened to meet Dakic, the clerk of the commune. Jakovljevic introduced me. Dakic is my relative, but I didn't know that, and we parted and I still did not know.[42]

Pr.: — Did you tell Dakic about your trip and intent?

Acc.: — No.

Pr.: — Did he find you a place to stay overnight?

Acc.: — Yes.

Pr.: — Did he recommend you?

Acc.: — He took me there and there was no one but a little girl. He told me that I could spend the night there.

Pr.: — Did Jakovljevic tell you when he took you to Veliki Zvornik that he would recommend you to Dakic?

Acc.: — No.

Pr.: — Did you know Dakic before?

Acc.: — I did not.

Pr.: — It is surprising that he recommended you precisely to Dakic, who, as it was discovered at the office of the customs officer in charge at Loznica, was really an agent of the Serbian government for the annexation crisis.

Acc.: — I didn't know that.

Pr.: — It is interesting that the connection came from the other side of the Drina.

Acc.: — I admit all that, but it was a completely accidental meeting. We came from one side, and Dakic came from the other. We introduced ourselves, and Jokovljevic asked Dakic to show me a cafe where I might pass the night, and he went back.

Pr.: — And what happened then?

Acc.: — I went to the cafe with Dakic and ordered coffee and supper.

Pros.: — You said that Milan Ciganovic told you that you would go through a tunnel?

Acc.: — Not a tunnel but a channel.

Pr.: — So you would go clear from Belgrade to Sarajevo through a channel?

Acc.: — Yes. There I passed the night and in the morning I went into the town where I again accidentally met Dakic and he told me where the station was and how much the trip from Zvornik to Tuzla cost. Then he went to his office. Meanwhile I did not wait for the stage, but I went on foot and on the way I took a seat in the stage.

Pr.: — Where did you stay overnight in Tuzla?

Acc.: — At Stevo Botic's.[43]

Pr.: — Did you have a letter?

Acc.: — Yes, from Grabez.

Pr.: — Did you tell him why you came?

Acc.: — No.

Pr.: — How many days did you spend in Tuzla?

Acc.: — Three days.

Pr.: — Did Ciganovic tell you anything about Misko Jovanovic?

Acc.: — No, nothing.

Pr.: — Did you see Grabez and Princip?

Acc.: — We met after two days.

Pr.: — Did they tell you where the weapons were?

Acc.: — No. We had quarrelled previously and they didn't trust me.

Pr.: — Then you travelled with them and on the railway you met a detective?[44]

Acc.: — Yes, already in the cafe, and he told me that just yesterday he had been with my father and talked with him.

Pr.: — Did he know that you had been expelled from Sarajevo?

Acc.: — I don't know. He told me that there were great preparations for the arrival of the Heir Apparent. I asked when he would come, and he said on the 28th of June. Til that moment I did not know when he would come. When I reached Sarajevo we separated. Grabez and Princip left together, and I went home.

Pr.: — Had you agreed as to where you would receive the weapons?

Acc.: — No. Princip wished to say nothing at all about that and didn't trust me. Whenever I said something about that to him, he always replied, "Shut up." Then we met three or four times in Sarajevo.

Pr.: — Did you talk about the assassination?

Acc.: — We did. But he did not tell me where the weapons were and I thought that there would not be an assassination.

Pr.: — Did you meet with Ilic?

Acc.: — Yes.

Pr.: — Did you talk about the assassination?

Acc.: — Yes.

Pr.: — Did he tell you that he had the weapons?

Acc.: — No.

Pr.: — Did he tell you that there were still others?

Acc.: — No.

Pr.: — How did you come to terms on the eve of the assassination?

Acc.: — Just two days before the assassination Princip and I met and he told me that there would be an assassination and told me to find him at Ilic's, that he would be in the editorial offices of *Zvono*. I went there, but there was no one there. Then we met. I looked for him in the *Srpska citaonica* (Serbian Reading-room) and we met about nine o'clock in the evening. Then he told me that he would give me a bomb in the morning, that I should come to Vlajnic's.[45] Then I came in the morning and got a bomb and cyanide.

Pr.: — What was the cyanide for and who recommended it to you?

Acc.: — Ciganovic. He said that it was very strong poison and that it could kill. Thus if we did not succeed we should kill ourselves.

Pr.: — Did he say that you had to kill yourselves?

Acc.: — We had decided that we would kill ourselves. Thus he told us that if we did not succeed that we should kill ourselves, that we should poison ourselves. I took a double dose and for several days after the assassination I couldn't eat. It made me sick, but it didn't work.

Pr.: — From whom did you get weapons?

Acc.: — From Ilic on the morning of St. Vitus' Day.

Pr.: — Did you meet Princip the day before?

Acc.: — Princip came to me in the printing plant and told me that we would meet in the evening. When we met, we went from the *Vereinshaus* (Social Hall)[46] to the Teacher's School. He told me that one person would stand before me below the Teacher's School and that I would be at the Bank,[47] that I should stand a little higher, and that the others were all lined up.

Pr.: — Did he tell you then that there were more?

Acc.: — Yes.

Pr.: — Did you know that Ilic would not participate?

Acc.: — No, I did not.

Pr.: — Clear up to the day of the assassination?

Acc.: — I did not.

Pr.: — How was it before the assassination?

Acc.: — I walked from the Austro-Hungarian Bank to the bridge.

Pr.: — Before that did you have a picture made of yourself?

Acc.: — Yes, so that something would remain of me.

Pr.: — Why did you give a false address in Zagreb to which to send the picture and who is the addressee?

Acc.: — It doesn't exist.[48]

Pr.: — What purpose did it serve to have the picture taken there?

Acc.: — I said that the person who had his picture taken with me should not take it.

Pr.: — You had money with you. Where did you get it?

Acc.: — I earned it. I gave grandma 20 crowns and my sister five.

Pr.: — What did you say on this occasion?

Acc.: — I gave it to grandma because I love her and because I promised her that I would help her. She used to give me money when I had none. She said, "Five forints is enough for me," but I gave her 20 crowns. I told my sister that I was going on a trip, that we would not see each other any more. I went and changed five forints, gave her five crowns, and she left. I remained there crying.

Pr.: — Why?

Acc.: — I was sorry for them.

Pr.: — You did not feel sorry for your father?

Acc.: — I felt sorry for all of them.

Pr.: — I could show you a letter from your father in which he complains about you.

Acc.: — I have not been satisfied with him either, and the raising he gave me brought me to this. But again I feel sorry for him.

Pr.: — How was it before the assassination?

Acc.: — I was strolling between the Austro-Hungarian Bank and the bridge. In order not to be obvious I took long strolls, because there were many detectives and spies. I chose a place where there wouldn't be many people. I was determined to kill only him.

Pr.: — You said that you don't like to lie, but in this case you didn't tell the truth. You knew that when the bomb exploded she would die too.

Acc.: — We were determined to kill only him, but if that were not possible, then we would sacrifice her and all the others. I did not know that there would be some from his escort. I thought that there would be only Potiorek, and his wife and him and that he would be killed. I didn't know that there were still others. When they approached I was pretty far from the others.

Pr.: — Were you on the sunny side of the Miljacka river?

Acc.: — Yes. I was about 20 paces further so I wouldn't hurt others, and I couldn't go any further. I had to stand by a lamppost in order to arm the bomb.

Pr.: — Did you unscrew the bomb before?

Acc.: — Yes. Then I hid it behind my belt and I held it with my hand all the time. When he approached I saw only a green cap and nothing else. I hit the bomb against the lamppost. It broke and I threw it.

Pr.: — When you struck it against the lamppost did it sound like a shot?

Acc.: — Yes. Like a weak shot. I threw it and then I saw

how the late Ferdinand turned toward me and looked at me with a cold, inflexible gaze. At that moment the bomb fell on the folded roof of the automobile, bounced off the automobile and fell on the ground. I turned around, took the poison, and jumped into the Miljacka.

Pr.: — You took the poison there above?

Acc.: — Yes.

Pr.: — Did you have a revolver?

Acc.: — No.

Pr.: — So then they caught you?

Acc.: — Yes.

Pr.: — Do you know that because of your bomb many people suffered?

Acc.: — I heard, and I am very sorry. I never intended to hurt them too.

Pr.: — You should have foreseen that when a bomb bursts everybody in the vicinity would be wounded.

Acc.: — I stood pretty far away and I intended to go still further, but it was too late, and so I could not go further.

Pr.: — Are you sorry that you were involved in this affair?

Acc.: — I would be very happy if I could say that I am not sorry. But this brought with it unanticipated consequences which no one could in any way have foreseen. If I had foreseen it I would have sat on those bombs, so that they would have blown me to pieces.

Pr.: — You feel sorry with regard to the others, but are you sorry with regard to your victims?

Acc.: — I didn't kill him and I console myself with that.

Pr.: — But you were in the conspiracy?

Acc.: — Yes, but again I console myself. I am glad that the bombs did not explode by my will. I was already sorry when I heard that there were many arrests. I thought that would have only the same consequences as under the "exceptional measures."

Pr.: — Did you not expect that after this assassination Serbia would occupy Bosnia and Hercegovina, if you did away with the best military leader, who according to your opinion was like Napoleon?

Acc.: — To the question of the honorable investigating judge: "Did you think that Serbia could seize Bosnia and

Hercegovina more easily if there were no Heir Apparent Ferdinand?", I replied that I thought so. But I was never of the opinion that Serbia could take Bosnia and Hercegovina easily. Serbia would not get Bosnia and Hercegovina after the assassination. As soon as I was jailed and saw what kind of consequences the assassination brought, I was sorry. Only for that reason I remained silent and did not want to betray the culprits. I am very pleased that there is no one in the prisoner's dock because of me.

Pr.: — Let's go back to the late Major Vasic. You said that he was in the *Narodna odbrana* and received you. Here you said that Vasic played some role in Sarajevo. Do you know whether he had ever been here?

Acc.: — I heard by accounts in Serbia that he was a Serbian spy here, that he had been a waiter and that he carried stones to the fortresses.

Pr.: — He was in the *Narodna odbrana*?

Acc.: — Yes, he was the secretary.

Pr.: — When you passed through Sabac, did you notice anything unusual in Sabac, any movements of the Serbian army?

Acc.: — There was mobilization.

Pr.: — Was that only in Sabac, or in all of Serbia?

Acc.: — Everything moved to Sabac. That was the Drina division.

Pr.: — How did you know that there was a mobilization?

Acc.: — I knew because there were people travelling with me who were going to report to the headquarters.

Pr.: — That was at the end of May?

Acc.: — Yes, the 28th of May.

Pr.: — Did you talk in the train with those who were called up, as to why they were mobilized?

Acc.: — We knew that there was a confused situation and that the Bulgarians threatened to attack in the spring. They went to Sabac to the headquarters in order to arm themselves.

Pr.: — So they armed themselves against Bulgaria? Were there "exceptional measures" also in Loznica and Ljesnica?

Acc.: — None.

Pr.: — You say that you were not very interested in the fact that Austria would be weakened by that assassination and that Serbia would acquire Bosnia and Hercegovina, but you also explicitly said as follows: "The Heir Apparent is ready and capable. Such an assassination is a precursor of revolution, and one revolution would be enough to annihilate Austria."

Acc.: — Yes.

Pr.: — You see that in your opinion the assassination is closely connected with the collapse of Austria.

Acc.: — That is not so. I asked myself: why are there no assassinations in France, Germany and England? Why only in Austria?

Pr.: — In Austria there were none of them.

Acc.: — Look, in Poland there was Sicinski; in Sarajevo, Zerajic, and then Jukic, Dojcic, Njegus.[49] Here I know of five or six assassinations.

Pr.: — Also in Italy King Humbert was killed.

Acc.: — Those were rare occasions. The Greek king was also killed, but that was one assassination, and here there are six from all parts of the country. I compared Austria with Poland. In Poland also before the revolution there were assassinations and espionage affairs.

Pr.: — So you had the notion that Austria could be broken up because of the assassinations. That was the beginning?

Acc.: — She couldn't because of the assassinations.

Counsellor Naumowicz: — You said that Ciganovic gave you cyanide to poison yourself. What was the purpose of poisoning yourself after the assassination?

Acc.: — In the first place I thought that I could not live as a slave, although I did not know that the law protects me as a minor. But I could not be a slave one single day.

Naumowicz: — How was it that it was Ciganovic that gave you the cyanide?

Acc.: — He did that for other reasons; maybe so that one would not reveal the other participants.

Naum.: — What do you care if Ciganovic is known to have a hand in the assassination?

Acc.: — That is not the same. He would suffer consequences.

Naum.: — In what way?

Acc.: — Maybe arrest. For now, if there were no war, he

would be arrested and handed over to Austria.

Naum.: — He certainly cared that nothing be known about that. Because of that he gave you cyanide.

Counsellor Hoffman: — You said that Dakic was your relative. How come you did not visit him at home?

Acc.: — I didn't know him. Only in Sarajevo did I learn that I have a relative in Zvornik who is a clerk of the commune.

Hoffman: — You visited him and did not tell him of your purpose?

Acc.: — He was a clerk of the commune. How did I know who he was? I couldn't tell him anything. It was the first time I met him.

Hoffman: — In the morning you said that you are an anarchist, and Princip a nationalist. You said that you got a clipping from a newspaper that the Heir Apparent was coming, that you did not intend to carry out an assassination at that time, and then Princip came and said that you would do it. You said that you were not connected with Princip before, that actually you knew him only by sight.

Acc.: — Who said that? We were acquainted.

Hoffman: — Did you talk about these things?

Acc.: — In the cafe.

Hoffman: — With whom were you more friendly than with Princip?

Acc.: — Princip was my closest friend.

Hoffman: — Who else was your friend?

Pr.: — Is there still another student who is an intermediary?

Acc.: — That is Djulaga Bukovac;[50] he did not mediate among us.

Hoffman: — You said that you agreed when Princip said that he would carry out an assassination. Then you later said that you did not have it in mind to kill the Heir Apparent because you were an anarchist.

Acc.: — I said it, of course. I just wanted to kill him.

Hoffman: — Why?

Acc.: — I wanted to kill him out of vengeance.

Pros.: — Tell us why you did not contact the *Narodna odbrana* when you were in Belgrade in 1912?

Acc.: — Up to then I did not know anything about the

Narodna odbrana, only that a member in the *Zeleni Vijenac* suggested that if I pay him a liter of *rakija* (native brandy) that he would take me there.

Pros.: — Didn't you know that it would give you financial support?

Acc.: — No.

Pr.: — You don't know where the bombs came from?

Acc.: — No.

Pr.: — You didn't know that they came from Kragujevac?[51]

Acc.: — I didn't know.

Pr.: — I don't understand about this Djoko Bajic. You said that you were afraid that he was a spy and that he was paid because he didn't work, and on the other hand that he incited you to the assassination. Wasn't he an *agent provocateur*?

Acc.: — In any case there was something mysterious about him. I didn't know, but I thought that he was an Austrian spy.

Pr.: — If he had been an Austrian spy he would have alerted us and there would have been no assassination.

Acc.: — Maybe he didn't know. I said that I was going to Skoplje, and Princip said that he was going into a monastery to prepare for the final examinations.

Pr.: — Did you get acquainted with Boza Milanovic[52] in Sabac?

Acc.: — No.

Pr.: — Did you hear of him?

Acc.: — He is an agent of the *Narodna odbrana* and a businessman.

Pr.: — Didn't you hear that he also has another occupation? Did you know that he was the center of all espionage in Bosnia?

Acc.: — I didn't know. We were in need of money when we were in Sabac and we figured: how would it be to turn to him? But we didn't because he didn't know us, nor did we know him, and we did not have a letter from the *Narodna odbrana* and therefore we didn't even report to him.

Pr.: — Did you meet with Grabez before the assassination?

Acc.: — I don't know how many days before. I was sitting in front of my house when he passed by. We greeted each other and he told me where he was going, to his home at Pale, and nothing else.

Dr. Feldbauer: — You said before the investigating judge that some third person influenced Princip to carry out the assassination.

Acc.: — I don't remember.

Feldb.: — Do you know who that third person was? You, as an intimate friend of Princip's, do you know who influenced him to carry out the assassination?

Acc.: — Our whole association.

Feldb.: — Do you know some kind of living person with whom Princip associated and who had some kind of influence on him? Did Princip later say to you: so and so talked me into it?

Acc.: — After our decision they influenced us.

Pr.: — Who?

Acc.: — Ciganovic and Djuro Sarac.[53]

Pr.: — Who is he?

Acc.: — He finished the seminary. And besides that, the Moslem Djulaga Bukovac.

Pr.: — Did you speak openly in the cafe?

Acc.: — Not with Bukovac, but with Sarac.

Pr.: — Was there anyone else present?

Acc.: — No.

Feldb.: — Were you aware that this was an influence?

Acc.: — No.

Pr.: — You said earlier that the first time, when you showed the clipping from the newspapers, Ciganovic said, "Here is a chance!"

Acc.: — Yes.

Pr.: — Then he was the first to give the stimulus for the assassination?

Acc.: — But we already had decided.

Malek: — On Saturday on the eve of the assassination did Princip or Ilic tell you where Ilic would stand?

Acc.: — No.

Malek: — Did you know for sure on Saturday that Ilic would participate actively?

Acc.: — No.

Malek: — You know Ilic. What were his opinions?

Acc.: — He had socialistic ideas. Princip once said that he

was afraid that Ilic would turn into a socialist.

Malek: — Ilic worked as a journalist. Did you read anything he wrote?

Acc.: — He wrote lead editorials in *Zvono*.

Malek: — Was that concerned with politics?

Acc.: — No.

Malek: — Did you hear that any article that he wrote was confiscated?

Acc.: — No.

Malek: — When you were in Belgrade, did anyone ask you about Ilic? For instance, Ciganovic?

Acc.: — Nobody.

Malek: — Did nobody mention him?

Acc.: — No.

Malek: — Did you read the letter which Princip wrote to Ilic?

Acc.: — No.

Malek: — Did Princip receive any kind of answer to that?

Acc.: — I don't know.

Malek: — Was it Princip's idea or yours to invite Ilic to participate?

Acc.: — They were close friends.

Malek: — At one place in the hearing you said that Princip told you while you were still in Belgrade that Ilic seemed to him to be unreliable, that he didn't trust him at all.

Acc.: — Princip told me that when we came to Sarajevo. I asked him what's wrong with Ilic, and he answered, "It seems to me that Ilic is a snob."

Malek: — You said that during your stay in Sarajevo that you complained to Ilic as to when the assassination would be, and Ilic answered: "There's time."

Acc.: — He said, "There's time. We'll meet."

Malek: — Did you think that Ilic himself decided on the assassination?

Acc.: — No.

Malek: — It is important that you didn't think that Ilic was a participant.

Acc.: — Yes.

Pr.: — Earlier he said that the fourth would be Ilic.

Acc.: — In Belgrade we thought that there would be four of us, namely: Princip, me, Grabez, and Ilic.

Pr.: — In Belgrade you believed that there was also Ilic.

Acc.: — I knew that Princip had written him about that.

Malek: — In the inquiry he said that he thought there would be four. Now he says that he didn't know whether there would be Ilic also. Were you convinced that Ilic would be with you?

Acc.: — I wasn't.

Prem.: — In the papers which circulated among the youth in Sarajevo did you find anything which was of decisive importance for your intentions?

Acc.: — I found only *Smrt jednoga heroja* (Death of a Hero),[54] namely Zerajic's, and then there were still more papers which I don't remember.

Pr.: — So Zerajic was your model?

Acc.: — Yes.

Prem.: — You told me when we talked about *Zora* (Dawn) that just then you wavered.

Acc.: — Yes.

Pr.: — I would ask that the accused tell us that content from *Zora*.

Acc.: — In one place a young Serbian professor killed himself. That was foolish, because with his own life he could have killed at least one enemy. When he decided to do so, he should have killed at least one enemy.[55]

Pr.: — Have you been in such a position that you would kill yourself? Did the idea of that ever come to you?

Acc.: — Yes.

Prem.: — I request that the way in which he was raised be taken into consideration.

Acc.: — Something else. They talk about Jesus and the Christian faith. Here they say: "Love your enemies. Whoever throws a stone at you, give him bread," and there they say: "Hate your enemies, and to whomever throws a stone at you, repay him more."

Pr.: — What is that *Zora*?

Prem.: — A paper which appeared in Prague in 1912.

Pr.: — Who edits it?

Prem.: — There are several of them.

Pr.: — What is its orientation?

Prem.: — Purely Freemason. Its intention is to poison young people.

Naumowicz: — What did you understand by it when Princip said of Ilic that he was a "snob," that he would not participate in the assassination?

Acc.: — That is said of someone a little higher, who holds himself a little higher.

Pr.: — The hearing is recessed for five minutes.

After the recess

Pros.: — Before noon you said that because of weapons you wanted to turn to the *Narodna odbrana*.

Acc.: — To get weapons.

Pros.: — How is it that *Narodna odbrana* gives arms?

Acc.: — Because we thought that they would give us means for the assassination.

Pr.: — Why just the *Narodna odbrana*?

Acc.: — We turned to them, whether they gave or not.

Pros.: — How come it gives arms for assassinations?

Acc.: — The *Narodna odbrana*, besides having a cultural orientation, has also a revolutionary one. It is a revolutionary organization.

Pros.: — What kind of revolution does it promote?

Acc.: — I don't know the details.

Pros.: — But you have to know at least something.

Acc.: — We assumed that the *Narodna odbrana* would give us the means for the assassination, so we thought to go there and ask.

Pros.: — Why did you turn to the *Narodna odbrana*? Does it have weapons at its disposition?

Acc.: — Yes. It organized guerrilla bands.

Pros.: — From where does the *Narodna odbrana* get weapons?

Acc.: — I don't know that, but I know that the *Narodna odbrana* prepared guerrilla bands for the Balkan wars.

Pros.: — Who gave it weapons? Do you know?

Acc.: — I don't know.

Pros.: — So you turned to the *Narodna odbrana*? But would you have to say that you would carry out an assassination?

Acc.: — We would.

Pros.: — Do you think it would have agreed to this?

Acc.: — I don't know. We assumed so.

Pros.: — Was there perhaps talk in the *Zeleni Vijenac* that the *Narodna odbrana* would give arms?

Acc.: — Yes, Djoko Bajic said so.

Pros.: — Let it be noted that they contacted the *Narodna odbrana*.

Acc.: — We did not contact them.

Pros.: — That you wanted to turn to them in order that they give you weapons because it has revolutionary goals. Djoko Bajic said that one could find weapons there.

Acc.: — Djoko Bajic said if we wanted to do it. For example, when I told him about Nastic, that I would very much like to kill him, he said to me, "Don't do it, I will take you to the *Narodna odbrana* and there you will get weapons." But we did not know for sure.

Perisic: — Did you know Cvjetko Popovic? (Yes.) You didn't see him when you came to Sarajevo? (No.) Where did you receive the bombs?

Acc.: — At Vlajnic's.

Pr.: — Who was there?

Acc.: — Ilic, Princip, and Grabez.

Perisic: — So he[56] wasn't there? (No.)

Malek: — And did you know Lazar Djukic? (No.) Why did you do the assassination with a bomb? Why didn't they give you a Browning?

Acc.: — That was the arrangement.

Malek: — Or was it because you were not well-trained?

Acc.: — With a Browning I would have to commit suicide, and I knew that.

Malek: — Did you practice? (No.) Didn't you practice with the bombs? Didn't you read the instructions?

Acc.: — I talked about it.

Malek: — Is it possible that someone who had no instruction would undertake an assassination with bombs?

Acc.: — It's possible.

THE HEARING OF GAVRILO PRINCIP
12 OCTOBER 1914
In the afternoon

Pr.: — Call Gavrilo Princip. (He is brought in.) Do you consider yourself guilty?

Acc.: — I am not a criminal, because I destroyed that which was evil. I think that I am good.

Pr.: — And what about her?

Acc.: — I did not wish to kill her, I killed her accidentally.

Pr.: — So you don't consider yourself guilty? (No.) Then tell us in detail from the beginning how you developed your ideas of killing the Heir Apparent. To begin, what schools did you attend?

Acc.: — Three classes of the Business School, then I passed an examination for the fourth class of the gymnasium and then I was here and in Tuzla for some time.

Pr.: — Which years?

Acc.: — More than four years ago.

Pr.: — Did you fail?

Acc.: — No, rather in Tuzla I passed the examination from the Business School into the gymnasium. I came here from Tuzla.

Pr.: — How long did you study here at the gymnasium?

Acc.: — I attended the fifth class here for two months, then I was sick for two months and continued as a private student. I did not wish to take the examinations here, so I went to Belgrade.

Pr.: — Why?

Acc.: — That is my private affair.

Pr.: — Did you have the means to go?

Acc.: — No, nor did I have the means to maintain myself here. I always lived on credit and therefore I went there. Then in Belgrade I continued as a private student and I finished the fifth, sixth, and seventh classes. I wished to attend the eighth class this winter, but in the meantime I wanted to carry out the assassination and I returned to Sarajevo and did it. Ask whatever you wish.

Pr.: — Tell us your life story. Where you worked, what your thoughts were and so on. In which year did you go to Belgrade?

Acc.: — In May of 1912.

Pr.: — Did you pass your examinations right away?

Acc.: — I did not pass the examinations that year.

Pr.: — Did you enlist in the guerrilla bands that year?

Acc.: — I went when the Balkan war broke out.

Pr.: — To which one?

Acc.: — To the *Narodna odbrana*.

Pr.: — Who was that? To whom did you go?

Acc.: — There was some secretary, I don't remember who, who was registering.

Pr.: — Did he accept you?

Acc.: — The late Major Milan Vasic accepted me. Then I went to Prokuplje near the border and there I trained for some time under arms. At the time they decided on those who should go across the border, I became ill and they rejected me.

Pr.: — Then you returned to Belgrade? How did you live?

Acc.: — My father and brother sent me money.

Pr.: — Did you father know that you would join the guerrillas?

Acc.: — I was with them for some time.

Pr.: — Then you returned from Belgrade to Hadzici.[57] How long did you stay in Hadzici?

Acc.: — I was there until March of last year.

Pr.: — Did you study?

Acc.: — I took some books and prepared myself for the examinations for the fifth and sixth classes.

Pr.: — Could one take both examinations at once?

Acc.: — One could take three or four. It was possible to take two examinations at one time.

Pr.: — Here you left from the fifth class. Why did you leave the Sarajevo gymnasium?

Acc.: — I was sick for a month.

Pr.: — Did you have some sort of clash with the teachers?

Acc.: — No.

Pr.: — You returned to Belgrade in Serbia and took an examination; for which class?

Acc.: — For the fifth and sixth, and then I was in Belgrade for three months and at the end of the year I passed the examination for the seventh class. Then I returned to Hadzici in October. I was there in Hadzici until February last winter, and I studied for the eighth class, and then I came back for the eighth class.

Pr.: — What did you read aside from the prescribed subjects? Did you concern yourself with politics and journalism?

Acc.: — No.

Pr.: — What kind of ideas did you have?

Acc.: — I am a Yugoslav nationalist and I believe in the unification of all South Slavs in whatever form of state and that it be free of Austria.

Pr.: — That was your aspiration. How did you think to realize it?

Acc.: — By means of terror.

Pr.: — What does that signify?

Acc.: — That means in general to destroy from above, to do away with those who obstruct and do evil, who stand in the way of the idea of unification.

Pr.: — How did you think that you might realize your objectives?

Acc.: — Still another principal motive was revenge for all torments which Austria imposed upon the people.

Pr.: — Then in March you were again in Belgrade. Did you study for the eighth class then? Which cafe did you frequent?

Acc.: — The *Pozorisna Kafana* (Theater Cafe), *Zirovni Venac*, and (the cafe) *Amerika*.

Pr.: — Were there other students there?

Acc.: — There were Bosnians.

Pr.: — What was their thinking?

Acc.: — For the most part they were nationalists.

Pr.: — Then, they were all of the same opinions as yourself?

Acc.: — Not all exactly like myself. It was not necessary for all to be of the same opinions in the carrying out of his own ideas, nor was it necessary that everyone employ the same means.

Pr.: — What was the feeling about Austria in your circles?

Acc.: — It was the opinion that Austria behaved badly to our people, which is true, and certainly that she (Austria) is not necessary.

Pr.: — What was the opinion about Serbia, that it would be to the advantage of Bosnia to be annexed to Serbia?

Acc.: — The plan was to unite all South Slavs. It was understood that Serbia as the free part of the South Slavs had the moral duty to help with the unification, to be to the South Slavs as the Piedmont was to Italy.

Pr.: — Tell me now, when did you first learn that the late Heir Apparent would come to Sarajevo?

Acc.: — When I came to Belgrade in the month of March I read it in the newspapers. I think the German ones.

Pr.: — Did you then come up with the idea of carrying out an assassination?

Acc.: — Yes.

Pr.: — Was that before you spoke with Cabrinovic?

Acc.: — Yes, before.

Pr.: — How long before?

Acc.: — A few days before. Then I talked with him later because I knew that we were of the same opinions. I said, "How about arranging an assassination?" — after which he showed me some newspaper clippings.

Pr.: — What was in those clippings?

Acc.: — They confirmed the news that the Heir Apparent was coming to Bosnia. At that we definitely decided to carry out the assassination.

Pr.: — But for the assassination you needed the means?

Acc.: — We thought about how to obtain them. If there were no means at all, we might at least manage to buy a revolver.

Pr.: — To whom did you turn?

Acc.: — We spoke about the *Narodna odbrana*, but we knew that they would not give us the means because we were not known there.

Pr.: — To whom did you apply to get arms?

Acc.: — Then I tried to turn to someone in order to become acquainted with Ciganovic. I had known him earlier, but not well enough to speak of the assassination. Thus Bukovac introduced me, and I told Ciganovic what I wished to do, but that I did not have the means. I asked him to give us bombs because I knew he had them, and that we would take care of the revolvers ourselves. He was quiet for a while and then he said, "We'll see." In the main he agreed at once to give them to me.

Pr.: — Did you mention the purpose?

Acc.: — Yes. He agreed completely.

Pr.: — What was Ciganovic?

Acc.: — A railway clerk.

Pr.: — How was it possible for a railway clerk to agree at once to an assassination?

Acc.: — He was a refugee from Bosnia, and visited those cafes. He was a Serb.

Pr.: — Do you think that it is enough that a man be a Serb and right away be an enemy of Austria?

Acc.: — In my opinion every Serb, Croat and Slovene should be an enemy of Austria.

Pr.: — But enough to give arms at once? How come Ciganovic agreed at once? Had you ever before discussed with him the necessity of carrying out an assassination?

Acc.: — I had never discussed an assassination, but I had talked about the situation of the people and on conditions in Bosnia and in general in Austria. I had never been intimate enough with him to make it possible for me to talk about carrying out an assassination.

Pr.: — Tell us more.

Acc.: — After some time Ciganovic said to me that he would give me bombs. Because those bombs exploded after several seconds, success with them was not certain. I told him that we needed revolvers. He told me to take care of that ourselves, but because I am poor he would see to supplying arms. He told me that he would see to it later. I don't know how he came to that. I don't know what he said to Tankosic.

Pr.: — And Tankosic knew about the assassination?

Acc.: — I don't know. I think Ciganovic talked with him.

Pr.: — What about Grabez?

Acc.: — Ciganovic said that Tankosic summoned him.

Pr.: — Did Grabez not tell you?

Acc.: — Yes. He said that he was interested but that

Tankosic made a bad impression on him. Tankosic sent for one of us, and we decided that Grabez would go.

Pr.: — Why did Tankosic send for you?

Acc.: — To see whether we were capable. For the rest, I have told all before. It is inconvenient for me to talk when I am standing here.

Pr.: — Then when Grabez was at Tankosic's, did he say what Tankosic asked him?

Acc.: — I don't remember.

Pr.: — What did Grabez think about the whole thing? How did he come to decide in favor of the assassination?

Acc.: — He was of the same opinion as we. We studied together and so on, and we knew each other.

Pr.: — Yet when he returned, he said that Tankosic had not made the best impression on him? When did you receive the bombs and revolvers?

Acc.: — Before our departure.

Pr.: — Had you ever before had a bomb and revolver in your hands?

Acc.: — I examined them when I was at Ciganovic's.

Pr.: — How many bombs did Ciganovic have?

Acc.: — He had about twelve pieces before the Bulgarian war (1913).

Pr.: — Had you ever fired?

Acc.: — I had in Prokuplje and Belgrade. I had trained with Brownings on the Drina frontier and at Topcider.

Pr.: — Who took you there?

Acc.: — Ciganovic.

Pr.: — Was Grabez there? (Yes.) Cabrinovic? (No.) When did you leave Belgrade?

Acc.: — On Ascension Day (28 May 1914, N.S.).

Pr.: — How many days before that did he give you the bombs and revolvers?

Acc.: — Two days before.

Pr.: — Did you receive money?

Acc.: — I got 150 dinars from Ciganovic.

Pr.: — Did he tell you, or did you already know yourself where you would go?

Acc.: — He didn't have to tell me, I had passed out of

Serbia several times.

Pr.: — You knew which way you would go?

Acc.: — I did not know where we would cross the Drina, but I knew that we would go to Loznica. I asked him, and he told me that he did not know how, but that he would send us to a Captain Popovic at Sabac.

Pr.: — Did he send you there?

Acc.: — Yes, he said that we should ask him to put us across somewhere. He gave us a note with two initials. I don't know which they were. I think M.C., the initial letter of his name and surname.

Pr.: — Was the note open or sealed?

Acc.: — Open in a small envelope. I stuck it in my pocket.

Pr.: — Did you travel together?

Acc.: — We did.

Pr.: — What happened when you got to Sabac?

Acc.: — Then we looked up the captain and found him at a cafe. We went with him to the headquarters and he said to us, "You can go across at Klenak." I told him that we had reasons not to. He shrugged his shoulders and said, "I don't know another place, but I can send you to the captain of the border guards." Before that he gave us a railway pass and he gave us a short letter to the captain in Loznica. He asked him to receive us and give us a hand. We stayed overnight in Sabac, and then in the morning at 7 o'clock we went to the railway station and got a discount ticket for the trip.

Pr.: — Were the transit permits he gave you issued in your own names or false ones?

Acc.: — In the name of some revenue official.

Pr.: — Then when you got to Loznica you showed your permits?

Acc.: — We said that we were Bosnian students, but we did not give our names.

Pr.: — Did you show the letter?

Acc.: — He asked what we wanted. The letter said: "Receive these people and see that you help them." He asked us where we were going and we kept quiet and said that we wanted to go to Bosnia, and he said we could easily get across. We said that we had to go across unobserved, because otherwise the gendarmes would arrest us. He said that he didn't know a way, but that he would call the revenue officers to ask whether it was possible. He called them on the telephone and told us to come tomorrow. We said our good-byes and went into the market. Then the next day we went together to the captain and the revenue officials came. The two of them said that we could not safely cross over with them, but one said that he would find a peasant who could pass us over unobserved. Before we had gone to the captain we went with the revenue officers to an inn and there we had decided that Cabrinovic would cross at Mali Zvornik without arms.

Pr.: — Why?

Acc.: — Because he had a passport.

Pr.: — You hadn't quarreled.

Acc.: — No. That was a normal quarrel, friendly. So he went to Mali Zvornik. We sat with Grbic in a cart and went to Loznica to the guardhouse and spent the night there. In the morning we passed over the Drina at Isakovic's Island and fired the revolver. There at the guardhouse we fired too.

Pr.: — At that island did you find some sort of hut?

Acc.: — We spent the night with some peasant named Milan.

Pr.: — Did you find another peasant? Was Grbic with you?

Acc.: — Yes. Later someone came whom we learned was called Micic. Grbic talked some with him, saying that we wished to pass over unobserved. He said that he would get us a cart, and we said that we could not use a cart, because we wished to pass over unobserved. He didn't know what to answer. Then he said that he would send us a peasant named Jakov Milovic. He promised that he would call him. Meanwhile Grbic said to him when he left, "See to it that this remains a secret; otherwise you will lose your heads." Then Micic left, and later the pair returned. We were there then. Grbic asked Milovic whether we could pass over, and he said that he could take us across.

Pr.: — Did you ask Milovic to take you directly to Tuzla? Did you speak of one Misko?

Acc.: — No.

Pr.: — Did not Ciganovic say in Belgrade that you should go to Misko?

Acc.: — No. I knew nothing positively of it at that time;

besides, I had known him at Tuzla. Then in the evening when it turned dark we crossed the border. Milovic and Micic were with us. Grabez and I carried arms. The weather was damp and we wandered across several fields. What time it was when we got to his house, I don't know. After a while Micic left without saying good-bye. He left unobserved. Then Jakov went with us. We came to his house and there we rested. Then we turned toward some woods and we hardly came out of them because it was dark and we passed the night in a hut on the edge of the forest.

Pr.: — There was no one in the hut?

Acc.: — No. It was an ordinary stable.

Pr.: — Did you set out by day or by night?

Acc.: — By day.

Pr.: — Presumably secretly?

Acc.: — Not exactly secretly, but not by an open road either. Then we came to Obren, and Jakov went to see who was at home. There was no one there. We waited. It was cold and we went into the house. There they offered us coffee, and because we had heavy things, each of us had two bombs and two revolvers, we asked for bags. It was hard for us to decide to show our arms. We wrapped the weapons in the rags.

Pr.: — Did Obren Milosevic see the weapons?

Acc.: — I think not. I said, "You can't tell anyone that we have passed, otherwise your house will be destroyed." Those words were not intended seriously. I did not believe that anything would happen to them. I knew that it would work on him when he was threatened. Then all three of us set out. They went ahead and carried things in two bags, and with greater caution, we went behind by forest roads. Because we saw some footprints, perhaps of gendarmes, we were constantly checking our pace out of caution, and the peasants became fearful. We came near to Priboj in the village of Tobut. There we turned aside into the bushes in a field and took those things from the peasants. I don't know Veljko Cubrilovic and how it happened that they went for him. They set off to get him.

Pr.: — You did not have a letter for him?

Acc.: — Milovic talked, and Grbic also talked about him. We thought that the peasants would take us to Tuzla. Because they looked for excuses and did not wish to join us, we waited and we heard a commotion. That was Veljko Cubrilovic, a priest and a couple of peasants. We heard someone take his leave. We were in the bushes. A peasant came up to us and we came out of the brush. Veljko awaited us and we introduced ourselves to him. We said that we were from Bosnia and that we had just arrived. Then we paid the peasants five crowns.

Pr.: — The peasants did not know your exact intentions?

Acc.: — They knew absolutely nothing. Then I said to them again, "Look out, because you know what I have said," and they left. We talked with Veljko as to how we would get into Tuzla with those things. He put them in a saddlebag and then he said, "Come along with me." He kept pestering us the whole time with questions. I don't know how it came about that we told him that we were going to Sarajevo. He said something and then he asked us whether we were going to carry out an assassination. We said that we would. I don't remember which of us said it, but I incidentally told him, that although he had conducted himself in a completely friendly way that nevertheless we would destroy everything if he said anything. He told us to go with him and we went by some paths. It was muddy and we came to some huts. Then he went on ahead and we waited outside. A peasant youth named Nedjo Kerovic came to us and we went into the house of Kerovic. There we rested, had supper, and slept.

Pr.: — What did you do with the bags?

Acc.: — Veljko took them and carried them with him in the saddlebags. He rode ahead on a horse, and we went after him. They took off the saddlebags and arms and carried them into the house. Veljko began to drink with the peasants. They talked about the weather and so on, about ordinary things. Because we were tired, we fell asleep. Some peasant came, and Veljko jumped up to show him the things. Because I was sleepy I don't know how that all was, but I saw that Veljko showed them. Jovo Kerovic didn't see the things at all. Then we talked about how to get to Tuzla. One Cvijan Stjepanovic said that he was going to Tuzla and we could go with him. It was most difficult with the things. So we agreed to go by night. But before that both Grabez and I warned them to tell no one that we had been with them, otherwise they would lose their lives. We warned them only as a formality. Blagoje became afraid and therefore we threatened him most harshly.

Pr.: — You decided to go only to Tuzla. Who took the bombs and revolvers?

Acc.: — We gave those to them and they carried them. I put them around their waists.

Pr.: — Didn't they ask for what purpose you carried them?

Acc.: — They didn't ask us, nor did we talk about that to them. Then we set out at eleven o'clock by cart. We went down to the main road. They told us that there was a gendarmes' barracks there, and I said that we should get acquainted with the neighborhood. So we looked over the barracks, and then we got into the cart again and slept in the cart until we were near Tuzla. Then we went down into *Simin-Han* (Simo's Inn), and because we were dirty we washed up. Meanwhile they went on to Tuzla to Misko Jovanovic's to hand over the things. We agreed that we would go to Misko so that he could introduce us. In Tuzla we went to a cafe and sat down, but not together. After nine o'clock we went out and I bought trousers. Grabez also left. Then we later set out for Jovanovic's apartment in the *Srpska citaonica* (Serbian Reading Room), and there Stjepanovic introduced Misko to us. Because there was no one there we introduced ourselves and he conducted us to a sideroom where we talked. He asked us, "What's up?" We said that we were students. We said nothing about the assassination or the things.

Pr.: — You prepared weapons for him, and he didn't ask why. How did you imagine that he could accept things when he didn't know what you would use them for?

Acc.: — Since that fellow[58] wrote him as a friend I was sure that he would join us. When I trusted the one, I had to trust the other too.

Pr.: — How could he believe you?

Acc.: — He was frightened, but he accepted it anyway. Then we talked with him and asked him how to transmit the weapons.

Pr.: — He talked with you about how to transmit them, and did not ask for what purpose?

Acc.: — We said that we had to, and he did not ask us for what purpose. No one asked us. No one spoke to us about it.

Pr.: — Then that means he knew?

Acc.: — No.

Pr.: — And did Veljko Cubrilovic know?

Acc.: — Yes.

Pr.: — Did you read the letter that Veljko sent?

Acc.: — I don't remember. I know that there was nothing about the assassination in it. Later we asked him whether it would be possible to take the things to Sarajevo, and he said that he could not and that he was afraid. Then we said that they would stay with him, that we could not take them with us because there would be controls in Sarajevo. I told him that one of us would come, either Ilic, or I.

Pr.: — How did you know Ilic?

Acc.: — From when I was in Sarajevo before. Since I was in the second class.

Pr.: — Had you come to terms previously?

Acc.: — I had written him about Easter of that year that we would carry out an assassination, but in a sort of allegorical form.

Pr.: — How did you come to terms?

Acc.: — I did not exactly say that we would carry out an assassination, but in a way so that it was understood.

Pr.: — Say the words.

Acc.: — I don't remember the contents.

Pr.: — He received your letter and right away he started looking for others.

Acc.: — He did not look for others until we came.

Pr.: — Yes. It says explicitly that he spoke with Veljko[59] Cubrilovic at the beginning of May, and you arrived at the beginning of June.

Acc.: — I said that there would be more of us.

Pr.: — That was explicit that you would carry out an assassination, and that he should look for others.

Acc.: — I don't remember whether there were others.

Pr.: — Thus, you made arrangements with Jovanovic in that way and then you left?

Acc.: — Yes.

Pr.: — Did you meet regularly with Cubrilovic?

Acc.: — Yes, in a cafe.

Pr.: — Did you know those students?

Acc.: — Yes. They were my colleagues.

Pr.: — Do you know what their opinions were?

Acc.: — I don't know, because there I was in the fourth class.

Pr.: — You don't know what kind of spirit governed there?

Acc.: — No.

Pr.: — You don't know how it was in Sarajevo, where you lived?

Acc.: — From Sarajevo I went to Hadzici. I was at my brother's one day and then I went back to Sarajevo to attend a festival of the *Omladina* (Youth).[60] I took a room at Ilic's and I talked with him about the assassination.

Pr.: — Did he tell you that he was looking for others?

Acc.: — Yes. Because I said to him to find reliable people, he said, "Good." Because I believed that he was reliable, I believed that he would also find trustworthy companions.

Pr.: — What kind of political opinions did Ilic have?

Acc.: — He was a nationalist like me. A Yugoslav.

Pr.: — So he was of the same opinions as yourself?

Acc.: — He was. That all the Yugoslavs had to be unified.

Pr.: — Under Austria?

Acc.: — God forbid. I was not for the dynasty. We didn't think that far, but we thought: unification, by whatever means.

Pr.: — Did you discuss how to go to Tuzla for the bombs?

Acc.: — We decided that one of us would go. Because I had already gone once we decided that he should go. He went several days later. I told him how to meet with Jovanovic and what to say to him and he left.

Pr.: — Did you have a sign?

Acc.: — Yes, a box of *Stefanija* cigarettes.

Pr.: — Ilic didn't know Jovanovic?

Acc.: — No. Then he came back to Sarajevo. He didn't tell me who he saw. I stayed with him until the assassination and we talked the whole time. On the last day he did not wish to carry out the assassination. He wanted to dissuade me, but I insisted that we had to carry it out. Because he saw that it would be useless to talk to me, he stopped. I only said to him to see to it that the people to whom we gave arms to perform the assassination were reliable.

Pr.: — Who distributed the weapons?

Acc.: — He. I didn't, because I didn't know the people.

Pr.: — When did you receive the weapons?

Acc.: — On the day of the assassination. From Ilic's house.

Pr.: — How was that?

Acc.: — I took them from the house about eight o'clock and took a walk. He also took some and I don't know who he gave them to or where they had agreed to meet. Some got them a day or so earlier.

Pr.: — Did you know that there was a Moslem?

Acc.: — I knew, but he didn't tell me. I saw him one evening. On the day of the assassination I wanted to find someone who would not be conspicuous, and I found the son of the prosecutor, Svara, and one Spiric. First I walked with Spiric. Then we invited Svara and we walked and talked about ordinary things. At first we were in the park and I wanted to stay there, but they wanted to go to the *Korso* (a promenade). I didn't want to stay there because I had to go to my place. So I returned there and I walked on the quay and I was at my assigned place. The automobile arrived and I heard the blast of a bomb. I knew that that was one of ours, but I didn't know which one. The mob started to run, and I ran a little too and the automobile stopped. I thought that it was over and I saw that they had Cabrinovic. I thought that I would kill him so that no one would know anything further, and then kill myself, too. I abandoned that idea, because I saw that the automobiles passed by. Up to then I had not seen the Archduke. I went to the Latin Bridge and then I heard that the assassination had not succeeded. Then I took thought as to where to stand, because I knew where he would pass from having read it in the *Bosanska Posta* (Bosnian Post) and the *Tagblatt*. Then I saw that a lady was sitting with him, but because they passed so fast I did not know whether she was sitting. Then I stood and one Pusar came up to me and talked with me and said, "Do you see how dumb they are?" I was silent. He called me aside and because I thought he was a spy I thought that he wanted to get something out of me. A relative of his is a spy, so I thought that he was too. I don't know whether or not he was near me, but then the automobile came and I took out the revolver and I shot at Ferdinand twice from the distance of four or five paces.

Pr.: — The second time you did not aim at the lady?

Acc.: — No. I saw that someone else sat there; I wanted to kill Potiorek.

Pr.: — Did you know that you had struck a mortal blow?

Acc.: — I did not know whether I had struck home. At that time I didn't even know how many shots I had fired. Because I wanted to kill myself I raised my arm but the policemen and some officers grabbed me and beat me. Then, bloody as I was, they took me to the police station. Then they beat me again in order not to be unrevenged.

Pr.: — So you intentionally shot to kill him and Potiorek?

Acc.: — Yes. Because he was with them, I thought also of him and I am not sorry about that, because I believe that I did away with one evil and I thought that was good. In general he did evil to all things. He is the initiator of the "exceptional measures" and of the high treason trial.

Pr.: — The high treason trial is no kind of evil whatever.

Acc.: — Those are all consequences from which the people suffer.

Pr.: — Of what do the sufferings of the people consist?

Acc.: — That they are completely impoverished; that they are treated like cattle. The peasant is impoverished. They destroy him completely. I am a villager's son and I know how it is in the villages. Therefore I wanted to take revenge, and I am not sorry.

Pr.: — How about the "exceptional measures"?

Acc.: — They especially affected the Serbs. Thus all that influenced me. I knew that he is an enemy of the Slavs. As the prosecutor said, I did not think that he is a genius, but I thought that he would interfere with and harm the Slavs.

Pr.: — Interfere with what?

Acc.: — As the future ruler, with our unification. He would introduce certain reforms, which, you understand, would be harmful to us.

Pr.: — We will postpone this question until tomorrow.

The court is recessed until 7:45 o'clock in the morning.

The Second Day

CONTINUATION OF THE MAIN HEARING
13 OCTOBER 1914
Beginning at 8:10
REHEARING OF NEDELJKO CABRINOVIC

(Nedeljko Cabrinovic is called again).

Pr.: — The President points out to the defendant Cabrinovic that he had said during the investigation on 28 June that he alone carried out this action, and that he had hidden the bomb in the courtyard; furthermore, that he got the bomb from a Serb and that he had no accomplices.

Acc.: — Admits that he said so.

Pr.: — For what reasons did you say that?

Acc.: — I did not want to reveal more.

Hoffman: — For what purpose did Grabez write to Stevan Botic?[61]

Acc.: — To let me stay overnight.

Hoffman: — What was in the letter?

Acc.: — To let me stay overnight.

Hoffman: — How long did you stay in Tuzla?

Acc.: — Three days.

Hoffman: — Did you talk to Grabez?

Acc.: — Yes.

Hoffman: — Did Grabez tell you that he had a meeting with Jovanovic in the Serbian reading-room?

Acc.: — No.

CONTINUATION OF THE HEARING OF
GAVRILO PRINCIP
13 OCTOBER 1914

The President points out that on June 28th when he was questioned for the first time he said that he did not have accomplices and that he was surprised when he heard the bomb explode. Furthermore, that nobody tried to persuade him in the assassination, nor was he in collaboration with anyone.

Acc.: — I said that in order to cover up for the others. It is true that no one talked me into it.

Pr.: — In what inns did you stay in Belgrade?

Acc.: — I used to frequent the cafes *Zirovni* (Vijenac) and *Zeleni Vijenac*.

Pres.: — With whom did you meet?

Acc.: — With Bosnian students.

Pr.: — What political opinions did the group which you frequented have?

Acc.: — I cannot speak for everyone.

Pr.: — You said earlier that those students were excited about the union of Bosnia and Hercegovina with Serbia?

Acc.: — But they were divided as to the manner of carrying out the ideas.

Pr.: — Were they with you in the guerrilla bands?

Acc.: — They were. They were mostly civil servants, people with jobs.

Pr.: — Were there people among them who didn't have jobs and so passed the time with you?

Acc.: — A former waiter named Djoka Bajic.

Pr.: — Were you close to him?

Acc.: — Because he was unemployed and had money, I suspected that he was an Austrian spy.

Pr.: — Is that enough in Serbia to suspect someone of being a spy? Was he excited about terroristic ideas? Did he say that you had to carry out an assassination on the late lamented Heir?

Acc.: — Yes, he said so once.

Pr.: — Was that before you made your decision, or after?

Acc.: — After. I think Cabrinovic told me about that. Therefore I avoided him and joked about it.

Pr.: — Are you a close friend of Cabrinovic?

Acc.: — Yes.

Pr.: — How long?

Acc.: — We have been acquainted for four or five years, but we have been close for only two or three years.

Pr.: — Are you good friends then because you and he have the same ideas?

Acc.: — We agreed insofar as to use the same means for the unification of the South Slavs.

Pr.: — What kind of means are those?

Acc.: — I already said. The killing and removal of all those who do evil. Evil to the South Slav people.

Pr.: — Was that your opinion or Cabrinovic's ?

Acc.: — We discussed it often, and in most cases are agreed, though not always.

Pr.: — He wished to unify Bosnia and Hercegovina with Serbia by force?

Acc.: — To unify the South Slav lands.

Pr.: — But in no case under Austria?

Acc.: — No.

Pr.: — Was he of that opinion?

Acc.: — I think he was.

Pr.: — Did he not suggest some other motive for the act arising from religious views? In fact, do you believe in God?

Acc.: — Why are you asking?

Pr.: — You have the right to answer or remain silent.

Acc.: — I won't answer that.

Pr.: — Did you know that they are Freemasons?

Acc.: — In the cafe *Moruna* Ciganovic once said, when he talked about the assassination, that the Freemasons in such and such a year had condemned Franz Ferdinand to death.

Pr.: — That circumstance did not influence your decision?

Acc.: — No. Ciganovic himself said that he is a Freemason and I am surprised that Cabrinovic didn't know anything about that. I didn't pay attention to that and I suggested that he talk with someone from whom we might get the means.

Pr.: — You are not a Freemason, or are you?

Acc.: — I am not a Freemason.

Pr.: — Did you know Cabrinovic is a Freemason?

Acc.: — He said that he would join that lodge, but I don't know whether he did.

Pr.: — What is the name of that lodge?

Acc.: — The lodge of Freemasons.

Pr.: — Doesn't it have a specific name?

Acc.: — I don't know.

Pr.: — It is of decisive importance that that circumstance about the Freemasons had no influence on your decision.

Acc.: — As far as I am personally concerned, the first time Ciganovic did not agree to give weapons, and the second time he did. He said that he would discuss the details with someone else.

Pr.: — You received a letter from Popovic. In the letter were two words. Wasn't that some kind of code?

Acc.: — Those were two ordinary words. When Popovic asked who sent us, we said Ciganovic and Tankosic.

Pr.: — Did Tankosic and Ciganovic come to the steamboat when you left?

Acc.: — No.

Pr.: — Did Ciganovic tell you in Belgrade that there is some kind of "channel" from Belgrade to Sarajevo?

Acc.: — I don't remember.

Pr.: — Cabrinovic said that Tankosic told him that that channel leads directly from Belgrade to Sarajevo. We know what has to be understood by that: that they have agents.

Acc.: — I crossed back and forth into Serbia so many times that I could have done it this time without their help, but I wanted to be even more secure.

Pr.: — Do you know anything about the *Narodna odbrana* in Serbia? What objective it has? Who is the president of that association?

Acc.: — I know that its principal goal is the raising and strengthening of the national consciousness of the Serbian people.

Pr.: — What do you understand by the word "Serbia"? Only the kingdom?

Acc.: — Yes. But as the prosecutor put it in the indictment, the activity did not exist in those dimensions in Bosnia.

Pres.: — How did you know this? Are you a member of the executive council?

Acc.: — No.

Pr.: — How do you know that?

Acc.: — Because I talked to a man who said that there is no organization in Bosnia, that they had still not decided how they would work.

The President points out to the accused that among the official papers of the captain in Loznica was found a list of all the agents in Bosnia, or at least one part. There a very active member of the *Narodna odbrana* is listed, a teacher who enjoys an excellent reputation and confidence, one of the very best agitators against Austria.

Acc.: — That might be some individual. That does not mean that such work was spread in all parts. That is significant work.

Pr.: — Do you know the objectives of the *Narodna odbrana*?

Acc.: — No.

Pr.: — What kind of tasks did the *Narodna odbrana* have at the time of the Serbo-Turkish war?

Acc.: — It armed volunteers from its own means.

Pres.: — Did Ciganovic together with Tankosic decide to provide the bombs?

Acc.: — He told me about a man with whom he would come to terms on these things, but he didn't give me his name.

Pr.: — What does *covjek* (man) mean in your language?

Acc.: — It has no special meaning.

Pr.: — What did the peasant tell you who came with you all the way from Isakovic's Island to Priboj?

Acc.: — He told me his name, but I don't remember it.

Pr.: — You asked him his name, and he answered "a man" (covjek). (It is confirmed that Grabez said that.)

Naum.: — Did you say of Misko Jovanovic that he would receive bombs "because he is a good man" (jer je dobar covjek)? At least with us it is not the custom that "a good man" receives bombs and revolvers.

Acc.: — "A good man" doesn't have any special meaning.

Naum.: — Did you tell Grbic what was going on?

Acc.: — I told no one but Cubrilovic.

Naum.: — Why did you say that the trip from Belgrade to Priboj was mystical (misticno)? Was it because the people whom you met helped you? Maybe you wished to say mysterious (misteriozno).

Acc.: — That expression doesn't mean anything.

Naum.: — You said that Obren Milosevic gave you rags in which you wrapped the bombs, and then that he was present, that he saw them. He himself says that he saw them.

Acc.: — I myself wrapped them. I cannot be sure whether he saw them.

At that **The President** pointed out to him that statement at the inquiry where it said that Milosevic asked, "What do you need these for?" That means that he saw them.

Acc.: — I don't know that. Maybe he saw them and asked, but I know I didn't tell him anything.

Pr.: — Jovo wasn't in Kerovic's house at all?

Acc.: — He wasn't.

Pr.: — Did Mitar see the revolvers and bombs?

Acc.: — Nobody showed them to him.

Pr.: — You played with the bombs and threw them. That was on Isakovic's Island?

Acc.: — I don't know where that was.

Pr.: — Did you receive cyanide?

Acc.: — Yes.

Pr.: — Did you swallow it?

Acc.: — Yes, but it didn't work. I vomited it.

The President points out to the defendant that in the inquiry he said that the idea of unification developed among the youth in the South Slav states. In your opinion what kind of mission should Serbia have?

Acc.: — To help in the splitting-off from Austria.

Pr.: — Is that a common opinion in Serbia?

Acc.: — I am talking about myself.

Pr.: — In the inquiry you said that that is the opinion of every honest Serb and Croat.

Acc.: — I said that that is natural, that one expected it.

The President points out that statement in which he said: "That is my thinking and the thought of the youth, but there is trash who think differently."

Acc.: — I think that all South Slavs will unify in the way which I intimated.

Pr.: — Why didn't you expect that from Austria?

Acc.: — Why do we need Austria?

Pr.: — Do you think it is necessary to sacrifice even life for unification?

Acc.: — I think so. My principal motive was enlightenment, the enlightenment of the people.

Naum.: — Did you know Veljko Cubrilovic before?

Acc.: — No, I didn't know him at all.

Naum.: — When did you hear about him and from whom?

Acc.: — When Grabez talked about him.

Naum.: —Where was that?

Acc.: —When we set out from Isakovic's Island.

Naum.: — Did Grbic say anything about Cubrilovic when
he came to the island?

Acc.: — Absolutely nothing.

Naum.: — Now, Milovic says that he got orders from Grbic
to take you to Cubrilovic.

Acc.: — I don't know.

Naum.: — Did you ask him to take you to Cubrilovic when
you were in the vicinity of Priboj?

Acc.: — I told him to take us to Tuzla. I wanted to be
secure.

Naum.: — Obren Milosevic said that you stated that you
would go no further, and that you sent him directly to fetch
Cubrilovic.

Acc.: — Because he did not want to go with us to Tuzla.

Naum.: — How did you know that Cubrilovic was not
going to question you?

Acc.: — Because Milovic said that he knew him.

Naum.: — Did Milovic talk about Misko Jovanovic?

Acc.: — I don't know.

Naum.: — Where did you first hear about him?

Acc.: — In Kerovic's house.

Naum.: — On the way Obren Milosevic asked whether you
knew him?

Acc.: — Maybe he asked Grabez.

Naum.: — Did you receive two bags from Obren and did
you not pay him for them?

Acc.: — We thought we would return them to him.

Naum.: — As I know peasants, they would not give such
bags to anyone.

Acc.: — When we told him that the bags would be returned,
he believed it.

Naum.: — At night by your order he drove you to Tuzla in a cart.

Acc.: — Because he wanted to go the next day, but we asked him to go by night.

Naum.: — For them it is hard work when they go by night and drive for free. Did you give him two crowns for coffee?

Acc.: — We gave him four crowns, I think.

Naum.: — You gave that to those first ones, but to Stjepanovic you gave two crowns.

Acc.: — I gave Kerovic two crowns.

Naum.: — How come those people drove you for free?

Acc.: — Veljko Cubrilovic said that he would pay ten crowns.

Naum.: — How come that stranger whom you never saw before promised to pay ten crowns for your transportation, when he knew that you wished to carry out an assassination?

Acc.: — Once we begin to believe one, we believe all.

Naum.: — Did you read the letter which Popovic wrote to the captain in Loznica?

Acc.: — Only three lines.

Naum.: — Was it printed?

Acc.: — No.

Naum.: — Grabez says that it was.

Acc.: — It was written in slanted handwriting.

Naum.: — What was written?

Acc.: — "See to it that you accept these people and conduct them to you know where." For the railroad he wrote that we were revenue officers.

Naum.: — Grabez said that he received a permit which requested all districts along the way not to hinder these people and to give them help.

Acc.: — It was written that we were revenue officers. That was for the railroad, in order to receive half-fare.

Naum.: — It is remarkable that you went to Bosnia and did not say why you went, and that strange people who never saw you before gave you a permit in which all authorities along the way were requested to give you a hand.

Acc.: — We had to give that to the railroad.

Naum.: — What did you give to the captain in Loznica?

Acc.: — That note to receive us.

Naum.: — How come Popovic wrote that you were revenue officers if he didn't know what you wanted?

Acc.: — We asked that we be given financial help for the railway fare.

Naum.: — How was it that he believed you right away?

Acc.: — We said that we were students.

Naum.: — How was it that the captain who was playing cards, as soon as he saw you, got up right away and went to you? One doesn't do that with strangers.

Acc.: — When we came into the cafe he was sitting and playing cards. When we told him that we wanted to talk with him, he said that we should wait a little.

Naum.: — It surprises me that he came immediately as soon as you commanded it.

Pr.: — Do you know whether Veljko Cubrilovic told Nedjo and Blagoje Kerovic that you were going to Sarajevo to carry out an assassination?

Acc.: — He did not say.

Pr.: — They admitted it.

Acc.: — We didn't hear that.

Pr.: — Did Ciganovic tell you that there was someone whom you would contact when you crossed Bosnian border?

Acc.: — No. I asked Ciganovic whether he knew someone, and he said that he didn't.

Pr.: — One of you said that Cigo said in Belgrade that you could leave the weapons at Misko Jovanovic's. You asked Cubrilovic to take you to Jovanovic?

Acc.: — Maybe because he knew Misko.

Hoffman: — You said that in Belgrade you associated with the secretary of the *Narodna odbrana*?

Acc.: — I did not associate with him.

Hoffman: — What then?

Acc.: — At the secretary's I enrolled in the guerrilla bands.

Hoffman: — Did Joca Prvanovic give you a letter for Veljko Cubrilovic?

Acc.: — No.

Hoffman: — Is Ciganovic a clerk of high or low rank?

Acc.: — He has a salary of about 240 dinars.

Hoffman: — Is he rich or poor?

Acc.: — So-so.

Hoffman: — From where could he give you 150 dinars?

Acc.: — I don't know. I think he collected them from friends. It is said that it was some sort of promissory note.

Hoffman: — Who gave that note?

Acc.: — Tankosic.

Hoffman: — Who received the 150 dinars?

Acc.: — Ciganovic gave them to us. At first we received 130 dinars, and later, because it was not enough, we asked for more. We did not receive our own money because we couldn't telegraph home.

Hoffman: — How much did Cabrinovic get?

Acc.: — Forty. Cabrinovic had his own money.

Hoffman: — Where did Ciganovic hand over the Brownings and bombs to you?

Acc.: — In front of the cafe *Moruna*.

Hoffman: — Did he bring them himself, or did you go to him in his office?

Acc.: — He did not bring them all at once, rather at one time he brought the bombs, and the second time the revolvers.

Hoffman: — How much time passed from the time when you received the arms up to the time when you went to Sabac?

Acc.: — One day.

Hoffman: — Did you talk about that with Ciganovic?

Acc.: — Yes, we talked about the assassination.

Hoffman: — What instructions did he give you?

Acc.: — I said that after the assassination I would kill myself, and he said that that was good.

Hoffman: — When you went from Isakovic's Island to Obrezje, Jokov Milovic accompanied you. How long did the trip take? Did you talk on the way?

Acc.: — I don't know how long it took. It was raining and muddy. We didn't talk at all because we didn't go together but we walked separately, bent over.

The President shows the defendant the bomb and asks where it came from.

Acc.: — From Ciganovic.

Pr.: — Where did he get it?

Acc.: — He was a guerrilla. When the war was over every guerrilla could keep his bombs.

Pr.: — Where were those bombs made?

Acc.: — I don't know.

Pr.: — One guerrilla said that after the war everybody had to return all the arms he had received under threat of severe punishment.

Acc.: — That applied only to those who misused[62] them.

Pr.: — Were the bombs with or without this sort of iron ring?

Acc.: — They were all the same. It served only for attachment.

Then **The President** shows the defendant a Browning.

Acc.: — I know. Number 19.75.

Pr.: — How do you know it?

Acc.: — I saw it.

Hoffman: — You said that you had supper at Mitar Kerovic's. Who was at the table?

Acc.: — Grabez, Cubrilovic and Mitar Kerovic and I.

Hoffman: — And Blagoje and Jovo?

Acc.: — They weren't there.

Hoffman: — How come they called Cvijo Stjepanovic?

Acc.: — Maybe in order to go to Tuzla because Blagoje could not go. He had an invitation.

Hoffman: — Where was Jovo?

Acc.: — I don't know. Maybe he was doing something outside.

Hoffman: — One doesn't work at night.

Acc.: — He left and he didn't see anything.

Hoffman: — Did Nedjo Kerovic and Cvijo Stjepanovic know that you would carry out an assassination?

Acc.: — We didn't tell them.

Hoffman: — You left the cart before Lopare, and after you passed Lopare you took the cart again. That already shows that they could know.

Acc.: — They only saw that we carried arms and that we hid them.

Hoffman: — Why did you hide them?

Acc.: — We had reasons.

Hoffman: — When you got to Tuzla, who told you that you had a meeting in the Serbian reading-room?

Acc.: — It was agreed that the peasants tell Misko.

Hoffman: — Did you know about Veljko Cubrilovic's letter to Jovanovic?

Acc.: — Yes.

Hoffman: — What did he write?

Acc.: — It was very short: that he should accept the arms . . .

Hoffman: — The next day you met with him in a side room. Did he know that you wanted to carry out an assassination?

Pr.: — I have already asked him that.

Hoffman: — When you got to Sarajevo did you stay at Ilic's?

Acc.: — Yes.

Hoffman: — Do you know about Laza Djukic?

Acc.: — I didn't know about Laza Djukic.

Naum.: —You said that at the time of the assassination you went to the place assigned to you?

Acc.: — Yes, Ilic and Grabez worked out the plan where each of us would stand.

Feldb.: — Did your family take care of your raising while you were studying?

Acc.: — My brother supported me because he was in good circumstances.

Feldb.: — In Serbia did you see the allegorical picture of the liberation and unification of the South Slavs? Did you see the geographical map of Croatia, Slavonia, Backa, Banat all in one frame?

Acc.: — I never did.

Feldb.: — Did any one teach you how to shoot?

Acc.: — No one.

Feldb.: — Did Grabez and you shoot the same Browning? Did anyone in Serbia teach you how to shoot?

Acc.: — We got one revolver, and we fired with it. Later we got three.

Feldb.: — What induced you, four days after the assassination, to tell the investigating judge that you wanted to see Grabez and Cabrinovic?

Acc.: — I didn't want to reveal anything; but when I saw that innocent ones suffered as well as many friends who accidentally associated with me, I wanted the peasants to be left out of it. That's why I wanted to meet with Grabez and Cabrinovic.

Feldb.: — How old is Ciganovic?

Acc.: — Twenty-eight.

Feldb.: — When were you born?

Acc.: — 13 July 1894.

Pr.: — We will talk about that when we proceed to the presentation of evidence.

Feldb.: — You said in the record that Vojin Tankosic helped Ciganovic in this matter. How did you know that?

Acc.: — Because he was on good terms with Vojin Tankosic. He said that he is a Freemason, and so I understood that they are close friends.

Feldb.: — Cabrinovic admitted that other persons had influence on you.

Acc.: — No one had an influence on me.

Feldb.: — Do you know Djuro Sarac?

Acc.: — Yes.

Feldb.: — Did you talk with him about the assassination?

Acc.: — Recently, after the decision had been made. Maybe Ciganovic talked about that to him.

Feldb.: — Did Djulaga Bukovac have some influence on you?

Acc.: — No.

Feldb.: — Did you read revolutionary works?

Acc.: — I read Krapotkin and the Russian socialist literature.

Feldb.: — When did you begin to read Russian revolutionary books?

Acc.: — Three years ago.

Premuzic: — When did you begin to have nationalistic thoughts?

Acc.: — Two years ago.

Prem.: — How and where did you get those ideas?

Acc.: — Already in Sarajevo.

Prem.: — Who helped you in Hadzici with the reading?

Acc.: — My brother.

Prem.: — Anybody else?

Acc.: — No one.

Prem.: — Do you remember what you stated in the record of the hearing about the behavior of Misko Jovanovic when you were with him?

Acc.: — That he was timid. I even forbade him to make jokes.

Prem.: — Is what you said in the record true?

Acc.: — It is.

Zistler: — Yesterday you stated that you met with Cubrilovic and that you said that you all would kill him and his family. How did you meet? What did you say to him? What did he reply? How did you threaten him, and was he afraid of your threats?

Acc.: — When I talked with him, I noticed that he was merely surprised at our arrival and curious. Everything affected us. So we admitted the assassination because we could not keep a secret. I told him to be sure that everything would be kept secret. I talked as if someone stood behind us and as if someone would kill his family if he said anything.

Zistler: — Who was that someone?

Acc.: — I just said that in order to impress him.

Zistler: — Do you know that there are revolutionary organizations in Serbia which take revenge on those who do not voluntarily collaborate in their undertakings?

Acc.: — That exists in Russian circles, but not in Serbia.

Zistler: — Did you perceive that you frightened Cubrilovic?

Acc.: — It seems as if that affected him.

Zistler: — Did you talk about this before you got to Kerovic's or later?

Acc.: — When I rose to take leave of Kerovic I only said, "See to it that what I said remains a secret."

Zistler: — Do you employ terroristic means when you look for help? Could you evoke such fear in Cubrilovic that he would act from fear alone?

Pr.: — That is a leading question.

Zistler: — I would like to stress the mood which governed Cubrilovic.

Acc.: — I talked with Ilic earlier about the means to found

an organization which would act so that we could get money, as revolutionaries do. But in this case it wasn't necessary.

Zistler: — Was Nedjo Kerovic present when the head of household chose him to go to Tuzla?

Acc.: — He wanted to go anyway because his hand was sore.

Perisic: — Do you know Cvijan Stjepanovic?

Acc.: — I know him.

Per.: — Did you meet him at Kerovic's house?

Acc.: — Yes.

Per.: — Who invited him to Kerovic's?

Acc.: — Veljko Cubrilovic.

Per.: — Were you present in the room when Cvijan Stjepanovic arrived?

Acc.: — Yes.

Per.: — Did someone show Stjepanovic the weapons and tell him what purpose they served?

Acc.: — Veljko showed the weapons and said that they were bombs. Veljko knew that they were bombs.

Per.: — Did Cvijan Stjepanovic ask where you were going and why you were carrying bombs?

Acc.: — No. We were tired. We didn't talk about that.

Per.: — In your nationalistic concept, hating Austria, did you assume that the unification of all South Slavs could not take place otherwise than beneath the Karadjeordjevic dynasty?

Acc.: — I did not think of the Karadjeordjevic dynasty. I never thought that after the assassination there would be a war. I thought that it would have an impact on the youth and that they would spread these ideas further.

Pr.: — **The President** shows to the accused the statement in the inquiry in which he said that Germany and Italy served as examples: "It is the moral duty of Serbia to free the South Slavs from Austria. We heard that from every honest Serb and Croat."

Acc.: — I said that Serbia and the South Slavs were strong enough, but I did not believe that the assassination would be followed by a war.

Pr.: — Did you associate with officers in Serbia? Did you hear that they expected a war this year?

Acc.: — I didn't even know any officers.

CONFRONTATION OF PRINCIP AND CABRINOVIC
13 OCTOBER 1914

Pr.: — Cabrinovic, your friend Princip says that you, who were of the same opinions as he, wished to unify the South Slavs into one state?

Princip: — That was my opinion.

Cabrinovic: — Those were our ideas. Yugoslavia was my ideal.

Pr.: — Princip, you were the instigator of the assassination?

Princip: — I talked with him in the *Zirovni Vijenac* about the assassination, but he decided on the assassination himself.

Pr.: — Cabrinovic, you said explicitly, when you received the note —

Cabr.: — I received an anonymous note. However Gavro insists —

Pr.: — That he was already in agreement with you.

Cabr.: — I don't remember.

Princip: — I know positively.

Cabr.: — Princip insists that the idea of the assassination came to him before I showed him the clipping from the newspaper.

Pr.: — He says that he decided before.

Cabr.: — There was often talk of the assassination among us, but I don't remember the final decision.

Princ.: — The final decision fell at the time when we received the newspaper clipping. Before that I thought of the assassination for myself.

Pr.: — Do you know anything about Zerajic?

Princ.: — He was my first model. At night I used to go to his grave and vow that I would do the same as he.

Cabr.: — I did the same thing when I came to Sarajevo. I carved his name on the grave.

Princ.: — The grave was neglected and we put it in order.

Malek: — Points out to the defendant Princip that in the inquiry he confessed that he carried out the assassination and said that "revenge is bloody and sweet." Then he repeated at the main hearing that he carried out the assassination out of revenge, and later he said that he did it for the unification of the South Slavs. Later he said that he did not think there would be a war after the assassination. Which prevails with you: the idea of revenge, hatred, or the idea of the unification of the South Slavs?

Princ.: — Both were equal.

Malek: — Why did you take lodgings with Ilic when you returned to Sarajevo?

Princ.: — Because it was a back street, he is a quiet young fellow who does not attract attention.

Malek: — Did you have your own room?

Princ.: — Together.

Malek: — Where were the bombs?

Princ.: — In some kind of suitcase under the bed.

Malek: — How much money did you have when you returned from Serbia?

Princ.: — 50 dinars.

Malek: — How much did you agree to pay for the room?

Princ.: — I made no agreement.

Malek: — Did you borrow money from Ilic?

Princ.: — Yes, 30 to 49 crowns.

Malek: — You stated that Ilic said it would be better to give up the assassination?

Princ.: — He said that now was not the time for an assassination and that it could have bad consequences, that there would be persecution of the people. I thought that it would not be of such dimensions as happened after the assassination and I did not let him influence me.

Pr.: — When you wrote him from Belgrade to Sarajevo, did you think that he might collaborate?

Acc.: — I thought so if suitable people were not to be found.

Pr.: — It is surprising that he (Ilic) chose a youth under 20, although he is older.

Acc.: — One didn't think too much about that.

Pr.: — Did Ciganovic or others in Belgrade know that Ilic would participate?

Acc.: — I said that I had Ilic and that I could count on him.

Pr.: — Did you say that you knew him?

Acc.: — Only Sarac knew him, not Ciganovic.

Pr.: — When you passed from Serbia to Bosnia, did you

hear about Obren Milosevic? Did someone in Serbia say that he knew him?

Acc.: — No one.

Pr.: — Did you know that Milovic[63] was a smuggler?

Acc.: — It seemed so from what Grbic said.

Pr.: — In the inquiry you did not say that you threatened Obren Milosevic.

Acc.: — I know well that I threatened him. Maybe the interrogating judge just didn't ask me.

Pr.: — When the peasants came to the teacher Veljko he asked: "What are you carrying?" You said, "Arms," and when he asked further, you said, "Time."

Acc.: — "Wait a little," I said.

Pros.: — Where did you exchange the 150 dinars?

Acc.: — In Belgrade we changed all the money into crowns, but we were accustomed to say "dinars."

Pros.: — Do you know that in 1908 Austria almost had war with Serbia?

Acc.: — I know it.

Pros.: — How then could you think that you would kill the Heir Apparent, that you would be hanged, and that there would be no further consequences?

Acc.: — Because Serbia could not be held responsible if weapons are found in the possession of private persons.

The President recesses the hearing for five minutes.

After the recess

CONTINUATION OF THE HEARING OF GAVRILO PRINCIP

Premuzic: — Do you believe in God, or are you more an atheist?

Princ.: — Atheist.

Prem.: — When you travelled, did you notice troop movements?

Acc.: — I didn't see a single soldier.

Prem.: — Did you see a train with recruits who had been called up?

Acc.: — No.

Pr.: — Cabrinovic, did you talk about it?

Cab.: — I talked with acquaintances who went to Sabac to present themselves at headquarters.

Pros.: — Did you have the means to obtain arms?

Princ.: — I would have sent a telegram home for the examination fee if I had.

Pros.: — And those others?

Acc.: — Cabrinovic had money, and Grabez is well off.

Pros.: — Why did you contact the *Narodna odbrana*?

Acc.: — Just in a conversation I mentioned, "How about contacting the *Narodna odbrana*, which gives support to impoverished students."

Pros.: — Which gives support for revolution. You said that arose in your mind. How do you explain the fact that Tankosic is a prominent leader of the *Narodna odbrana*?

Acc.: — He has absolutely nothing to do with the *Narodna odbrana*; on the contrary he is in conflict with the secretary and with the executive committee in general.

Pros.: — He is a prominent man in the *Narodna odbrana*.

Acc.: — He was as a volunteer. Otherwise he is nothing in the *Narodna odbrana*.

Pros.: — Major Tankosic is also a Serbian major. How does it happen that a Serbian major helps in an assassination project?

Acc.: — That was a personal affair.

Pros.: — How did it happen that captains in Loznica and Sabac gave you a hand? They are prominent Serbian people.

Acc.: — They are ordinary officers.

Pros.: — Do you see that in our army?

Acc.: — Our army is completely different, and the Serbian is different.

Premuzic: — Do you know the association *Prosvjeta* (Culture) in Belgrade?

Acc.: — No.

Pr.: — With whom did you first agree about the assassination, with Grabez or Cabrinovic?

Acc.: — With Cabrinovic.

THE HEARING OF TRIFKO GRABEZ
13 OCTOBER 1914

Pr.: — Call Trifko Grabez.
Pr.: — Are you guilty?
Acc.: — Yes.
Pr.: — Of what?
Acc.: — Of assassination.
Pr.: — Where did you go to school?
Acc.: — Belgrade.
Pr.: — Why not here?
Acc.: — I was expelled because I slapped Professor Truhelka in Tuzla.
Pr.: — When was that?
Acc.: — In 1912.
Pr.: — In what class?
Acc.: — In the fifth. Then I went home, and from there to Belgrade. In Belgrade I finished the fifth and sixth classes.
Pr.: — How many months were you in the fifth class in Tuzla?
Acc.: — Three.
Pr.: — When did you pass the examination for the fifth class?
Acc.: — In the month of May.
Pr.: — And for the sixth?
Acc.: — In the month of July.
Pr.: — According to that you gained one year. When did you take the examination for the seventh year?
Acc.: — This year at our Easter.
Pr.: — How is it possible that in Serbia they accept students expelled from here and that they can skip classes in school? Is it that our schools are better than those in Serbia, or that students from Bosnia have privileges there?
Acc.: — There the spirit of instruction is different. They don't study Latin for 5 to 6 hours. They don't have Greek. The curriculum is arranged differently.
Pr.: — How could you prepare for the fifth and sixth classes in nine months?
Acc.: — Because I was prepared and actually worked seriously.

Pr.: — Where did you stay?

Acc.: — I changed my rooms often.

Pr.: — Tell me something about your student life. With whom did you associate? What did you talk about? Who was your friend and companion?

Acc.: — In Belgrade I came into the company of Gavrilo Princip. I knew him before. That was when I went the first time to Belgrade. When I went to Belgrade the second time I came into contact with Nedeljko Cabrinovic.

Pr.: — In what year?

Acc.: — 1913. I associated with all the other Bosnians.

Pr.: — Where did you eat?

Acc.: — In restaurants.

Pr.: — Did you eat in the *Zirovni Vijenac*?

Acc.: — It was expensive there. I used to go to the cafes *Zirovni Vijenac* and *Moruna*. So living, I stayed for some time with Princip in Carigrad Street. And of course, expelled, I thought about my own country. We talked about conditions in our country and we watched what was happening there. When we heard that the Heir Apparent Ferdinand was coming to our country, and knowing our troubles and what is done to the Serbian people in Bosnia, we had to conclude that Austria had to pay handsomely for her wrongdoing. Especially Ferdinand. And so I got the idea of the assassination at Easter and we agreed in principle.

Pr.: — Who made the decision?

Acc.: — Princip and I.

Pr.: — Did you know Cabrinovic?

Acc.: — Yes.

Pr.: — Did you talk with him?

Acc.: — I didn't discuss anything with him.

Pr.: — Who first had the idea of the assassination?

Acc.: — We both came to the idea of the assassination, but whether of Ferdinand or Potiorek, we didn't know. I went home for Easter and decided to return to enter the eighth class.

Pr.: — Did you return before you decided on the assassination?

Acc.: — Before that. That was around Easter, maybe in April. After I passed the examination I went home to Bosnia.

At that time there still wasn't any talk about the assassination of the Heir. I knew I was capable of it. That I would do it no matter what. We discussed the arrival of Ferdinand and that it would be the duty of Bosnians to "welcome" him. I was at home for one and a half months. Meanwhile I was in Sarajevo and read in the paper *Istina* (Truth) that Ferdinand was coming to Bosnia and that maneuvers would be held for a counterattack on Serbia. At that time I definitely decided that he had to be destroyed.

Pr.: — What did you have against him?

Acc.: — I had against him that in general he was one of those who brought all evil to Bosnia. He was a Nemesis of the Slavs, a German fellow of the sort who could be an opponent of the great idea of South Slavdom, and therefore according to Princip's and my opinions, he had to be destroyed.

Pr.: — On what basis did you form this judgment?

Acc.: — On the basis of what happened in the Slavic South.

Pr.: — But he was not responsible for that.

Acc.: — Neither was Potiorek. He only carried out orders from Vienna.

Pr.: — In Vienna there are ministers, but how can you hold the late lamented Heir Apparent responsible for what happened in Bosnia? He was the inspector-general of the armed forces and nothing else.

Acc.: — As such he was the enemy of Slavdom.

Pr.: — In the armed forces there are many Slavs who fight for Austria.

Acc.: — When the Slavic soldiers fight for the Austrian heir they are an unawakened mass.

Pros.: — I request that this be substantiated because I will prosecute him for that.

Pr.: — You considered him a very capable military leader and therefore you were afraid of him in case of war with Serbia.

Acc.: — I wasn't afraid. I was not guided by Serbia's interests, but only by Bosnia's. If I had known that the consequences would be a European war, I would never have participated in the assassination.

Pr.: — Is it your opinion that Bosnia and Hercegovina must be annexed to Serbia?

Acc.: — Yes.

Pr.: — Was that your ideal?

Acc.: — Yes.

Pr.: — Is that your ideal now?

Acc.: — Yes. And that exclusively in the form of the Karadjeordjevic dynasty, under the single name of Yugoslavia, be it a republic or a federative republic.

Pr.: — On what basis do you judge that the South Slavs in Austria are so unhapppy?

Acc.: — On the basis of experience.

Pr.: — Inasmuch as you have only gone through the fifth class, what kind of experience can you claim to have had?

Acc.: — I lived in Serbia. I saw the "exceptional measures," the commissionership of Cuvaj in Croatia, the high treason trials of the Serbs in Zagreb in which innocent people suffered.

Pr.: — Do you consider yourself innocent?

Acc.: — I do not consider myself innocent.

Pr.: — Those others had their own political scandals.

Acc.: — The Pjanic[64] scandal.

Pr.: — You said before that in Belgrade you learned about such a difficult situation.

Acc.: — Yes. From Serbian and Croatian newspapers. The Croatian newspapers also wrote about those things occasionally.

Pr.: — You said in the inquiry that the whole time in Belgrade there developed such a militant spirit that you were ready to sacrifice your life. Did you think that would be of any use?

Acc.: — I think that the Slavs as a people equal with the other peoples in the Monarchy must be given the most elementary political rights.

Pr.: — For example?

Acc.: — Political freedom.

Pr.: — What does political freedom mean?

Acc.: — I am not familiar with the matter.

Pr.: — What are you talking about?

Acc.: — Cultural and free development, schools, and universities, gymnasium.

Pr.: — Don't you have them here?

Acc.: — There are those which you want. Why don't you allow autonomous schools?

Pr.: — There are.

Acc.: — Every cultural movement is regarded with the greatest abhorrence.

Pr.: — You have church communes which are completely autonomous.[65] In what lies the repression of which you speak?

Acc.: — That you are destroying that which every honorable man thinks.

Pr.: — I would like you to cite facts.

Acc.: — The "exceptional measures." Why did we deserve them? You destroyed the *Soko* . . . (Falcon)[66]

Pr.: — It was not destroyed.

Acc.: — Each association had to request separately, but in Serbia each application was handled in two or three days.[67]

Pr.: — Are you religious or are you an atheist?

Acc.: — I am a believer.

Pr.: — How can you reconcile religion with the destruction of God's creation?

Acc.: — Faith doesn't go that far.

Pr.: — Your father is a priest. What kind of raising did he give you?

Acc.: — He gave me a purely religious raising within the framework of Holy Scripture.

Pr.: — How do you follow his teachings?

Acc.: — As a child I obeyed them, but other things influence a man when he leaves childhood.

Pr.: — Among the youth there is no faith?

Acc.: — There is, National faith, much of it.

Pr.: — How long did you stay at home after the agreement with Princip and before you talked with him about the assassination of the late esteemed Ferdinand?

Acc.: — I came home. I stayed a month and a half, and returned to Belgrade to take the examinations for the eighth class. About then I read in *Istina* that the Heir Apparent Ferdinand was coming to Bosnia and intended to hold maneuvers around Sarajevo. Princip said that he was completely determined to carry out an assassination. I asked about Cabrinovic, and he said that he was good.

Pr.: — Didn't you say that Cabrinovic was good? Did you not draw Princip's attention to Cabrinovic?

Acc.: — I don't remember exactly. I asked him what Cabrinovic thought, and he said that he had made up his mind. At that we decided that the assassination had to be carried out. There remained the question of arms. Princip said that he talked with Ciganovic and that he asked for material to carry out the assassination. Ciganovic had been a guerrilla, and as a Bosnian knew the conditions. Naturally, he agreed at once and promised to give us the necessary bombs. He had many bombs because as a soldier he had as many as he wished at his disposition.

Pr.: — Did you see bombs at his place?

Acc.: — Yes. We left it at that. We waited for Ciganovic. He said that I had nothing to fear. He was connected with Major Tankosic who was of secondary importance. The main culprit, if you must take this as criminal, was Ciganovic. When the time came to go to Sarajevo we knew that we must go to Sarajevo 20 to 30 days beforehand to put things in order.

Pr.: — Did you know that still others wanted to participate in the assassination?

Acc.: — I didn't know.

Pr.: — Did Princip tell you that he wrote Ilic?

Acc.: — I didn't know what he wrote. I only knew that he did write.

Pr.: — Did you know whether Ilic would participate?

Acc.: — I didn't know in Belgrade, I only knew that he knew about it.

Pr.: — Did Tankosic express a wish to meet you?

Acc.: — I don't know. Ciganovic said so. He told me to go. We wished to send Cabrinovic, but they said to me, "You go to Grabez!" I left with Ciganovic.

Pr.: — Where did you meet?

Acc.: — In the cafe *Moruna*. Then we went to his place. He came later.

Pr.: — Was he alone in the room or were there other officers?

Acc.: — There were Ciganovic, Tankosic, and I.

Pr.: — What did he ask you?

Acc.: — "Are you one of them, are you ready?" "I am." "Are you determined?" "I am." "Do you know how to shoot a revolver?" "No." "Do you know how to handle one?" "No."

Then he said to Ciganovic, "Here is a revolver. Teach them to shoot on the firing range!" Ciganovic went with Princip and me to Topcider and there we learned to shoot.

Pr.: — Did Cabrinovic learn to shoot?

Acc.: — I don't know.

Pr.: — What did you say about Mojic in the inquiry?

Acc.: — I said that in my confusion.

Pr.: — On Topcider, what did you shoot at?

Acc.: — At trees in the forest.

Pr.: — Could you tell who shot best? What did Mojic say?

Acc.: — I said at the inquiry that Ciganovic said that Princip shot better than I. As far as Cabrinovic goes, I don't know whether he shot. He said that he knew how to handle arms.

The President showed the accused the statement of 4 June in which it said that the last three days before he set out to Sarajevo he learned to shoot, that one Major Mojic, also an official, taught Cabrinovic "because he could not come to the training-ground where we shot. Because we shot at a target, Princip was the best marksman." You said that.

Acc.: — Perhaps I made it up, because I cannot say that Mojic taught Cabrinovic.

Pr.: — It is not possible that you invented such fine details.

Acc.: — I don't know.

Pr.: — Before you left, did you meet with Ciganovic?

Acc.: — Yes, he gave us the bombs, revolvers and a letter to the captain in Sabac.

Pr.: — What did he write?

Acc.: — Two words.

Pr.: — You didn't see what they were?

Acc.: — No. Then we left Belgrade by boat for Sabac. When we arrived in Sabac, we went to Captain Popovic. He was in a cafe and was playing cards. We introduced ourselves to him, and asked him for a few words if he had the time.

Pr.: — Did you say this to him in the cafe?

Acc.: — In the cafe, alone. In a corner of the cafe. We told him that we were travelling to Bosnia and that we had reasons to travel secretly and if possible that he give us half-fare tickets to Loznica, permits, and that he direct us to the captain in Loznica in order that we be passed over into Bosnia.

Pr.: — You told him to direct you to the captain in Loznica?

Acc.: — We especially said that.

Pr.: — How did you know that you had to go by way of Loznica?

Acc.: — Ciganovic said so. He wrote a note that we go to Loznica. I don't know what it said. Princip gave that letter to the captain in Loznica. We received half-fare train tickets and we went by train to Loznica. When we came to the captain he told us that he could pass us into Bosnia, that he had a man who could take us over, and that we should wait in Loznica until he came. The next day, when we went to Loznica, we went to the captain who invited us to a cafe where we found three Serbian revenue officers. We went inside and the captain ordered one of them, Grbic, to take us to Bosnia. I had decided that Cabrinovic in any case should go separately. I looked at my passport and saw that he looked very much like me,[68] so that he would be able to go via Zvornik. I gave him the passport.

Pr.: — Why did you decide that?

Acc.: — Because it would be inconvenient for the three of us to go together. I gave Cabrinovic the passport, and Princip and I went to the barracks of the revenue officers, from where the next day he would take us to the patch of Serbian ground, Isakovic's Island. We crossed over to the island and we were at the peasant Milan Cula's, as the indictment says. Then Franjo Grbic came to get us, but he couldn't find anyone.

Pr.: — By whom did he send a message to the other?

Acc.: — I don't know, Mico Micic just arrived.

Pr.: — What did you talk about?

Acc.: — Nothing, I was tired.

Pr.: — And the others?

Acc.: — I don't know. Grbic said that he would come to the island to take us to Bosnia. Milovic came and we crossed the border between seven and eight in the evening, carrying bombs and revolvers on our belts. At once we moved by mountains and side-roads and came to the house of Milovic. Because we were afraid to go further because of the gendarmes and because we were dirty, we ordered them to give us the bags and for them to carry the bombs and revolvers.

Pr.: — How could you give them orders?

Acc.: — When you have a revolver, then that decides.

Pr.: — Did you threaten them?

Acc.: — "Since you decided to take us, you must do as we say," and they went with us up to Priboj. They wanted to return.

Pr.: — Did Micic and Milovic see that you had revolvers and bombs?

Acc.: — Yes, they saw it.

Pr.: — Did you talk about the assassination?

Acc.: — No, we didn't. Princip told us in general to say nothing to anyone.

Pr.: — Did they ask you what you needed them for?

Acc.: — They didn't ask about the bombs at all. They had to follow orders.

Pr.: — They did not want to stay at Obren Milosevic's, but they wanted to go right on?

Acc.: — "Let's go during the day," and I said, "You still have to find a peasant to carry the revolvers for us." "Don't be afraid about anything."

Pr.: — Did Obren Milosevic see the revolvers and bombs?

Acc.: — Yes. We came to his house. He and Jakov Milovic went ahead, and we behind them, about one or two hundred paces, so that if the gendarmes caught us they wouldn't find anything suspicious.

Pr.: — Did you tell them that was out of caution?

Acc.: — We told them: "Go ahead of us!"

Pr.: — They had the weapons, bombs and revolvers, so for them there was danger of death?

Acc.: — There was no danger for them, but for us.

Pr.: — You said: "When we have revolvers, then they have to listen; but when they have revolvers, then one would have to obey their orders."

Acc.: — The peasant is not so conscious that he could use the means against us.

Pr.: — They voluntarily went on with you?

Acc.: — By our orders.

Pr.: — When they had the weapons they did not have to. They could have reported to the gendarmes that students have revolvers. How do you interpret that?

Acc.: — They were in danger of their lives if they reported

us, because then they would suffer for it. I would have said that they were with Grbic, and that Jakov Milovic was working by orders of Grbic. From this it is possible that he was in contact with Grbic. How could he order someone whom he did not know? I concluded that on the basis of the indictment.

Pr.: — When you threatened him, you didn't know the indictment.

Acc.: — Now on the basis of the indictment I conclude that he was in contact with Grbic. He said himself that he went there several times. He knew what he was doing. He knew that if the gendarmes reported him he would already have to be sentenced as a smuggler.

Pr.: — If he reported the assassination, they would let him go.

Acc.: — If Jakov Milovic were stronger than Milosevic, if he had said "You have to go!", that would have settled it.

Pr.: — That would mean that there was some kind of compulsion to submit to the word of others and to carry out their orders.

Acc.: — Jakov did not want to report it. And if one did not want to, then the other could not either.

Pr.: — How about Veljko Cubrilovic?

Acc.: — He wanted to conduct us to Priboj. We saw a larger place that had a gendarmes' barracks, so that we were afraid that the gendarmes would notice us. I did not have a permit, I had only a worker's book and because of that we said that they had to go with us to Tuzla. They said, "We can't. We don't know the way."

Pr.: — Why to Tuzla? To whom did you wish to go in Tuzla?

Acc.: — We had no further objectives.

Pr.: — Didn't Ciganovic tell you anything?

Acc.: — Ciganovic said that in Tuzla he knew Misko Jovanovic as a good Serb and that he would not reject us if we should turn to him.

Pr.: — And you demanded that they lead you to Jovanovic?

Acc.: — We did not demand it.

Pr.: — They said so.

Acc.: — It isn't true. We demanded that they take us to

Tuzla, or up to Tuzla, depending on the situation. They said that they did not know the way and they could not go. We realized that people who do not know the way would be dangerous for us and we looked for someone else who would lead us. I asked to whom we could turn. We didn't know, but we first sent them to Priboj.

Pr.: — Who was the first to advise you to go to Priboj?

Acc.: — No one gave us instructions. We told them, "Go to Priboj and see whether there are gendarmes."

Pr.: — When you left Obren Milosevic's house did you know that you would go to Priboj? Didn't Milovic tell you?

Acc.: — He didn't say anything. We thought that we would go in the direction of Tuzla. We didn't know that we couldn't go further than Priboj. Princip and I hid ourselves in the bushes, and we sent them to see whether there were gendarmes. They left and returned quickly, and Princip jumped over the barrier and after several minutes also called me. When I came, I saw Princip with the teacher Cubrilovic whom I did not know up to then.

Pr.: — Nor his opinion?

Acc.: — I got acquainted with him. He said that his name was Cubrilovic. We put the bombs and revolver in those bags.

Pr.: — In which bags?

Acc.: — We hid in the underbrush, we put the bombs and revolvers into the bags and put them on the horse. He asked me, "What do you need that for?" and I said, "It's the times, the times (tempora)," and he shut up.

Pr.: — It's curious how they obeyed you. Did you tell him that he had to obey, or did he just obey?

Acc.: — I said, "The times (tempora)," and they felt forced to obey. I paid Milovic seven or eight crowns and we went into a fenced area.

Pr.: — This word "tempora," was that a password which you received in Belgrade?

Acc.: — God forbid! I was surprised by that stupid question, "What do you need that for?"

Pr.: — You were looking for help to transport the bombs? Why didn't you tell him?

Acc.: — Without a doubt a stupid question, because that would hurt him.

Pr.: — He had to know that you had bad intentions.

Acc.: — Why did that have to interest him?

Pr.: — When you asked for help, he must have been interested in why.

Acc.: — Veljko Cubrilovic asked further whether that was to carry out an assassination of Franz Ferdinand.

Pr.: — You told him right away.

Acc.: — I simply said, "The times." If by that was meant "to kill," I didn't tell him.

Pr.: — Did Princip say it?

Acc.: — I don't know.

Pr.: — Who was the leader?

Acc.: — Princip.

Pr.: — You don't remember, but he says it explicitly.

Acc.: — He put the bombs in the saddle-bag, the saddle-bag on the horse, and we went across some mountains to the village house of Kerovic. I was wet and muddy. I took off my socks and lay down to sleep. Later I woke up, ate and afterwards slept again because I was tired. We had marched for 21 hours. Then I was sick and I threw up. What they talked about, whether anyone showed the bombs, I don't know.

Pr.: — At what time did you leave from Priboj?

Acc.: — We hadn't even been in Priboj.

Pr.: — I mean from Kerovic's house.

Acc.: — About nine o'clock.

Pr.: — You didn't tell anybody anything on your departure? Did you tell them to be quiet?

Acc.: — I threatened them.

Pr.: — What did you say?

Acc.: — It seemed to me that they had seen the bombs. Whether they saw the bombs, I don't know. I said it.

Pr.: — To whom?

Acc.: — To Blagoje, that he was not to tell anybody that we were there, "because you will suffer terribly, people will come who are stronger than Austria and the gendarmes, and they will kill all the males."

Pr.: — Did you have any instructions from anywhere?

Acc.: — I've already answered that as far as I am concerned. Nothing was positively stated and the peasant naturally was afraid.

Pr.: — Who travelled with you to Tuzla?

Acc.: — The young Kerovic, the one with the injured arm, and Stjepanovic.

The President shows the accused the statement of 15 July, in which it was said, "The peasant asked whether we knew the teacher Cubrilovic, and we replied to the peasant that we didn't know him, but that two students of Cubrilovic's were in Sarajevo, and then we agreed on it."

Acc.: — He said: "I will find a peasant." Probably he was acquainted with Cubrilovic and asked him if he could take us further.

Pr.: — Who held the bombs and revolvers when you travelled by cart?

Acc.: — I didn't hold them. They were in the saddle-bags.

Pr.: — Did you see whether Cubrilovic gave a letter to someone else?

Acc.: — No.

Pr.: — Did you know with whom you would stay in Tuzla?

Acc.: — No. Cubrilovic had been saying that in Tuzla he had a godfather, Misko Jovanovic: "I think that he will not turn you away," but I don't remember that well.

Pr.: — Probably in the cart he was discussing with Princip as to who would take the bombs?

Acc.: — He said nothing, only that we would get out before Tuzla. In the evening they woke me up: "Let's go, we're ready!" I got up and in the same way I threatened Blagoje and later Stjepanovic, and then we sat in a cart and went by some kind of path until we came to a paved road. There we came to the village of Lopare and avoided a gendarme barracks. Later we sat in the cart. When we passed Lopare, it was a beautiful night and I said to Stjepanovic to watch out. He kept silent and smiled. We travelled that way the whole night and we arrived before Tuzla at about four o'clock in the morning. I got out with Princip and gave Stjepanovic a forint. We went to the river Jala and washed ourselves. Later we went into Tuzla and sat in the *Kavana Bosna* (Cafe Bosnia). At nine o'clock I bought new trousers, got dressed at my colleague's and went to the Serbian reading room. Gavro Princip came too and there we found Misko Jovanovic. With him we came into the room and said that the bombs and revolvers had arrived. At that he asked us: "For what purpose?"

Pr.: — Did you threaten him?

Acc.: — I didn't threaten him with anything. We discussed as to how to take the bombs to Sarajevo. We told him that he could bring them to Sarajevo. Certainly for him that would not be suspicious. He said that one could not accept such risky things so we asked him to keep the things at his place.

Pr.: — Did he agree?

Acc.: — Yes.

Pr.: — Did you agree that someone would come?

Acc.: — We agreed that someone would come. Whoever brought a box of *Stefanija* cigarettes, he should know that he is one of us. In the evening we left from Tuzla for Sarajevo, Princip, Cabrinovic, and I. We arrived in Sarajevo in the morning. Then we split up in Sarajevo. I went to Pale. Princip remained here and so it was until the assassination. I came two or three times from Pale to Sarajevo and I agreed with them about the things to be done.

Pr.: — Did you find out whether the bombs had been brought?

Acc.: — Ilic brought them and he told me that the things were here. He told me that one should postpone the assassination because the results would be terrible for the Serbs. Princip and I were the only ones against that. And so I arrived in Sarajevo three days before the assassination and there I conferred with Princip. Ilic was strongly against the assassination and was urging me not to participate in any way. I told him that there was no sense in that, and that the assassination had to be carried out. Ilic thought that I would not carry out the assassination because he said that there were five people. He had his three, I did not know any of them, and he told me not to carry out the assassination. It is possible that he was convinced that I would not carry it out. I was firmly decided to carry it out.

Pr.: — When you were in Sarajevo the last few days and when you heard that the Heir Apparent was coming, did you know that his wife would arrive with him?

Acc.: — No.

Pr.: — But it was in the press the last few days before.

Acc.: — I didn't know, and I never intended to kill her.

Pr.: — Princip, was that your wish?

Princip: — I didn't think about her. I hit her by accident.

Acc. (Grabez): — On the day of the assassination I came to Sarajevo. At Basagic's book store I met with Cabrinovic who told me to come at eight o'clock to Vlajnic's sweet-shop. I came and there I saw Ilic and Cabrinovic. After that I went home with Ilic. He gave me the bomb and revolver, and I promised him that I would not carry out the assassination, that I would remain for further work and that I would work in the same spirit for revolutionary ideas. However, I went to carry out the assassination. I knew that Princip had to be standing at Siler's and I was looking for him. I intended to use the bomb, to confuse the chauffeur and the public, while Princip had to shoot the revolver. I walked along the quay, but Princip was not at the place mentioned, and I went toward the Magistrate's. He wasn't on either side. I walked several times along the quay, and because I didn't see him I was convinced that he had been arrested. I thought: if Cabrinovic does not succeed with the assassination, without a doubt the chauffeur would turn toward the Konak (City Hall) and he would not leave there the whole day. Therefore it was imperatively necessary that someone be at the place of Zerajic,[69] where the car would go more slowly. I was thinking of standing at the place of the turn-off for the Konak. I was thinking to find Princip at the old place and go toward the Latin Bridge. There were many people, and the detectives were cruising. It was even more difficult to go because two detectives noticed me. At that I thought of turning by the Emperor's Bridge and coming to the same place. However, when I came to the Emperor's Bridge there was such a crowd that one couldn't go any further and the police were blocking it. I decided to remain, and I stood there. After several minutes I heard the explosion of the bomb. I didn't know who threw it, because I knew that there were several assassins, but I thought that it was Cabrinovic, because I knew that the other assassins were of weaker quality.

Pr.: — How did you know that the other assassins were of weaker quality?

Acc.: — I knew the Bosnian youth here well enough. However, I thought that the assassination had succeeded because the automobile did not come for a long time. Suddenly the first, second and third cars came. I turned. I saw that the Heir Apparent was alive, and I thought that the others had let us down because I did not see anyone else shoot. Just where I was standing the car went slowly and I regretted that I had changed my place. When the automobile returned from the city hall, I thought that it would pass the Emperor's Bridge. However, the car went further and after several minutes one could hear the first shot, and then the second. Immediately after that, one heard that Ferdinand was dead.

Pr.: — In case the late esteemed Ferdinand returned by the Emperor's Bridge, had you decided to carry out the assassination?

Acc.: — Yes. The news that the Heir was dead spread rapidly and my first thought was to flee. I went across the road next to Gazi Isabeg's bath and I went around Filopovic's park to my uncle Gavro Crnogorcevic. I went into the bathroom and put the bomb under the seat in the bathroom, and the revolver under the roof and I leisurely went into the street to the place where the assassination took place. I observed the parts of the bomb. That day I was at Uncle Gavro Gasic's, the national delegate, and I spent the night there. The next day I went to Pale and went home and decided that if someone asked me where I was, I would tell them. Naturally, at that place no one would think that I was among the assassins. At home I was completely calm. Father thought that I was arrested.

Pr.: — Did you know that the Archduchess was killed?

Acc.: — I read it in special editions of Croatian and German newspapers. I wished that General Potiorek had been killed. At our house there was a female friend,[70] who wanted to go to Rudo the next day, to the Kroupal's. I thought about running away. It would have been convenient to leave with her because I would not be noticed by the gendarmes, and because there I had a friend Rista Todorovic, and I would not have been suspected. I didn't tell father that I was going. The next day I left the house for the Koran station, and around ten o'clock I left for Visegrad. Not having a permit, I was stopped in Praci by the gendarmes and taken to the jail in Sarajevo.

The President called for a recess of five minutes.

After the Recess

Pr.: — Now you will explain to us why you said something different before the court in the inquiry (shows him the statement of 15 July).

Acc.: — When I left the Emperor's Bridge after the assassination I thought that the assassins would be arrested, that many things would be discovered, and that I would be exposed. I thought that if I were exposed, I would not be exposed as an assassin. I would cover up the assassination by saying that I stood at that same place and I should be convicted only as an accomplice. When I came to the interrogating judge I saw that they didn't have the evidence to make a good case against me, because they tortured me,[71] and if they had had convincing evidence they wouldn't have done that.

Pr.: — Where?

Acc.: — At the police station. After I was taken to the court the judge confronted me with Princip. There, I don't know why, I admitted that I participated in the assassination. No doubt that was weakness, thinking that I could help myself that way. However, today when I say that every assassin was equally guilty, I told the exact truth.

Pr.: — You were in Pale all the time until several days before the assassination?

Acc.: — Yes.

Pr.: — Did you not go to Tuzla?

Acc.: — That isn't true. You can confirm that by the citizens of Pale.

Pr.: — About 22 or 23 June the following persons saw you in Tuzla (Reads a list of some witnesses who saw him in Tuzla.) If one person said that, I could believe that he was mistaken, but they explicitly say that they know you.

Acc.: — I said at the investigation that he could convince himself of that by the citizens of Pale and by my family, that I was at the most gone from home one day.

Pr.: — Did you not have an agreement with the students? Do you know that in Tuzla they excel in ideas of high treason?

Acc.: — I don't know that at all. I can only say that I was not in Tuzla.

The President then shows a Browning and bombs to the accused: Do you know where these came from?

Acc.: — I don't know.

Pr.: — Who made them?

Acc.: — I don't know.

Pr.: — Where can they be bought?

Acc.: — In great arsenals in Serbia.

Pr.: — Do they have bombs there?

Acc.: — They have containers there which can be filled with explosives.

Pr.: — How can one get explosives? It is said on the contrary that all guerrillas who had bombs had to return them to the state.

Acc.: — They did not have to.

Pr.: — Did you know what goals the *Narodna odbrana* had?

Acc.: — I know it as a cultural association.

Pr.: — What kind of role did that cultural organization have in Serbia's war?

Acc.: — It sent many guerrillas to Turkey, but did not give them arms. There is no doubt about that. It recruited candidates, and the state equipped them.

Pr.: — Others say that the *Narodna odbrana* supplied arms.

Acc.: — So far as I know, no.

Pr.: — Have you been a member?

Acc.: — No.

Pr.: — Did you know members?

Acc.: — No.

Pr.: — Tankosic and Ciganovic were not members?

Acc.: — Tankosic wasn't a member.

Pr.: —Did you talk with Tankosic?

Acc.: — Only once. I knew Tankosic through Ciganovic. Ciganovic and Tankosic were good friends. Ciganovic said that Tankosic was the greatest opponent of *Narodna odbrana* and of Milan Pribicevic and it is not true that he is a founder of the *Narodna odbrana*, nor that Milan Ciganovic is an active member.

Pr.: — Did you receive cyanide?

Acc.: — I didn't receive it at all. Ilic was convinced that I wouldn't carry out the assassination, so he didn't give it to me.

Pr.: — Why did Cabrinovic not receive a revolver?

Acc.: — I don't know.

Pr.: — Did Ciganovic tell you anything about Misko Jovanovic?

Acc.: — He said that he was a good man and an honest worker.

Pr.: — Did he tell you anything about Veljko Cubrilovic?

Acc.: — No.

The President shows the defendant the statement of 15 July.

Acc.: — Probably I said what is in the indictment.

Pr.: — What does it mean if you say to someone that he is *a man* (covjek)?

Acc.: — That he is a good man; that he works in the national field.

Pr.: — That he helps others to carry out assassinations. You were sure that he would help you.

Acc.: — We were not sure. It was my idea to threaten Misko Jovanovic.

The President shows the defendant the statement of 10 July where the accused says that Ciganovic told him that Jovanovic was a good man.

Acc.: — It is true that he is a good man and that he would not kill us.

Pr.: — And Veljko Cubrilovic also says that Misko Jovanovic is a good man. What kind of attitude do the peasants in Serbia have toward Austria?

Acc.: — Badly disposed.

Pr.: — What do they think of Austria?

Acc.: — That she is a strong empire, but they are decidedly hostile toward her.

Pr.: — Peasants should concern themselves with affairs at home. How come the Serbian peasant thinks about politics?

Acc.: — The Serbian peasant is of average intelligence. He knows what Austria wants to do to Serbia. He learns it from the newspapers and in school. The hatred against Austria is cultivated.

Pr.: — Is that your conviction?

Acc.: — Yes.

Pr.: — Did the captains in Loznica and Sabac know that you had bombs and weapons?

Acc.: — We didn't tell them. What they thought we didn't know.

Pr.: — Is every student given a half-fare ticket on the railroad and is he sent to the revenue officers so that they deal with him for two or three days?

Acc.: — I don't know what is involved. I wasn't able to tell that they knew the situation.

Pr.: — Didn't you notice that they asked what you wished? Did you tell them names?

Acc.: — Yes. I said Trifko Grabez, and I could have said Mihajlo Popovic.

Pr.: — You don't know where the bombs came from, but in the inquiry of 1 July you confirmed that they were Kragujevac bombs.

Acc.: — That is true. The bombs from Kragujevac are similar. Whether they really are Kragujevac bombs, I don't know, because there are bombs of different kinds, and all are modeled on those bombs.

Pr.: — What did you discuss with Ciganovic about the assassination?

Acc.: — I did not talk with him about the assassination. I associated with him recently, but Princip associated the most with him.

Naum.: — Do you know what Captain Popovic wrote to the captain in Loznica?

Acc.: — I don't know. He wrote something but I do not know what.

Naum.: — You stated exactly: that all authorities had to lend you a hand, and that they should not hinder you.

Acc.: — That was written on a small card. That was written for the railway ticket.

Naum.: — You come to the captain in Sabac. You have to cross over secretly and everyone has to help you. How do you explain that?

Acc.: — That the districts along the way come to our aid as regards transportation and roads.

Naum.: — And to pass you secretly across the border.

Acc.: — That was not written.

Naum.: — They didn't write that, but they arranged it. The captain in Loznica did not know you, but nevertheless he saw to it that you were passed secretly over the border. Is not an official suspicious of people who have to pass secretly across the border?

Acc.: — Prince Mihailo was killed by an Austrian bomb.

The President shows the accused the statement in which he said that he almost decided not to use the bombs because there is a 12-second delay in their explosion.

Acc.: — That statement is false. There are also bombs which explode in 18 seconds. Those are for war, and those are more practical. These are private.

Pr.: — And where is the factory in Serbia which makes private bombs?

Acc.: — I don't know the name.

Pr.: — But you know where the factory is?

Acc.: — I don't know.

Pr.: — On what basis did you conclude that?

Acc.: — I saw the same kind of bombs in many stores.

Pr.: — What was the name of the merchant where you saw them?

Acc.: — There are many. I don't know the names.

Naumowicz: — There is not a word in the inquiry about these threats of which you spoke today. How is it that you are stressing it now?

Acc.: — Those were not important things.

Naum.: — How did you know that you had to contact Cubrilovic?

Acc.: — I didn't know.

Naum.: — Grbic sent Milovic to lead you to Cubrilovic?

Acc.: — I don't know.

Naum.: — You explicitly told Milovic to summon Cubrilovic?

Acc.: — Milovic said on the way that he knew Cubrilovic.

Naum.: — The peasant who told you about Cubrilovic might also have been a detective, and you believed him at once.

Acc.: — We were in the mountains, and so we had to reckon on the worst that could happen.

Naum.: — When you went to Pale why did your father say that he thought that you had been arrested?

Acc.: — Because they arrested hundreds of Serbs.

Naum.: — Did your father suspect you?

Acc.: — My father thought that as a student in Belgrade I would certainly be arrested.

Naum.: — You go to Obren Milosevic's house. He gives you saddle-bags for nothing. How is that?

Acc.: — We told Milovic, "You must find a man who will carry those things for us."

Naum.: — Are you an adherent of terrorism?

Acc.: — I don't know exactly how to say it. I am.

Naum.: — You applied terrorism to your adherents, because you threatened every peasant whom you encountered.

Acc.: — That kind of thing requires many helpers. That was the most revolutionary act which was ever carried out in history.

Naum.: — Why do you consider the assassination to be the most important act in history?

Acc.: — According to the consequences, it was the most important.

Naum.: — Did you know that it would have that kind of consequences?

Acc.: — I didn't think so.

Naum.: — How was it that you threatened those people since at the time you still didn't know that the assassination would be such an important act?

Acc.: — He was a very important person. Napoleon, Alexander II, and then Ferdinand.

Pros.: — In Sabac did you get acquainted with Bozo Milanovic?

Acc.: — No.

Pros.: — Weren't you in Lopare?

Acc.: — No.

Pros.: — Who told you that there were gendarmes there?

Acc.: — I had a map in Belgrade on which all the gendarme garrisons were marked.

Pros.: — Did you determine the itinerary in Belgrade?

Acc.: — I planned the route where two gendarme garrisons were marked on the map.

Pr.: — Where did you get that map?

Acc.: — It was a special map, of course.

Pr.: — I never heard that the maps mark the revenue and gendarme garrisons.

Acc.: — Only specially made maps mark the gendarme and customs posts.

Pr.: — Probably from the book: *The Austrian Army?*

Acc.: — No.

Pr.: — Do you know that book?

Acc.: — I do.

Pr.: — Do you know the book which contains the program of the *Narodna odbrana?*

Acc.: — I read the program of the *Narodna odbrana* of the year 1908 as a cultural association.

Pr.: — And after the reorganization?

Acc.: — I don't know it.

Premuzic: — How did Jovanovic act when you were at his place together with Princip?

Acc.: — When we came there we got acquainted and immediately came to the point that the things should be transported to Sarajevo. We weren't at his place more than five minutes.

Prem.: — Did he say that the plan did not suit him?

Acc.: — Yes. We asked that he transport them, and he said he couldn't.

Prem.: — Did he protest against keeping the weapons at his house?

Acc.: — He didn't. He remained silent. We spoke.

Prem.: — He agreed at once. Did you threaten him?

Acc.: — I don't remember. Princip said that he took leave of him in an unfriendly way.

Strupl: — Do you know Jovo Kerovic?

Acc.: — I don't know all the Kerovics. Is that the one with the hand?

Feldbauer: — Jakov Milovic said that you told him that you had a permit from Sarajevo to travel in Bosnia.

Acc.: — I don't recall. I don't remember.

Pr.: — You said that Misko Jovanovic must have thought that you were preparing an assassination.

Acc.: — That is understood. We weren't going to play with those bombs and revolvers.

Pr.: — That is important, because he says that he didn't know what they would be used for.

Acc.: — As an intelligent person he could have figured it out.

Malek: — You said in the inquiry that Ilic said to you, "Take those things away from my place!"

Acc.: — Yes, he said that.

Malek: — He did not give you bombs to carry out an assassination?

Acc.: — He gave them to me to carry away.

Malek: — Did you tell Obren Milosevic that the Heir Apparent was coming to Sarajevo?

Acc.: — No.

Pr.: — Princip! Grabez says that you talked with him about the assassination before he returned to Serbia.

Princ.: — We talked in general about assassinations, but not about the assassination of the Heir Apparent.

Grabez: — Only when I returned, then.

The President calls for a recess.

Adjournment at 12 o'clock

CONTINUATION OF THE MAIN HEARING
13 OCTOBER 1914
In the afternoon
THE HEARING OF TRIFKO GRABEZ — CONTINUATION

Pr.: — (Shows Grabez a drawing of the place where he stood, and Grabez points out the place where he stood.) Tell us here, do you know who the Freemasons are? Did you talk about that in Belgrade?

Acc.: — I heard about that, and also Ciganovic talked about it. Cabrinovic told me that he belonged to them, and Ciganovic said that Tankosic also belonged to them. As to Ciganovic, I don't know.

Pr.: — What kind of goals do they have?

Acc.: — It is my impression that they have very liberal religious ideas.

Pr.: — Did Ciganovic or Cabrinovic not tell you about the death sentence against the Heir Apparent?

Acc.: — I don't remember.

Pr.: — Did that influence your decision? Are you perhaps a Freemason?

Acc.: — I am not. I don't belong to the association.

Pr.: — So that institution did not give the order to carry out the assassination?

Acc.: — It did not.

Premuzic: — In Sarajevo, did you know about Mehmedbasic?

Acc.: — No. I knew that there would be a Moslem, but I didn't know that it would be Mehmedbasic.

Pr.: — Were you surprised when you heard that there was also a Moslem?

Acc.: — I was not surprised.

Pr.: — Did that please you?

Acc.: — Yes.

Pr.: — Why?

Acc.: — Because the matter should be a matter of all Bosnia. It should not be a special matter of the Serbian people.

Pr.: — Why?

Acc.: — The Serbs are sufficiently compromised with respect to Austria, and with that they would to some extent be protected.

Pr.: — Was there discussion among you that in case Mehmedbasic succeeded in the assassination you would kill him?

Acc.: — I never spoke of that. I don't remember.

Pr.: — Had you decided to commit suicide if the assassination succeeded?

Acc.: — Yes.

Pr.: — With what?

Acc.: — With a revolver, of course.

THE HEARING OF DANILO ILIC
13 OCTOBER 1914

Pr.: — Call Danilo Ilic. (He is brought in.) You are Danilo Ilic. Do you want to tell us everything about the assassination? First say whether you are guilty.

Acc.: — I feel guilty, insofar as I participated.

Pr.: — Why do you feel guilty? Are you sorry that it happened, or are you sorry that it had consequences?

Acc.: — Both that it happened and that it had consequences. Especially that it had consequences.

Pr.: — Tell us everything from the very beginning.

Acc.: — When I finished the Teacher's School, I took a position in Avtovac and I was there for two months. Then I was transferred to Foca, where I stayed one month. Then I resigned and came to Sarajevo.

Pr.: — Why?

Acc.: — I didn't like that profession, and besides I was physically weak. Then I came to Sarajevo and I was in the service of the *Srpska Narodna Banka* (Serbian National Bank) for five months. Then I went to Serbia in July of 1913. I didn't find satisfactory work there, and I came back after I spent two and one-half months there. Then I was in the hospital for one and one-half days because of my stomach. Then I was without work for several months.

Pr.: — How did you live?

Acc.: — I have a house and mother in Sarajevo.

Pr.: — How much rent?

Acc.: — Sixty crowns.

Pr.: — Does your mother also live from that rent?

Acc.: — Yes.

Pr.: — Do you have mobile property or does your mother have cash?

Acc.: — I don't. Whether Mother has money, I don't know, but Mother is very thrifty and maybe she has.

Pr.: — Did you have to ask her for money when you needed it?

Acc.: — Yes, but rarely.

Pr.: — Did you give her money?

Acc.: — When I was in the Teacher's School.

Pr.: — What kind of occupation did you find?

Acc.: — For one month I was proof-reader at the *Srpska Rijec*, and then I was at *Zvono* as a journalist.

Pr.: — What was your pay?

Acc.: — Nothing. I received an honorarium.

Pr.: — Therefore one might say that for the past year after you left service you lived as a burden on your mother.

Acc.: — Yes.

Pr.: — When did your father die?

Acc.: — Twenty years ago.

Pr.: — Probably your mother lived only on the income from the house?

Acc.: — She earned money by washing linens for others. I had a stipend in the Teacher's School, one year from *Prosveta* and three years from the government.

Pr.: — On the occasion of the search some money was found at your mother's. I would like to know, how it was that she had so much money?

Acc.: — She saved it. She was very thrifty. She saved that before. Not when she fed me. She saved that up to 1913.

Pr.: — Isn't that your money?

Acc.: — Where would I get so much money? If I had money, I would have run away and not waited for them to arrest me.

Pr.: — Then you don't know where it came from?

Acc.: — I don't know.

Pr.: — And you knew she had it?

Acc.: — I thought so, because she saved a lot.

Pr.: — What kind of political ideals do you have? Are you a friend of Princip's?

Acc.: — Yes, since 1908.

Pr.: — You were also in agreement insofar as political opinions were concerned?

Acc.: — To some extent, yes.

Pr.: — What are your opinions?

Acc.: — I can't completely explain my own political beliefs. However I can say that we agreed in assassination as a means of protest against bad government.

Pr.: — What do you think about the South Slavs?

Acc.: — I spoke of that earlier. I cannot talk about that now. Since earlier I was against the assassination, and since I worked to prevent it, I cannot speak about the motives of the act.

Pr.: — But now we are talking about your political ideals. Don't you want to talk about that?

Acc.: — I stated earlier in the record what I previously said.

Pr.: — I wanted to present the record to you anyway. Here it says: "Our ideals are the unification of the whole South Slav people whether it be under a crown or if possible, under a republic." (He reads further.)

Pr.: — Did you say that? Does it correspond to your ideas?

Acc.: — To some extent it does. What is most important is that that was not the motive for the assassination itself. It was not the reason that I agreed. Later I gave another statement.

Pr.: — You said on August 4th that you met with Mehmedbasic and that you talked about your political ideals. (Reads): "We agreed that an assassination would help us the most," etc. (Reads further.) You already agreed at a time when it was not known that the Heir Apparent would come. You already had those ideas.

Acc.: — I defended that as a means of protest.

Pr.: — Here it says: The manner of carrying out one's ideas and not as a "protest" as you say now. For what purpose did you carry out the assassination?

Acc.: — There is still another of my statements in that respect.

Malek: — I can bring to your attention the statement of 13 July, where it says: "I have the following changes: I can't remember what I discussed with Princip . . ." (He reads further.)

Pr.: — Is that so?

Acc.: — Yes.

Pr.: — Tell us more. You were acquainted with Mehmedbasic. How was it with him?

Acc.: — We two discussed everything and agreed in the defense of assassination. We were especially dissatisfied with the government of Bosnia and Hercegovina.

Pr.: — Didn't you talk against anyone?

Acc.: — No.

Pr.: — Just generally that assassination was needed?

Acc.: — Yes.

Pr.: — How was it at the beginning of April, or when you received some sort of letter?

Acc.: — About Easter I received a letter from Princip in

which he said that he intended an assassination against the Heir Apparent and that he would have arms.

Pr.: — Did he write something else?

Acc.: — I don't remember exactly whether he wrote that I find someone else, but that seems to be the reason that I later looked for other people.

Pr.: — What did you do when you got that letter?

Acc.: — I met with Mehmedbasic. I don't know whether I already had Princip's letter. I said in the record[72] that I invited him, but that is not true. From the first when I made the statement I wanted to talk as if I had sought him out, but that was not true. Rather he looked me up, and he gave me the idea for the assassination before Princip did.

Pr.: — What did he say?

Acc.: — He asked me by letter to come to Mostar, that there were some important reasons. There we met in the Hotel Jelic and he said that one had to carry out an assassination on the Heir Apparent. I don't know exactly whether that was before Princip's letter.

Pr.: — Didn't you tell him that others also had the same intentions?

Acc.: — No. We separated with the proviso that the one who went first to Serbia bring back weapons and notify the other. When we separated, we agreed to write the other and tell him who would go to Serbia. I could not. Therefore we agreed that each of us would get ready at home and inform the other as to whether he would go or not. That's why we two agreed.

Pr.: — So anyway you decided that you could only get arms in Serbia. Why was that? Could you not also get them here?

Acc.: — We could not get them here.

Pr.: — Then one could, but not later.

Acc.: — We could not get them when we didn't have permits for arms.

Pr.: — You could have asked someone else to buy them for you. In the villages there are enough weapons. Every peasant has them.

Acc.: — Maybe they have them. I know absolutely that no one can get them here in any way, and there whoever wishes can buy them much cheaper.

Pr.: — There is freedom there so that everyone can arm himself.

Acc.: — I don't know whether there is freedom, I only know that one can buy them. Because of that we wanted to go there to buy weapons.

Pr.: — How was it that you wanted to go to Serbia, and then to come back with the arms, only because you could not buy arms here. There had to be something else.

Acc.: — Actually in order to get bombs, not only arms.

Pr.: — It is better that you admit the truth. So you wanted to go to Serbia to get bombs also?

Acc.: — Yes. I was in Serbia before that and as I stated at the inquiry I used to go to cafes in which there were guerrillas. I saw that some of the guerrillas could have bombs and we could get them from them. At that time I wrote Mehmedbasic that the arms would come, that he should wait a little, that is, until I got a letter from Princip. Meanwhile Princip came to Sarajevo and told me that he had arms.

Pr.: — From whom?

Acc.: — From Milan Ciganovic. He didn't say that he got them from someone. He only said that he gave them to him. He talked enough to me about Tankosic that I understood that Tankosic knew about the assassination.

Pr.: — Didn't he say that he met with him?

Acc.: — I don't know exactly. I stated that at the inquiry, but I don't know exactly. I stated that, and I do not deny it.

Pr.: — You stated thus (Reads.): "Then Princip said that he was at Tankosic's, who instructed him how to carry out the assassination in such a way that he who did it not be permitted to live . . ." Is it true that he said it in that way? Did Tankosic say that he had to commit suicide?

Acc.: — I came to that conclusion when Princip said that Tankosic knew about the assassination.

Pr.: — So that when you said Princip told you, he didn't really say. Rather that was your conclusion?

Acc.: — Yes.

Pr.: — How was it when Princip came? Where did he stay?

Acc.: — Before that I talked with Lazar Djukic about the assassination in general and I gave him to understand that he could get arms from me.

Pr.: — What did he say? Was he surprised?

Acc.: — I did not talk about the assassination of the Heir Apparent. Rather we talked about assassinations in general. I did not directly give him to understand that he could get arms from me. He said that it was hard to come by weapons, and I said to him that it was easy.

Pr.: — You explicitly said that it would come to assassination and that you did not know who would be accepted, and because of that he introduced Vaso Cubrilovic to you.

Acc.: — I talked about assassination with him, about the possibilities of assassination of the Heir Apparent.

Pr.: — That doesn't agree with your testimony. How was it when he introduced Vaso Cubrilovic to you?

Acc.: — Vaso Cubrilovic asked me whether I had arms for the assassination of the Heir, and I said that I did.

Pr.: — You told Cubrilovic, but Djukic didn't know?

Acc.: — He knew, but I did not tell him to look for someone directly. (The statement of 27 July is shown to the accused.)

Pr.: — Why do you change everything today? It is better that you admit the truth.

Acc.: — I admit it, but in general I was careful not to talk anyone into it directly, so that they would not say that I was guilty. I said it. In those days I was in a bad mood in general and I was not careful about the record.

Pr.: — Did you talk about the assassination directly with Vaso Cubrilovic? What did he tell you?

Acc.: — He said that he was ready, and that I should give him arms, and I said that I would give them. He found Cvjetko Popovic. I did not meet him because I did not intend to use him.

Pr.: — Then Princip came. Did he say anything about the arms?

Acc.: — He said that he was in Tuzla at Misko Jovanovic's, and after several days I went to Tuzla and came to Jovanovic's house.

Pr.: — Did you know him before?

Acc.: — I recognized him by the box of cigarettes. I stated that here when I talked about the assassination; however, I saw that the investigating judge asked me three times whether I had talked about the assassination. Later I came to the conclusion that we two had absolutely not talked about the assassination. I don't recall at all what we talked about. We talked the most about the transportation of the bombs.

Pr.: — When the means are transported, one certainly talks about the purpose. You said two or three times that you talked about the assassination (The accused is shown the statement of 4 July and 13 July where[73] it says: "In Tuzla I talked about the assassination of the Heir Apparent. Jovanovic knew about the assassination then . . .") Now you say he didn't.

Acc.: — I don't recall at all what we talked about.

Pr.: — When you arrived at Tuzla and sought the arms, did you have the impression that he knew about the assassination? For what purpose did he keep the arms?

Acc.: — I don't know at all what we two did and what we said. I know that we talked about the transportation of the arms. I was with him a short time. I thought that he knew about the assassination, and therefore I didn't talk about it.

Pr.: — What else? Where did you hide the bombs?

Acc.: — At home in a small suitcase under the sofa.[74]

Pr.: — Who cleaned the room?

Acc.: — Mother.

Pr.: — Could she have seen the arms?

Acc.: — The room was closed. Then I had Mehmedbasic, Popovic, and Vaso Cubrilovic.[75]

Pr.: — How did you agree to carry out the assassination?

Acc.: — Princip, and Cubrilovic and I discussed it. Grabez came to Sarajevo many times and talked about how to carry it out. We distributed ourselves from the Teacher's School to the Latin Bridge.

Pr.: — Where did each one have to stand?

Acc.: — I don't know exactly now. First Mehmedbasic had to be at the Austro-Hungarian Bank, then Cabrinovic a little further up toward the Teacher's School dormitory, a little further Cubrilovic and Popovic at the Emperor's Bridge, and then further up Princip and Grabez. I told them to stand further down and the others to stand where they pleased.

Pr.: — You said before that Mehmedbasic stood at the Mostar Garden, and Cabrinovic at the Austro-Hungarian Bank?

Acc.: — That's right.

Pr.: — How old was Mehmedbasic?

Acc.: — He was 26 or 27. However, I had already told him not to come for the assassination, but he came two days before the assassination.

Pr.: — Why?

Acc.: — Because I had become an opponent of the assassination and I began to prevent the assassination. At the hearing I did not tell everything I did. When Princip came and brought the arms I informed Mehmedbasic that Princip was here. Later I saw that the assassination would be harmful and began to prevent it. I talked with Princip as I also wanted to persuade him that there not be an assassination. I talked with him and he opposed it from the beginning, and later I said to him: let the other five do it, just you don't. Because I talked with him at length about that, he fell silent, but did not directly say: "I won't," but I understood that he agreed. I thought that he would not do it. Then Mehmedbasic himself announced that he would not come to Sarajevo at all because the assassination would fail, but later on he came anyway, two days before the assassination. Since I already had arms he wanted me to give him some of the weapons to take to Stolac. I did not say directly to Cubrilovic and Popovic that they should not perform the assassination, but I concluded that they were unfit for it. Because I had promised Princip that the other five would do it, later, if there were no assassination, I would have to prove that I was responsible that it did not take place. Therefore I gave the pair a bomb and revolver. I figured it out exactly. They wanted arms for training, because people who are not trained are probably not competent to do the assassination. I did not give them arms earlier than the eve of the assassination itself. I gave them to them on the Bembasa.

Pr.: — Did you come to a tunnel, when you gave them arms? Did any of them fire shots?

Acc.: — Not a one.

Pr.: — Thus none of them fired the revolver then?

Acc.: — Not a soul fired.

Pr.: — Didn't you show them how one fires a revolver?

Acc.: — I don't know whether that is in my statement. I don't remember now.

Pr.: — Did you show them how to handle the bomb?

Acc.: — Yes.

Pr.: — And the revolver?

Acc.: — Yes.

Pr.: — Yet you didn't fire a shot from the revolver?

Acc.: — I don't remember.

Pr.: — Here, it says thus (He reads.): "That afternoon before the assassination, Cubrilovic and Popovic waited for me at Bembasa . . ." (Statement of 12 July.) Did you know for sure that there were cartridges?

Acc.: — I don't recall exactly.

Pr.: — Did you load the revolvers?

Acc.: — They were loaded.

Pr.: — By whom?

Acc.: — I don't know.

Pr.: — Did you give them cyanide?

Acc.: — Yes.

Pr.: — Why?

Acc.: — I said, "That is for poisoning."

Pr.: — Why take it?

Acc.: — In order to poison themselves when they carried out the assassination.

Pr.: — You said that to them the day before the assassination and gave them arms, and now you want to say that you withdrew from the assassination.

Acc.: — I did not directly withdraw, but that is already a withdrawal when I did not give them the arms before.

Pr.: — Where could one train with the revolvers in Sarajevo?

Acc.: — There is a place outside of Sarajevo. Had I wanted them to practice I would have given them arms, but I had the ammunition with me. Otherwise one could not be sure the assassination would succeed.

Pr.: — Did you bring still more bombs to them at the sweet-shop the morning of the assassination?

Acc.: — That was on the same day as the assassination. Grabez and Princip told me about Cabrinovic, that he was a very naive fellow and that he was not fit for the assassination. I too believed that he would not do it. I intended not to give him any kind of arms at all because he would not carry out the assassination.

Pr.: — Did you show him how to use a bomb?

Acc.: — No, he knew.

Pr.: — You found Popovic and Djukic, Mehmedbasic and Cubrilovic. You talked with them and they were convinced that you also would accomplish the assassination. Why didn't you carry out the assassination yourself?

Acc.: — At first I was for the assassination and worked for it, but later I was an opponent and worked against it.

Pr.: — When you give bombs to someone, you don't work against assassination.

Acc.: — But I was convinced that they would not carry out the assassination.

Pr.: — But you certainly don't give arms to children because they can do harm.

Acc.: — Afterward the arms would be gathered.

Pr.: — Better admit the truth. It is obvious that you don't admit the truth. You didn't say a single word that you wanted to divert Cabrinovic, Cubrilovic, and Popovic.

Acc.: — I did not dissuade them, but I was firmly convinced that they would not carry out the assassination. I got the impression from conversation that they were not fit for the assassination. (The statement of 4 August is shown. Here you explicitly say: only when you received word from Princip did you remember Mehmedbasic, and that you wrote him concerning the assassination and that he wrote you.)

Acc.: — I wanted in general in the statement to speak as if I had been for the assassination, because I did not wish to say that I had been for the prevention of the assassination.

Pr.: — Had those bombs been at your place? (Shows him.)

Acc.: — Yes.

Pr.: — Had you shown them how they had to unscrew them and strike them on a hard object?

Acc.: — Yes.

Pr.: — Because you have fooled around enough today, say whether it is true, whether you, when you gave the revolvers to Cubrilovic and Popovic, showed them how to shoot those revolvers in a tunnel?

Acc.: — I don't remember now. I think I didn't.

Pr.: — In the record you said that you didn't shoot. Now say whether you did or not?

Acc.: — I didn't.

Pr.: — Call Princip. (He comes.) Did he discourage you from the assassination?

Princip: — Before the assassination he spoke to me many times and discouraged me, and I let him talk about that and then he stopped.

Pr. (to Ilic): — Did you tell Grabez to withdraw?

Ilic: — I also told Grabez.

Pr. (to Grabez): — Grabez, is that true?

Grabez: — Yes.

Princip: — I only know that I did not agree. I admit I also said to him when he talked to me, that I wouldn't agree and in the end I stopped talking about it.

Ilic: — I understood that he agreed.

Princip: — It is his business to defend himself as best he can, but I say what I think.

Naumowicz (to Ilic): — You said that Mehmedbasic invited you to Mostar because he had something important to tell you. Didn't he say anything about the assassination? You went to Mostar. You said that you are poor, but at that kind of letter you immediately travelled to Mostar and back.

Acc.: — I had saved 300 crowns from the time when I was a teacher. I said that also at the inquiry.

Naum.: — And you threw away this 300 crowns which you gathered by hard work just to learn that Mehmedbasic wanted to say something to you. It is much more likely what you said before: that you went to persuade him to participate in the assassination. Who introduced Cubrilovic to you?

Acc.: — Djukic.

Naum.: — For what purpose?

Acc.: — For the purpose of the assassination.

Naum.: — To participate?

Acc.: — I didn't directly ask him to participate but I talked in such a way that he could understand that I needed someone.

Naum.: — Cvijetko Popovic said explicitly that you shot.

Acc.: — I didn't.

Naum.: — You also said: "Where those bullets hit, no one will live."[76]

Acc.: — Maybe I said that, but I didn't shoot.

Feldbauer: — How long did Princip stay with you before the assassination?

Acc.: — One month.

Feldb.: — With whom did he arrange the rent? Did he pay something for the room?

Acc.: — He had to pay mother, not me.

Feldb.: — How is it that you don't know that?

Acc.: — I didn't ask.

Premuzic: — Where did you give the bomb to Princip, and where to Grabez?

Acc.: — I don't even know when Princip took the weapons from the apartment. Grabez received them in my room, and Cabrinovic at Vlajnic's.

Prem.: — Did you know Ciganovic?

Acc.: — By sight.

Prem.: — And Djuro Sarac?

Acc.: — I did.

Prem.: — Did you talk with him about the assassination?

Acc.: — No.

Prem.: — Did you know Djoka Bajic?

Acc.: — No.

Perisic: — You gave the bomb to Cabrinovic at Vlajnic's, and to Grabez at home. Did you take him home?

Acc.: — Yes.

Per.: — Was that the morning of the assassination?

Acc.: — Yes.

Per.: — He found Popovic as a third and brought him to you. Did you tell him what kind of consequences it would have? How could that kind of youngster agree to that? Did you know him?

Acc.: — I knew him for a long time.

Per.: — Did you talk about the assassination and about politics in general?

Acc.: — No.

Per.: — Thus he comes and at once he agrees?

Acc.: — Of course. I knew that he wouldn't shoot, that he is not capable.

Per.: — I know, when you gave the arms, but since you also were firm in your conviction that he (Popovic) would not do it, did you talk with him?

Acc.: — I did not talk with him at all until the eve of the assassination itself.

Malek: — You said that Cubrilovic told you that because of his sister he wouldn't participate in the assassination. He says that at that you answered him: "So what!"

Acc.: — I sure did!

Malek: — After that, when you said that Cubrilovic wouldn't participate in the assassination, did you look for someone else?

Acc.: — No.

Malek: — In the inquiry did you yourself call attention to Jovanovic from Tuzla?

Acc.: — Yes.

Malek: — It was not known before you said it that he gave you bombs. Thus, had you wanted to protect Jovanovic as you did today, you wouldn't have pointed him out.

Pr.: — I call a recess for five minutes until the next one comes.

After the Recess

Counsellor Hoffman (to Ilic): — Why did you run away from Sarajevo after the assassination?

Acc.: — I didn't run away.

Hoffm.: — You did. To Brod.

Acc.: — That was before.

Pr.: — Where were you at the moment of the assassination?

Acc.: — At the corner of Cumurija street and the quay.

Premuzic: — How often in your life have you been in Tuzla?

Acc.: — That was the first time.

Prem.: — Did you have an acquaintance?

Acc.: — No one.

Prem.: — You concerned yourself with politics. Didn't you know Dr. Stojanovic and others?

Acc.: — I heard of them, but I didn't know them personally.

Prem.: — Did some citizen of Tuzla write in *Zvono*?

Acc.: — I don't remember, maybe there was some contributor.

Prem.: — How did you travel from Sarajevo to Doboj?

Acc.: — By train.

Prem.: — When was that? Do you remember the date?

Acc.: — I don't know the exact date.

Prem.: — Did you travel alone?

Acc.: — I don't remember.

Prem.: — Today you answer everything: I don't know, it is not, etc. However you say things which have long been refuted. Better say how it was. Say once again, but absolutely truthfully, whether you talked with Misko Jovanovic about the assassination?

Acc.: — I do not know whether I did.

Pr.: — How many days before the assassination did you travel to Brod?

Acc.: — Ten days before.

Pr.: — For what purpose?

Acc.: — I do not know exactly what the purpose was. Perhaps because I was against the assassination. Then it first came to my mind not to participate in the assassination.

Pr.: — Was it not your intention to participate?

Acc.: — It was at the beginning when Princip wrote me the letter, since that time.

Pr.: — That very day perhaps, or the next you said that Djukic was looking for others. You see that you did not want to participate alone.

Acc.: — I wanted to have more.

Pr.: — What happened in Brod? Why did you come back?

Acc.: — To prevent the assassination.

Pr.: — Wasn't it mainly so as not to be here on the day of the assassination?

Acc.: — I wanted to leave Sarajevo for good.

Pr.: — But they had the bombs.

Acc.: — They didn't have them.

Pr.: — They were with you. Princip lived with you.

Acc.: — Yes.

Pr.: — Then you would have left, and they would have had the weapons.

Acc.: — The three of them had the weapons. Therefore I returned from Brod, in order to try to prevent the assassination.

Prem.: — Wasn't the question raised as to why Misko went from Tuzla to Doboj?

Pr.: — Why didn't Misko hand over the revolvers and bombs in Tuzla?

Acc.: — I was afraid that I would be arrested in Tuzla as a stranger. We agreed that he would carry them to Doboj and hand them over to me.

Pr.: — Why was it that when you left by train in the morning, you asked in the house in Tuzla whether Misko was there?

Acc.: — I missed the train. I wanted to travel together with him, but only so that he could carry the weapons in the train, and then I would have taken them from the train and taken them to Sarajevo.

Pr.: — Wasn't there an agreement that he travel to Doboj, rather than only to the train?

Acc.: — Yes.

Premuzic: — Did he want to go to Doboj on his own account?

Acc.: — I don't know how it was. I think he had business.

THE HEARING OF VASO CUBRILOVIC
13 OCTOBER 1914

Pr.: — Call Vaso Cubrilovic. (He enters.) How old are you?

Acc.: — Seventeen.

Pr.: — Are you guilty?

Acc.: — Yes.

Pr.: — Of what?

Acc.: — That I wanted to kill the Heir Apparent Franz Ferdinand.

Pr.: — And his wife?

Acc.: — I didn't want to kill his wife. Only him.

Pr.: — How is it that a youngster of seventeen can think of carrying out an assassination? Tell us.

Acc.: — I attended the gymnasium in Sarajevo.

Pr.: — Did you finish a class?

Acc.: — Yes, the sixth.

Pr.: — Was there some sort of association?[77]

Acc.: — Not of any kind.

Pr.: — In the gymnasium, as a whole?

Acc.: — There was no revolutionary organization in the gymnasium, but there was a nationalistic one.

Pr.: — Was it organized?

Acc.: — We had a council, but it didn't do anything.

Pr.: — Are you a member of the association?

Acc.: — The association didn't do anything. It was more literary. There were clerical elements, and those who were against national unity, and the Serbs. Thus we had to found our own organization in order to spread our idea.

Pr.: — What kind of idea?

Acc.: — I have in mind the political and cultural unity of the Serbs and Croats.

Pr.: — How would you achieve that?

Acc.: — In the course of events.

Pr.: — Did you want to participate in the unification?

Acc.: — We could not know whether we would participate.

Pr.: — Why then did you plan to carry out an assassination?

Acc.: — Because I considered the Heir to be an enemy of the Slavs and in general because he was a representative of the regime which most greatly oppressed Bosnia and Hercegovina by means of the "exceptional measures" and by all other harassments.

Pr.: — How can you bring the "exceptional measures" into connection with the Heir Apparent? He was not the governor of the province.

Acc.: — He had the greatest influence.

Pr.: — There was a parliament, ministry and other factors. He wasn't the government.

Acc.: — He had the greatest influence on the political situation in the Austro-Hungarian monarchy.

Pr.: — Are you a Serb or a Serbo-Croatian?

Acc.: — I am a Serbo-Croatian.

Pr.: — What does that mean?

Acc.: — That means that I do not consider myself only as a Serb and that I must not work only for Serbia, but for Croatia as well.

Pr.: — Are you a nationalist?

Acc.: — Yes.

Pr.: — What does that mean?

Acc.: — That means that one might fight until his people are brought to the same level as others.

Pr.: — In the inquiry you said something different.

Acc.: — I said that a nationalist must strive to elevate the people both culturally and politically.

Pr.: — You said: "I am a nationalist who is for the unification of all South Slavs. The goal is that they all be drawn into one state."

Acc.: — That is political.

Pr.: — I ask then, political?

Acc.: — I said that.

Pr.: — Does that agree with your opinion?

Acc.: — Yes.

Pr.: — Was that the goal of your association?

Acc.: — In our association we did not talk about that. Our program was not elaborated. That was my own opinion, and I don't know what the others thought.

Pr.: — You spoke for the association?

Acc.: — That was my own idea.

Pr.: — Tell us about the assassination.

Acc.: — When I learned that the Heir Ferdinand was coming, I thought of an assassination, only I didn't have weapons. Therefore I discussed that once with Djukic, with a second school colleague, and in the discussion I said to him, "Ferdinand is coming, we should lie in wait for him." He said, "If only there were people!" I said that I would be one, but I did not have arms.

Pr.: — You said: "We should lie in wait for him."

Acc.: — He understood what I said. He knew that I would not welcome him with the cheer: "Long live!" He said, "If only there were people!" and I said, "I would be, but I don't have arms." He said, "I will introduce to you a man who will give you weapons." He said that he would introduce me to Ilic and after several days we met with him on the quay. He acquainted me with Ilic, and after that I continued my conversation with Ilic.

Pr.: — What did Ilic say about the assassination?

Acc.: — We did not talk about the assassination.

Pr.: — Did you tell Ilic directly that you would participate?

Acc.: — Yes.

Pr.: — What did he say? Did he approve?

Acc.: — He said that he would give me weapons.

Pr.: — Did Ilic tell you at that time that there were special people?

Acc.: — He said that I would receive weapons in 20 days, many days before the assassination.

Pr.: — Didn't he tell you anything about the necessity to obtain arms?

Acc.: — No.

Pr.: — You said: "Right away that day Ilic told me that the arms would come from Serbia."

Acc.: — I don't know whether it was that day or later, but he said that they would come from Serbia.

Pr.: — Did he tell you that, or did you ask him?

Acc.: — I didn't ask him.

Pr.: — Then you said that he told you that the weapons would come but . . . .

Acc.: — I said that he would get them from unofficial sources in Serbia, he told me that. He said that he must be careful that official Serbia not learn about it.

Pr.: — Ilic, did you say to him that official circles in Serbia would not give arms?

Ilic: — I have talked so much about the assassination that I can't remember to whom I talked or what I said.

Pr.: — That was presented to you and then you said that you didn't know anything about it. But if you said that, then you said it in that way.

Ilic: — Maybe I said that I would reject him. Maybe I had weapons when I told him that.

Pr.: — Did you say it, or didn't you?

Ilic: — I don't know. In fact, I didn't have any reason to say that, if I talked with him in order to reject him.

Pr.: — Your statement of 13 July reads: "That official Serbia especially fears that an assassination could occur, which would be harmful for Serbia." Thus you only talked in order to mislead him?

Ilic: — Only that I not give weapons. Maybe I said it. I don't know exactly what I said.

Pr. (to Cubrilovic): — What happened then?

Cubrilovic: — Then we agreed as to when we would carry out the assassination. Ilic said that we needed someone else. I don't know whether he said it, but we still needed one more.

Pr.: — Did he say that still another was needed, or did you yourself come to that conclusion? You didn't know how many bombs there were, and you wouldn't have looked for others, if someone else hadn't said that another was needed.

Acc.: — It must have been Ilic that said it to me. I had to find someone, and I didn't know anybody. I knew some colleagues and Cvjetko Popovic. I heard that he had been jailed because of Pjanic and I asked him, "When Ferdinand comes something really should be done," and he said, "Nothing can be done." I said, "Something can be," and he agreed. I gave him the things.

Pr.: — When did you learn that the bombs were in Sarajevo?

Acc.: — Several days before the assassination.

Pr.: — When did you get them?

Acc.: — On Saturday afternoon at the Bembasa with Popovic.

Pr.: — Tell us about that.

Acc.: — Ilic told us to come and we met at the Bembasa. We went down to the park and Ilic at first gave me a bomb and revolver and showed me how to use them. Then he gave them to Popovic. Then he fired one shot at the Kozija Bridge in the tunnel.

Pr.: — Who fired?

Acc.: — Ilic.

Pr.: — Why?

Acc.: — He fired the revolver in order to show how to shoot. He fired a shot and returned the revolver to Popovic.

Pr.: — Was that all?

Acc.: — Yes.

Pr.: — Ilic, come here (He comes). Is that true?

Ilic: — It is possible, I admit it.

Pr.: — Is that true or not?

Ilic: — I don't know exactly how I stated it in the protocol.

Pr.: — Do you know whether you fired, or don't you?

Ilic: — I don't know whether I did. Maybe.

Pr.: — Is it possible? Earlier you explicitly said that you didn't.

Acc.: — I don't remember.

Pr.: — I asked you several times and you explicitly said that you didn't.

Acc.: — I don't remember exactly.

Pr.: (to Cubrilovic): — This is very important. What did you tell Kalember after the assassination about Cabrinovic's assassination?

Vaso Cubrilovic: — That I fired one shot.

Pr.: — And did you fire it?

Acc.: — No.

Pr.: — One shot was fired from your revolver. There are witnesses who heard that one shot was fired when Cabrinovic threw the bomb.

Acc.: — I did not fire. My revolver was full.

Pr.: — From which revolver was the shot in the tunnel fired?

Acc.: — The revolver was taken from Popovic's hand. I didn't know my revolver was in my pocket.

Pr.: — Then from which revolver did he fire?

Acc.: — From Popovic's.

Pr.: — When?

Acc.: — When we were in the tunnel.

Pr.: — Thus, he shot?

Acc.: — Yes.

Pr.: — Why did you tell Kalember that you fired a shot?

Acc.: — I was joking with him.

Pr.: — Where did Popovic stand?

Acc.: — Further up.

Pr.: — Where did you stand?

Acc.: — At Dimovic's house.

Pr.: — How was it that day? You had a bomb and revolver . . .

Acc.: — Then I went home and the next day I got up . . .

Pr.: — Did you tell anyone else in Sarajevo that you intended to carry out an assassination?

Acc.: — Ilic told me that he would give me the weapons. I asked my comrades Kalember and Perin whether I might leave some things with them and I said: a bomb and revolver.[78] He said, "I don't dare to get involved."

Pr.: — Did you say for what purpose?

Acc.: — First I told him that I had some things to leave and I asked, "May I leave them?" He said, "You may" and asked, "What kind of things are they?"

Pr.: — What did you say?

Acc.: — I said, "Bomb and revolver."

Pr.: — Did he ask you why you had them?

Acc.: — Yes. I told him, "For an assassination."

Pr.: — Of whom?

Acc.: — He knew. Of Ferdinand.

Pr.: — What did he say to that?

Acc.: — He said, "I won't accept them. Don't do it. I don't want to get involved."

Pr.: — Did you also tell others?

Acc.: — I told Perin the same as Kalember.

Pr.: — You explicitly told Perin that you had a bomb and revolver and that you would leave them at his place and that you intended to carry out an assassination against Ferdinand. Did you say those words?

Acc.: — Yes.

Pr.: — What did he say?

Acc.: — He was frightened and said that he didn't want to get involved.

Pr.: — What did you say to Zagorac?

Acc.: — I told him about the assassination and I didn't say anything more.

Pr.: — How?

Acc.: — I told him that there would be an assassination and nothing more.

Pr.: — Did you tell him that you would carry it out?

Acc.: — I did, but I didn't say by what means.

Pr.: — What about Kranjcevic?

Acc.: — Popovic told him. I was in Tuzla. Popovic said to me that he told Kranjcevic. I didn't tell the truth.

Pr.: — You said one thing to the investigating judge and

something else before Kranjcevic. You said: "One month before the assassination we became acquainted and I asked him to
take care of them . . ." How was it when you asked him?

Acc.: — Popovic talked with him. I talked after Popovic
had already made an agreement with him. I don't know what
he said. I only know that I agreed to leave the weapons with
him if I had to.

Pr.: — How was it with you?

Acc.: — I was standing at Dimovic's and I did not draw the
revolver because the duchess was there. I did not want to shoot.

Pr.: — And the bomb?

Acc.: — The bomb was on my belt.

Pr.: — Did you see how Cabrinovic threw the bomb?

Acc.: — Yes.

Pr.: — Did you recognize him?

Acc.: — No. I heard only that someone threw a bomb and
it exploded.

Pr.: — What happened with Kranjcevic?

Acc.: — He came later where we said to meet. I gave him
the revolver and he left with it. Popovic did not come but remained at the other place.

Pr.: — Did you see Popovic that day?

Acc.: — No.

Pr.: — How did it happen that you told Kalember that you
really fired the revolver?

Acc.: — I played a game with him. I joked.

Pr.: — How could you joke about such things?

Acc.: — It was just a joke.

Pr.: — You only decided at that place that you would not
carry out the assassination?

Acc.: — Yes. Once more I wanted to withdraw.

Pr.: — Why did you want to withdraw?

Acc.: — I thought that the duchess would not be there.

Pr.: — When you saw that she would be there too, you said
that you were sorry for him.

Acc.: — Not for him, but for her.

Pr.: — Thus it is an insult when someone says to you that
you did not wish to kill her, but him?[79]

Acc.: — It certainly is.

Pr.: — Did you know that there would be others besides you and Popovic?

Acc.: — I did, but I didn't know who they were.

Pr.: — You stated (Presents the statement of 5 July in that respect.): "I thought in general that someone who was ahead of me would carry out the assassination, because I did not intend to do it at all . . ."

Acc.: — Of that first one I did not say that I thought that he would do it. I don't remember that.

Pr. (Reads further.): — "When the Archduke came by in the automobile I did not draw the revolver because I was sorry for the Archduchess."

Acc.: — I did not spare him. I had prepared for the assassination one and one-half months before.

Pr.: — What about Dragan Kalember, Perin and Forkapic on the eve of the assassination?

Acc.: — I was not with Dragan, nor with Djukic. I was alone. I was strolling and came up to them, and they laughed about something, especially Forkapic, Djukic and Perin. I don't know what they laughed about. I only know that Forkapic said, I don't know whether with regard to the assassination or the defacing of businesses' signs,[80] when it appeared in the *Hrvatski Dnevnik* that anyone who denounced the perpetrators would be rewarded.

Pr.: — Did you have the bomb and revolver on that Saturday evening?

Acc.: — I had the revolver. Perin saw the revolver, and as to Kalember I am not sure.

Pr.: — Did you tell him anything about the quay?

Acc.: — I told him not to stand at Dimovic's house.

Pr.: — Why did you tell him not to stand there?

Acc.: — I certainly intended to carry out the assassination.

Pr.: — Did you say: "Because there will be an assassination there?"

Acc.: — I said: "Because there will be an assassination there."

Pr.: — Did you tell him that there would be still others?

Acc.: — I don't know.

Pr.: — You said that you had several comrades and that it would be best for them not to go to the quay.

Acc.: — Maybe I said that.

Pr.: — Immediately after the assassination, did you see one of them: Perin, Kalember, or the others?

Acc.: — I saw Perin. He asked me, "Did Cabrinovic throw the bomb?" I said, "I don't know," and I left.

Pr.: — Did you know that Princip carried out the assassination?

Acc.: — No.

Pr.: — Did you meet a second time with Perin?

Acc.: — No.

Pr.: — You said: "Later we met again."

Acc.: — Yes, we did the next day.

Pr.: — You also said to Perin that you fired the revolver?

Acc.: — Those two were together.

Pr.: — Besides the revolver, did you also receive cartridges, bullets?

Acc.: — No.

Naumowicz: — Did you have any kind of secret connection with Serbia? Did you know the route by which one could pass unobserved to and from Serbia?

Acc.: — No.

Naum.: — You are a brother of Veljko's?

Acc.: — Yes. I could not have had connections.

Pr.: — Did you know that your brother was involved in this affair?

Acc.: — No.

Pros.: — How did this Forkapic get involved?

Pr.: — Don't you know for sure whether he spoke about the assassination, or of the defacing of the signs?

Acc.: — That was a joke and nothing else. He mentioned, "It would be good if the one who reported it got 300 crowns." I don't know whether that concerned the assassination, or the other matter.

Feldbauer: — When was that conversation?

Acc.: — Ten days before the assassination.

Feldb.: — Was that conversation about the assassination, or about the defacing of the signs?

Acc.: — I don't know what the conversation was about.

Feldb.: — Try to remember a little. You're accusing that man.

Acc.: — I don't know about him.

Feldb.: — Was he involved in the matter of defacing the signs?

Acc.: — All the students joked about that.

Feldb.: — Were the students involved in that matter?

Acc.: — I don't know.

Prem.: — Did you say to Zagorac that you would carry out the assassination so that he would take it seriously?

Acc.: — I don't know how he took it.

Zistler: — Do you have parents? Are they alive?

Acc.: — No.

Zist.: — Who supports you?

Acc.: — My brothers and sisters.

Zist.: — With whom did you eat your meals?

Acc.: — At my sister's, with whom I stayed.

Zist.: — What kind of student were you in school? How did you succeed in individual subjects?

Acc.: — Until the war[81] I was a good student. Since then I have been weaker.

Zist.: — Did you ever fail a class?

Acc.: — No.

Zist.: — Did you receive a second grade[82] in any subject?

Acc.: — No.

Zist.: — You said that you received a second grade in mathematics and some other subjects and that you wanted to commit suicide?

Pr.: — Were you all the time convinced that you would carry out the assassination and that you would participate in it?

Acc.: — Yes.

Pr.: — In the interrogation you said that you forgot about the assassination, and only when you received the second grade did you decide to carry out the assassination.

Acc.: — I had agreed, but three or four days before the assassination I backed out again. The reasons were those subjects and the removal of the Serbian and Croatian flags at Ilidza.[83]

Pr.: — When the Heir Apparent arrived?

Acc.: — Yes.

Pr.: — What are your religious views? Are you an atheist, or do you believe in God?

Acc.: — I have to have some faith.

Pr.: — Then what faith do you have?

Acc.: — I believe everything.

Pr.: — A religious person never would go so far as to kill anyone, because he knows that the commandment is: "Thou shalt not kill!"

Acc.: — And why do millions die on European battlefields? I may feel pity for the Heir Apparent as a human being, but as the Austrian Heir I cannot. I can pity millions of our peasants.

Zist.: — You once said that you are a Serbo-Croat, another time a Yugoslav. What is a Serbo-Croat, and what is a Yugoslav? What do you understand by that? You develop theories, but can you understand what you are talking about?

Acc.: — Serbo-Croat. We are one people because we speak with one language.

Zist.: — You said that it is a cultural and political unity. What do you understand by political unity?

Acc.: — Political unity can be the unification of all South Slavs.

Zist.: — If you are a Serbo-Croat, then there cannot be the unification of all South Slavs. I see that you are talking about theories which you cannot explain to yourself. You talk about Yugoslavia. When they asked you what nationalism was, you said that Serbs, Croats, Bulgars and Slovenes should draw together into one state, be it inside or outside of Austria. How do you think that all of those nations will come into Austria, which are now outside of Austria?

Acc.: — To me it is all the same whether Bosnia be under Austria or under Serbia. The main thing is that it be good for the people.

Zist.: — When you carried out the assassination, did you envisage that Bosnia and Hercegovina would be separated from Austria?

Acc.: — I did not think of that.

Zist.: — Did you concern yourself with politics?

Acc.: — I read newspapers.

Zist.: — Where did you get your political ideas? Only from the newspapers? Do you know the structure of the Austro-Hungarian Monarchy?

Acc.: — I can say that in the Austro-Hungarian Monarchy only the Germans and Hungarians rule, and the Slavs are oppressed.

Naumowicz: — Kalember, Perin and Forkapic were your friends?

Acc.: — Yes.

Naum.: — Are they nationalists?

Acc.: — I don't know about Forkapic, but Perin and Kalember are.

Malek: — Do you remember that when you talked to Perin about the assassination under a girl's window, that he said that was Utopia.

Acc.: — Yes.

Malek: — Do you remember that you said that the students of Tuzla are heroes and that you would raise the whole Motajica in revolt?

Acc.: — That is not true.

Malek: — Do you remember that before the assassination you told the students that two great men would come?

Acc.: — I don't.

Malek: — Did Perin mock you: "This is the fellow who will kill Ferdinand?"

Acc.: — Yes.

Malek: — Did Kalember tutor you in mathematics?

Acc.: — I went from time to time to work with him.

Pr.: — I recess the court for 5 minutes.

After the Recess

Feldbauer: — You said of Forkapic that you don't remember exactly whether he or someone else said that one might receive money for denouncing the assassins?

Acc.: — I don't know about Forkapic.

Feldb.: — From when do you know him?

Acc.: — Up to that time I hadn't known him even for one month.

Feldb.: — Here you once said: "Forkapic said that." When you were brought before the court you said: "I don't know whether it was Forkapic or someone else."

Acc.: — I know that it was Forkapic, only I don't know whether it was about the assassination or about the defacing of the signs.

THE HEARING OF CJETKO POPOVIC
13 OCTOBER 1914

Pr.: — Call Cvjetko Popovic. (He enters.) How old are you?

Acc.: — Sixteen.[84]

Pr.: — Are you guilty?

Acc.: — Yes.

Pr.: — Of what?

Acc.: — Of the assassination.

Pr.: — So, tell us about it. When did you come to think of the assassination?

Acc.: — I don't know exactly which day. I remember that it was about the last of May, about the 20th. One afternoon I met Vaso Cubrilovic on the quay. Among other things we talked about the arrival of the Heir Apparent Ferdinand in Sarajevo. He said that he wanted to lie in wait for him, to assassinate him.

Pr.: — Did he say to assassinate him, or to lie in wait for him?

Acc.: — Between us an assassination was understood.

Pr.: — What are your political opinions?

Acc.: — That the Serbs and Croats are one people.

Pr.: — What kind of conclusions do you draw from that? That isn't enough.

Acc.: — They should be for themselves, independent.

Pr.: — Then did your principles and opinions in some way influence your decision toward the assassination?

Acc.: — No, merely revenge for the persecution of all the Slavs in the whole Monarchy.

Pr.: — Could you say where the persecution is and give examples?

Acc.: — In Bosnia and Hercegovina. For instance, the "exceptional measures." In Croatia the commissionership. In the Kranj the favoring of the Germans, and likewise in the Banat and Bcka the favoring of the colonists.

Pr.: — You felt yourself called to carry out revenge and gave no thought to the way in which the Serbs and Croats might be united?

Acc.: — I believed that they would be united, but I did not deal with that. I firmly believed that that was a matter of the distant future.

Pr.: — When you talked with Cubrilovic and he said that one must lie in wait for the Heir Apparent, did you immediately agree?

Acc.: — Yes.

Pr.: — In what way is the Heir Apparent related to the situation of the Slavs in Austro-Hungary?

Acc.: — I considered him the representative of force and I thought that was the best means to avenge the persecution.

Pr.: — He had no kind of power. He was only the military inspector. He was not the governor. Thus you could not consider him the representative of that government.

Acc.: — He had influence. As the Heir Apparent, he had some say.

Pr.: — Not so much that you must take revenge on him.

Acc.: — The greatest revenge was achieved by that.

Pr.: — I believe that you had some other kind of reason. How did you view the Heir Apparent: that he was good, industrious, especially in military matters?

Acc.: — I had the conviction that he inclined more toward us Slavs than toward the Hungarians.

Pr.: — Was that your conviction?

Acc.: — Yes.

Pr.: — According to that it should have been your intention that he remain alive. That would be better for the Slavs. You took revenge on just the man on whom depended the future of the people. Did you read the article in the *Hrvatski Dnevnik* that day when the late Heir Apparent came, where it said: "The Heir Apparent is our hope?" Thus the reason for revenge and all else that you state doesn't hold up.

Acc.: — I told my motive at once, as soon as the investigating judge asked me.

Pr.: — Just because of that I cannot understand your train of thought as to how you could come to the decision to kill him, although he was a friend of the Slavs. Weren't you merely interested in seeing to it that the Slavs would never be satisfied under Austria?

Acc.: — That was not my aspiration. I thought that it would be the strongest revenge if I took revenge on him as the Heir to the Austro-Hungarian Monarchy.

Pr.: — How could that be? You met with Cubrilovic and then he said that one should await him. What did he say? Whom did you have to turn to?

Acc.: — Then he mentioned that to me. He did not offer. Rather I accepted. I said, "How can we do it when there are no weapons?" He said that he knew a man who would take care of everything. Then we didn't talk about that any more. Later he said that man was Ilic and that we would accomplish the assassination with bombs and revolvers.

Pr.: — How did the whole thing go?

Acc.: — I was already acquainted with Ilic. I was in the first year of the Teacher's School, and he in the fourth, but I had never been friendly with him. I talked with him on Saturday. Cubrilovic said that we would get arms and then we left for the Bembasa and there Ilic gave us the weapons.

Pr.: — Did anyone shoot?

Acc.: — Yes, Ilic fired from my revolver.

Pr.: — Ilic says that he doesn't remember that he fired a shot.

Acc.: — He fired.

Pr.: — Was it not you who fired on the occasion of the assassination? Where did you wait?

Acc.: — At the corner of Cumurija street and the quay.

Pr.: — Thus a little further from the place where the bomb was thrown?

Acc.: — Yes.

Pr.: — So you did not shoot?

Acc.: — No.

Pr.: — Did you meet with other students and tell them?

Acc.: — I didn't meet with anyone but Kranjcevic. He is my friend and I had confided in him that we would carry out the assassination of the Heir Apparent. He said to be careful and that it was a thoughtless thing to do.

Pr.: — What did you ask of him?

Acc.: — I did not ask to leave the things with him, nor did he promise.

Pr.: — There are others who say that the two of you agreed that you would leave the things at his place, and then they left theirs too.

Acc.: — I didn't.

Pr.: — Did you decide that you would carry out the assassination?

Acc.: — Yes.

Pr.: — Why didn't you do it?

Acc.: — I didn't have the courage. I don't know what happened to me.

Pr.: — What did you do with the bomb?

Acc.: — As soon as I heard that Cabrinovic threw the bomb I thought that Cubrilovic threw it. I wanted to run home, but I returned and left the bomb in the basement of the *Prosvjetni Savjet* (Cultural Council).

Pr.: — You did not tell Kranjcevic to wait for you after the assassination so that you could give him the bomb?

Acc.: — No.

Pr.: — Did you receive cyanide?

Acc.: — Yes.

Pr.: — What did you do with it?

Acc.: — I left it in the basement.

Pr.: — Were you present when Cubrilovic said something to Kranjcevic?

Acc.: — Yes.

Pr.: — What did he say?

Acc.: — He asked whether he could leave some things at his home, and that he should wait for him in Skenderia.

Pr.: — Could you throw the bomb if you wished?

Acc.: — Yes.

Pr.: — You are a good student. An excellent one?

Acc.: — I always was.

Pr.: — Did it ever occur to you that an assassination was a frightful thing? Otherwise it is evident that you are better than all those whom we have investigated and that you allowed yourself to be seduced. How did that happen?

Acc.: — Since the time when I was jailed because of Pjanic, when I was innocent, I began to think of revenge. When the occasion presented itself, I thought that it was best.

Pr.: — Are you sorry?

Acc.: — Yes, because I did not think that the consequences would be a war.

Pr.: — Are you sorry for the people?

Acc.: — I am sorry for the duchess, but I am not sorry for him, because I had already decided that I would carry out the assassination.

Pr.: — How was it discovered that you participated in the assassination?

Acc.: — I don't know. When I came home, at 7 o'clock I arrived in Zemun, and at 11 o'clock they jailed and questioned me.

Pr.: — You travelled to Zemun the same day?

Acc.: — I left Tuesday morning at six o'clock.

Pr.: — Then they jailed you?

Acc.: — Yes.

Pr.: — You wanted to escape to Serbia?

Acc.: — No, but my parents live in Zemun.

Pr.: — Did you think that your participation would ever be disclosed?

Acc.: — Yes.

Pr.: — Did you promise not to betray each other?

Acc.: — I never thought that I would remain alive. I intended to kill myself.

Pr.: — Why did you not commit suicide when the others carried out the assassination? You had to know that you would fall under suspicion.

Acc.: — I thought that I would carry out the assassination.

Pr.: — Why didn't you escape to Serbia after the assassination?

Acc.: — I thought that no one would inform.

Pr.: — How did they find out?

Acc.: — I don't know who told, but I saw from the questions which the gentlemen in Zemun put to me that they knew everything and I admitted everything right away.

Pr.: — Are your parents alive?

Acc.: — Yes.

Pr.: — What is your father?

Acc.: — A retired school director.

Pr.: — And your mother?

Acc.: — I have a stepmother.

Pr.: — You had to keep in mind that your father and family would suffer. Didn't you know that you would make your father unhappy?

Acc.: — He cannot be responsible for me. What's more, he was in Zemun and I was in Sarajevo.

Pr.: — Are you a Bosnian?

Acc.: — I was born in Prnjavor, but my legal residence was in Bezanija near Zemun.

Pr.: — Concerning religion, what is your religion?

Acc.: — I have my own Orthodox faith.

Pr.: — But do you know that religion commands that one should not kill a man?

Acc.: — I know.

Pr.: — Do you take your religion seriously, or just so-so?

Acc.: — Oh, so-so.

Pr.: — So you do not believe firmly?

Acc.: — No.

Pr.: — Do you know anything about Tankosic and Ciganovic?

Acc.: — No.

Pr.: — Have you ever been in Serbia?

Acc.: — No.

Pr.: — Did you know Princip and Cabrinovic before?

Acc.: — Not Cabrinovic. Princip I did, but I didn't talk with him.

Pr.: — And Ilic?

Acc.: — I knew him from the Teacher's School, but I never was intimate with him. Of all of those, my closest friend was

Kranjcevic, and I had become acquainted with Cubrilovic only recently.

Naumowicz: — Did you discuss among yourselves that the late Heir Apparent was the military leader and because of that he could be dangerous for Serbia in case of war?

Acc.: — No.

Naum.: — Was that one of the reasons to remove him?

Acc.: — No.

Pr.: — How did you come to the conclusion that the late Heir Apparent was the initiator of the "exceptional measures"? Where did you hear that?

Acc.: — I don't assert that he was the initiator. I said that I decided on the assassination because the Slavs were persecuted in the Monarchy.

Pr.: — You do not assert that?

Acc.: — No.

Pr.: — You wanted the most decisive object?

Acc.: — Yes.

Perisic: — Tell me, what do you think about politics? Is your political belief outside the framework of the Austro-Hungarian Monarchy? Did you favor the separation of Bosnia and Hercegovina from the Monarchy and their annexation to Serbia?

Acc.: — I was never for that, nor did I talk about it.

Per.: — Have you been a member of any kind of association?

Acc.: — Recently I joined a progressive organization in the Teacher's School.

Per.: — In that organization did they talk about that?

Acc.: — I was never at a meeting.

Per.: — How did you conceive of that unity?[85]

Acc.: — I talked with my colleagues about that. We believed that the political unification of all South Slavs would come, but that was a thing of the distant future, and that we would never see it. Rather, we had to work all the harder to bring the Serbs and Croats together for cultural elevation as well, because we are the weakest in the cultural and educational field.

Per.: — After that, when the bomb was thrown, did the automobile pass slowly by you?

Acc.: — Yes.

Per.: — Were you given the opportunity to carry out the assassination?

Acc.: — Yes.

Malek: — How did Popovic get mixed up in this? Although he thought that he was safe, in the files, in the official memorandum of 2 June it says . . .

Pr.: — Please discuss that when we read the files. Have you any further questions?

PARTIAL HEARING OF NEDELJKO CABRINOVIC
13 OCTOBER 1914

Premuzic: — Cabrinovic, you heard, and you yourself also said two or three times that the word was dropped that you lost courage and that you thought that nothing would come of the assassination. You said this yourself. What inspired you again to carry out that assassination? On what basis?

Cabr.: — There were several things.

Prem.: — Tell me the truth. What influenced you? Perhaps the persons who influenced you?

Cabr.: — When I came home it was very pleasant for me, they welcomed me, which I had not expected. I felt very uncomfortable that they welcomed me in such a way. Later I was reconciled and felt good. Then when I asked Princip, "How goes it?" he waved his hand. I was completely reconciled to the situation. But recently I began quarrelling every day with my father about my staying out until nine or ten o'clock. He didn't like it and scolded me. He is a man of hasty temper and that angered me, so I thought about going on somewhere else. All the time I thought about suicide. What they said about the flags[86] made me angry and inflamed me. Also, the servile loyalty with which they welcomed the late Heir Apparent in Mostar offended me.

Prem.: — Did you talk with someone about that, about that servile loyalty?

Acc.: — I was angry and I did not understand why some Serbs acted like the government's mamelukes.

Prem.: — Perhaps you thought of Dimovic's party?[87]

Pr.: — I forbid such comments.

Cabr.: — That was not clear to me, I did not understand. I read only revolutionary books, so I could not understand why the Serbs published an organ which was for the government and furthermore that the paper was named *Istina* (Truth). In the publishing plant we laughed at it too.

Prem.: — There was no real instigator of the assassination?

Cabr.: — There was, St. Vitus' Day. When I heard that there was St. Vitus' Day, that too gave me impetus. Besides, they told me in Sarajevo that I was a spy and I wanted to show everyone that I am not a spy.

Prem.: — Did some person directly influence you?

Cabr.: — Let it be clear. I am on trial and no one has to answer for me. I alone will carry it to the grave with me.

Pr.: — You said before the interrogating judge that you know a good deal more, but that you will not tell it.

Cabr.: — That was a joke, because he thought that I knew much more. That was no kind of formal audience. I talked in a completely simple manner about the Heir Apparent. Then when the interrogating judge wanted to make something out of it, I said that I knew much more.

Princip: — About that shot which you say was fired. That isn't so. Rather, some bombs have a more powerful explosion when the cartridge bursts.

Malek: — Some of the students said concerning the shot that Cubrilovic was bragging about that he shot not one time but twice.

Pr.: — I recess the hearing until tomorrow at 8:45 o'clock.

The Third Day

PARTIAL HEARING OF CABRINOVIC, GRABEZ, AND ILIC

Pr.: — Cabrinovic, you said that when you came to Sabac that you went to the captain and that he gave you a permit for the railroad with a false name as if you were a revenue officer. How do you explain that a soldier, captain of a company and commander of the border guard, forged a certificate by writing a false name and for another Serbian administrative authority at that for your benefit, if he didn't know anything about your intentions, if he didn't know that you wanted to cross the border secretly.

Acc. Cabr.: — I was not aware that he knew anything.

Pr.: — How is it that one authority falsifies for another authority with the purpose of helping you to get across the border if nothing was known? The captain would have thrown you out of the cafe and into jail had he not known what was going on.

Cabr.: — We had brought him a note.

Pr.: — Was the name of Ciganovic enough? Was he such an important person? Were his initials sufficient that every officer did whatever anyone who brought him a note wanted?

Cabr.: — I am not responsible that those were two initials, and maybe there was something by which he could know who sent us. The permit which we received was not for the authorities but for the railroad so that we could get half-fare tickets.

Pr.: — Why did he falsify your names? Could he not have recorded your names as students, so that you could have received half-fare tickets just the same?

Cabr.: — He had before him a list of revenue guards and he took the names from that list.

Pr.: — That means that they didn't know at the railroad who passed over the border that day.

Cabr.: — That's possible. I never said that he didn't know anything. Maybe he knew, but I don't know whether he knew.

Pr.: — Is there some sort of political authority in Sabac?

Cabr.: — There is the district administration.

Pr.: — Why were you not at the political administration?

Cabr.: — We met with a man from the political administration who told us about military deserters: "We don't know what to do with them. Every day up to fifty of them come over."

Pr.: — Why did you not contact the political authorities?

Cabr.: — We had a note for the captain, so it didn't make sense to go to the political authorities. Ciganovic told us distinctly to be careful that Stojan Protic, minister of internal affairs, did not learn that we travelled to Bosnia.

Pr.: — That was concealed from the civil authorities?

Cabr.: — They would have arrested us at the border and taken us back. At first he wanted us to go to a certain deputy at the border, but out of caution, because the deputy might tell the chief or his party, he chose a means that we must reveal to no one.

Pr.: — And Ciganovic spoke about a *canal* between Sarajevo and Belgrade?

Cabr.: — I had understood that as *tunnel*.[88]

Pros.: — You said, and all of you have rejected the suggestion that you had a job with the *Narodna odbrana*. As you see, Ciganovic explicitly said, "in order that the minister of internal affairs not know."[89] Tell me, how it was that just such prominent members of the *Narodna odbrana* as Ciganovic and Tankosic gave you the means? Furthermore, note that this very Ciganovic sent you to the military administration. One military administration sent you to another. They sent you just to that Jakovljevic who is a prominent member of the *Narodna odbrana*.

Cabr.: — I don't know.

Pros.: — From Jakovljevic you went to Dakic who was an agent of the *Narodna odbrana*. Those others sent you to Veljko Cubrilovic and Misko Jovanovic, who are also agents of the *Narodna odbrana*. How do you explain that that was not an affair of the *Narodna odbrana*?

Cabr.: — I explain it this way. I did not know that Ciganovic and Tankosic were members of the *Narodna odbrana* and prominent leaders. As others said who knew Tankosic better than I, he was even in opposition to them and they had some sort of conflict. It is a fact that they gave us the means and helped us, but it is also a fact that they did not do that as members of the *Narodna odbrana*. They did that personally on their own account. Popovic was an intimate friend or colleague of Ciganovic's, so they might have arranged it in Belgrade.

Pr.: — You say that Captain Popovic was in Belgrade on the eve of that day?

Cabr.: — Yes, he asked us where we came from, and we said, "From Belgrade." He replied to that, "I came from Belgrade yesterday." Maybe Popovic misused his position as a colleague of Ciganovic's, and it might have been the same in Loznica with Grbic. Dakic and Misko Jovanovic were agents of the *Narodna odbrana* and they might have had strong connections.

Pros.: — Milovic and Micic confessed.

Cabr.: — Maybe they already had some sort of means by which they went, and now we accidentally went by the same means, although it doesn't have anything to do with the *Narodna odbrana*. Because they were agents of the *Narodna odbrana*, this affair is also brought into connection with the *Narodna odbrana* and thus it really seems that this was done by order.

Pros.: — That was not arranged, but it is true.

Cabr.: — You can say that, but it isn't true.

Pr.: — Grabez, you said something about a meeting at Topcider. Where did you fire?

Grabez: — In the woods.

Pr.: — Not on the firing range?

Grabez: — No, we didn't. Later a guard came and told us that we were not allowed to shoot in the woods. Because he forbade it, we left.

Pr.: — You did not shoot on the firing range?

Grabez: — No, because one can use it only on Sundays.

Pr.: — Princip, is that so?

Princip: — Yes, because we were not members of the *Streljacko drustvo* (Gun Club).

Pros.: — Why did you conceal from the beginning that you knew Tankosic and Ciganovic and didn't want us to know about that at all?

Grabez: — Because I stood on the principle that I would not disclose even little things, but I was forced to abandon this because of the disclosures of the others.

Feldbauer: — Princip wants to say something.

Princip: — That railroad wasn't a private one and I asked the captain not to issue the permits in our name. He asked, "How shall I issue them?" I said, "Give them to us in soldiers' names."

Pr.: — How was it possible that the military authorities issued false certificates on your request?

Princip: — He hesitated, but because we asked him, and he is a friend of Tankosic's, he did it.

Pr.: — How did he know that you came from Tankosic?

Princip: — I told him that Ciganovic sent us, and that Tankosic told him to accept us. No doubt he told him.

Pr.: — As soon as the captain heard that that was so, he immediately accepted you. Yes, now the matter is clear.

Pros.: — One question for Ilic. You said from the very beginning that you went down to Mostar to pick up Mehmed-basic, and yesterday you stated that he invited you down. Is it not possible that he had a guerrilla band which was supposed to kill the Heir in Mostar, and did not succeed?

Ilic: — I don't know.

Pros.: — You went to Brod. Wasn't there a guerrilla band there with the same goal? You knew about all that.

Ilic: — I did not.

Pros.: — You stated that you wanted to prevent the assassination. Then why didn't you hide the bombs instead of distributing them at the last moment? How do you explain that?

Ilic: — I was not allowed to take a forceful stand with respect to the assassination, because I knew myself that the bombs came from Ciganovic and that Tankosic was the leader of the guerrillas. I was afraid that by my conduct I would become the object of open hostility.

Pros.: — Perhaps you thought that the guerrillas would make some impression on us, that we would not be able to protect you.

Ilic: — I thought that I would have to go to Serbia again sometime.

Pros.: — If you had gone to Serbia they would have killed you.

THE HEARING OF VELJKO CUBRILOVIC
14 OCTOBER 1914

Pr.: — Call Veljko Cubrilovic. You are Veljko Cubrilovic? Are you guilty?

Acc.: — In the sense of the indictment, I am not, but I feel guilty in that to some extent I contributed to the killing.

Pr.: — Some say that they are not guilty precisely because they killed. Are you sorry?

Acc.: — I am sorry that all that happened.

Pr.: — With regard to the person, or to the consequences?

Acc.: — Both.

Pr.: — What are you sorry for?

Acc.: — I am an opponent of all assassination.

Pr.: — Since when? Since your arrest?

Acc.: — Also before that.

Pr.: — And do you feel sorry for the wife of the Heir?

Acc.: — Yes.

Pr.: — You are the teacher for the Serbian Orthodox community in Priboj. Where did you finish school?

Acc.: — Four classes in Novi Sad and four in Sombor.

Pr.: — Where are you from?

Acc.: — From Bosanska Gradiska.

Pr.: — Why didn't you teach here?

Acc.: — Because there were nine of us from Bosanska Gradiska in the gymnasium in Novi Sad.

Pr.: — Who supported you?

Acc.: — My merchant father, and later Vasilj Grdjic.[90] In August 1905 I was selected as a teacher in Tuzla and I was there for five years.

Pr.: — Did you get acquainted with Misko in Tuzla and did you make friends with him?

Acc.: — Yes.

Pr.: — Was he a good man then?
Acc.: — He lived as a bon-vivant.
Pr.: — What did he do?
Acc.: — He worked in the business with his father.
Pr.: — Did he concern himself with politics?
Acc.: — I don't know.
Pr.: — Did you concern yourself with politics?
Acc.: — I concerned myself with domestic affairs and followed political events.
Pr.: — To what party did you belong?
Acc.: — Petar Kocic's.
Pr.: — Then you went from Tuzla to Priboj?
Acc.: — Yes, in 1910 and I was there clear up to the arrest.
Pr.: — Have you travelled in Serbia?
Acc.: — I have been in Serbia twice since I became a teacher. In 1906 I was in Belgrade for two days at a teacher's congress. There were 40 teachers from Bosnia and Hercegovina. I was there for the second time in the summer of 1911 with my wife and sister and I went with the *Sokol* from Brcko. They gave a public performance in Banja Koviljaca and Sabac.
Pr.: — Did you get acquainted with anyone then?
Acc.: — Yes. Bozo Milanovic as the president of the *Narodna odbrana* awaited us in Sabac. He wanted to visit us. I was the leader of the *Srpski Sokol* in Priboj.
Pr.: — Did the *Srpski Sokol* exist in Priboj?
Acc.: — It existed in 1910 and 1911. I was the leader.
Pr.: — Who founded it?
Acc.: — I founded it.
Pr.: — How did it happen that you concerned yourself with the *sokol*?
Acc.: — I was in the *sokol* in Tuzla. Beginning in 1907 *sokol* associations were founded in Bosnia and Hercegovina. When the *soko* was founded in Tuzla, there was already a *soko* in Sarajevo and Mostar. The head of the *sokola* was Pero Stojanovic, and the leader was Professor Stevan Zakula.
Pr.: — Was he in Tuzla at the same time as you?
Acc.: — No. Misko Jovanovic was the assistant head, and later he was elected head.
Pr.: — What about Bozo Milanovic?

Acc.: — I went for a visit to Bozo Milanovic's. We were on the upper floor and a conversation about Bosnia and Hercegovina began. Bozo Milanovic was born a Bosnian. He talked about cultural matters in Bosnia and Hercegovina and it was observed that the situation was rather bad.

Pr.: — What did you understand by cultural affairs?

Acc.: — Literacy, the awakening of our own people, personal self-consciousness which among us is weakly developed. We said that the initiative for such work was weak. At that time courses in reading were begun.

Pr.: — Did you talk about political affairs in Bosnia?

Acc.: — No. We talked about how an association was needed which would organize cultural work in Bosnia and Hercegovina. Then he gave an example as to how they would do it. He brought in the *Narodna odbrana* and mentioned its structure. He told in what way it had been founded. In Belgrade, as the capital, there was the largest number of humanitarian and cultural associations. All of the presidents of the associations were members of the *Narodna odbrana* and they elected a special president. The headquarters was in Belgrade, and every man in Serbia was a member of the *Narodna odbrana* who was a member of at least one cultural association, whether it be the *sokol* . . .

Pr.: — Do you consider the *sokol* association to be cultural? Do anti-alcoholism associations also fall within the scope of the *Narodna odbrana*?

Acc.: — That would be the Central Committee. Likewise in larger cities there was a council made up of presidents of all associations which chose a president.

Pr.: — Did you talk about political tendencies?

Acc.: — Absolutely not.

Pr.: — Did he offer you a place as a representative?

Acc.: — I said that the provincial government in Bosnia would not permit such a concentration because on the occasion of the founding of *Prosvjeta* . . .

Pr.: — *Prosvjeta* already had the same goals as the *Narodna odbrana*. Why was it necessary to develop a *Narodna odbrana* here?

Acc.: — I don't know. *Prosvjeta* did not exist until 1901.

We talked in that sense. Later he asked me whether I wished to work; if necessary he would give me instructions. I said, "With pleasure."

Pr.: — How could the *Narodna odbrana* spread its activities outside the borders of Serbia? An association exclusively within the kingdom of Serbia? You volunteered at once to accept the position of a representative.

Acc.: — I did not perceive this in a political sense. If some kind of instructions were needed . . .

Pr.: — In what sense instructions?

Acc.: — Moral support, advice.

Pr.: — Was it necessary for that to found an organization as in Serbia?

Acc.: — I didn't think about it any further, nor did I work. I said, "I would be grateful if you would give me advice."

Pr.: — Did you agree that you would correspond?

Acc.: — It was necessary to maintain some connection. I said that I would keep in touch by mail. "You can send by mail," he answered, "but I will send a peasant who will lend you a hand if necessary."

Pr.: — How long does it take to go from Priboj to Sabac?

Acc.: — I don't know.

Pr.: — Three to four days. In any case, the mail is cheaper.

Acc.: — If it were necessary to transfer books, that is how I understood it.

Pr.: — One can also send books by mail. The only books which are confiscated by the censorship are the treasonous ones.[91]

Acc.: — What is forbidden interests a man. I did not think about that discussion at all. From 1911 until the arrest I had no kind of connection whatever with Bozo Milanovic. He was a utopian fellow, an idealist.

Pr.: — How do you know that?

Acc.: — I see that now.

Pr.: — What you say now, that is beautiful honorable work.

Acc.: — He is a man of 60, rejoices in secret connections, not thinking at all of the consequences; therefore I couldn't say to him, "I won't." Why should I say that to him? He said it in pretty words, and I knew that it would never come to reality.

Pr.: — Did you swear allegiance and did you give your word of honor?

Acc.: — I never did. I only said, "I will gladly accept advice from you in cultural matters."

Pr.: — Did you receive letters from him, or did he prepare clippings from newspapers for you?

Acc.: — Neither.

Pr.: — What about the connection?

Acc.: — In 1912 a peasant came to me and said, "If you need anything from Serbia, I will bring it." His name was Jakov Milovic.

Pr.: — Is he from Priboj, or further away?

Acc.: — Four hours away.

Pr.: — How did you call him?

Acc.: — He often passed through. He said that he would come, and if I should need anything he would bring it. I got the impression that he was a smuggler.

Pr.: — And letters?

Acc.: — I don't know anything about letters.

Pr.: — He states that he got letters from you.

Acc.: — I deny that, although Jakov Milovic admitted it. I never gave him any kind of letter whatsoever, I wouldn't know at all what to write.

Pr.: — Did you know that Bozo Milanovic had an important task in Sabac?

Acc.: — I didn't know.

Pr.: — He had a very important task at the same time that he was president of the *Narodna odbrana*.

Acc.: — I didn't know about that.

Pr.: — He was the chief of all espionage in Bosnia and Hercegovina. Everything was directed to his address and he sent it on to Belgrade.

Acc.: — I didn't know anything about that.

Pr.: — How did the meeting with the students take place?

Acc.: — The priest Jovo Jovanovic went to Mezgraja. The weather was partly good, partly bad. On the way I said to him, "If we get into very much water I wouldn't dare to go on, because I am not a very good horseman." He said that there wouldn't be much water, and I replied, "We'll see at the first place." When we turned from the main road I saw Jakov Milovic and a peasant whom I didn't know.

Pr.: — After two and one-half years you saw him and right away you recognized him?

Acc.: — He took off his cap. I saw him once or twice in Priboj after that meeting. He greeted me and I asked him, "where are you going?"

Pr.: — Didn't you know his name?

Acc.: — He said it, but I forgot. He said, "I was coming to you." "Why?" I asked him. He said, "I am not alone. There are two more" — I don't remember whether he said "students" or something else — "who want to meet you." At that I said to the priest, "Good-bye," because the water was too deep to cross. "Priest, I don't dare to go to Mezgraja because of the high water," and the priest smiled, "Why are you such a coward?" But I returned to the village. That was several days before Pentecost.[92] There was a mass in Priboj because it was the custom to celebrate that day and I wanted to buy a lamb. I excused myself from the priest and went with Jakov. The students went ahead of us. There were two of them. Now I know that the name of one was Princip and the other was Grabez. They were hidden in the underbrush. I didn't know where they were. As the country roads were crooked, when we drew very close, they came out in front of us and introduced themselves. I forgot their names but I recognized them again at the inquiry. I also introduced myself to them, and they asked whether they could get a cart to Tuzla. I replied, "You can go through the village. If I can find a cart, you will get it, and you can get out at the edge of the village on the main road." They agreed to that. Then they saw the peasants Milovic and Milosevic on their way.

Pr.: — At the parting, when the peasants left, did you say anything to them?

Acc.: — Nothing whatever.

Pr.: — Didn't you say to one to go up there, and the other down there?

Acc.: — I didn't say that.

Pr.: — Did the students before that say that they had something with them?

Acc.: — No. But when I agreed to find them a cart, then they asked me for saddle-bags.

Pr.: — Who carried the saddle-bags?

Acc.: — I don't know.

Pr.: — Didn't you ask them why they needed the saddle-bags?

Acc.: — No. We went up the hill and turned to the left. Grabez lagged behind; I offered him the horse and he didn't want it. Once I noticed that the saddle-bags were heavy. "What do you have here?" but Princip avoided an answer. What could that be? If they were books, he wouldn't hide them. If they were valuables, they would be packed in a box. That provoked my curiosity. He avoided an answer and I became suspicious. I wondered whether there were weapons inside, especially gunpowder, because I knew that it was very often smuggled, because gunpowder was cheaper in Serbia. He looked at me and the thought struck me like a lightning-bolt.

Pr.: — Did you know before that the Heir was coming to Sarajevo?

Acc.: — Yes, I had read it a few days before in the newspapers and so I wondered whether the weapons were not connected with the Heir. At that very place I told Princip my thought: "Please tell me, are not those weapons for the Heir Apparent, because he is coming?" Princip stopped and energetically said one thing which I did not say in the inquiry.

Pr.: — What did he say?

Acc.: — It's hard for me to tell you. Later, when he said it, I was compelled to keep silent.

Pr.: — Tell me, under what circumstances were you compelled?

Acc.: — It is hard for me, but finally I will say it. Princip glared at me and very forcefully said, "If you want to know, it is for that reason, and we are going to carry out an assassination of the Heir and if you know about it, you have to be quiet. If you betray it, you and your family will be destroyed."

Pr.: — Why didn't you want to say that before?

Acc.: — I didn't want to say it. I was afraid. At that time it was clear to me: that bombs were being carried, that two students were going, that behind Princip stood a revolutionary organization, and that there had to be somebody stronger, because inside there were bombs which they cannot buy.

Pr.: — Grabez says that they can be bought in Belgrade in any store.

Acc.: —I don't know. At once I remembered all that I had read about the work of the Serbian and Bulgarian revolutionary organizations and I had a hard struggle inside me. I had respect for him, and I would have had it even if a child of eight years had come. Under the influence of those words of Princip's, I did everything that they demanded of me. I told Princip that it wasn't nice or honorable to lead me to that without my own consent, and Princip said, "Whether you do it voluntarily or by force, just remember what I told you!" After that I shut up.

Pr.: — Had you discussed before with Bozo Milanovic that something might happen?

Acc.: — I never had.

The President shows the accused the statement of 23 July in which he said: "As soon as the peasants emerged with the students, I knew at once that they had important news from the *Narodna odbrana* to tell me, and I received the students."

Acc.: — I admitted that at the inquiry because I did not know all the circumstances. I was afraid of revenge against my family.

Pr.: — How do you explain that the *Narodna odbrana* is connected with the assassination?

Acc.: — I thought that it was a purely cultural organization. Had I known that it was for assassination, I would not have accepted it.

The President reads to the accused the above statement, in which it says: "I kept the word which I gave to Bozo Milanovic and without a second thought I accepted those students myself."

Acc.: — I said it because I thought it better to say that than admit those circumstances.

Pr.: — You did not dare to admit that the students threatened you, but to smear the work of the *Narodna odbrana*, that you could do.

Acc.: — I wasn't afraid for myself, but for my family.

Pr.: — There was no need to be afraid of the students.

Acc.: — I said that about the *Narodna odbrana* because I

knew from the newspapers that there are organizations which take revenge on entire families.

Pr.: — Did the students tell you that they were backed by an organization?

Acc.: — They led me to understand that by threatening me.

Princip: — I said that I told him that on the way.

Pr.: — When you heard that this was very dangerous, why did you involve other persons?

Veljko Cubrilovic: — I had to. I didn't have my own cart.

Pr.: — Whom did you ask? Your godfather?

Acc.: — I asked the one with whom I was most friendly. We parted before the house of Mitar Kerovic.

Pr.: — You said that Nedjo brought them secretly into the house.

Acc.: — I didn't say that. Mitar invited them into the house, not me.

Pr.: — What else?

Acc.: — We came to Kerovic's house. I intended to look for a cart at two places. If there were no cart at Kerovic's then I would go to Lopare. When I came to Kerovic's I saw Nedjo. The students remained on the mountain. Nedjo had a bandaged arm. When Mitar came he asked him, "Could you give a cart for the students?" and he said, "I could, and where are the students?" "Up over there!" At first he said no. I thought: If he doesn't want to give one, then I'll have to take them further. When he agreed, Nedjo went for the students and Mitar went into the house and took off the saddle-bags. I was very upset and asked for water and *rakija* (native brandy). He took it out and I drank one glass after another. At that moment Grabez and Princip came in and sat down. I carried the weapons into the house and put them on the bed. We were just sitting there and Nedjo came.

Pr.: — Who was in the room?

Acc.: — Mitar and Nedjo. The main question was who would go to Tuzla.

Pr.: — Did Mitar say that they needed a cart?

Acc.: — Yes. Mitar promised a cart. "Nedjo," said Mitar, "go to Cvijan Stjepanovic and make an agreement!" The conversation went on between Nedjo and me to call Blagoje and

Jovan at once. Nedjo called them, and at the same time he called
Cvijan Stjepanovic. Meanwhile we sat down. The women
served coffee, and Mitar gave orders to set the table. We sat and
talked. Then Blagoje and Cvijan arrived. As to Jovan I don't
remember whether he came into the room. We talked about
ordinary things: about the elections, because there was an elec-
tion in the neighboring district and a struggle between adherents
of the Kocic party and the *Narodna stranke* (National Party).
It turned out that I am an adherent of Kocic's party and Princip
was neutral. Grabez was sleeping. Then Vlaho and Jovan arrived.[94] I told them that weapons were to be smuggled into
Tuzla. I told them that the weapons had to be taken into Tuzla
and that they had to do it. I don't recall the exact expression.

Pr.: — Did you show the weapons?

Acc.: — Yes.

Pr.: — What did you take out?

Acc.: — Bombs. I wanted to open them but I didn't know
how. Then Princip stood up and showed them.

Pr.: — And they voluntarily listened. That was interesting
for them.

Acc.: — By all means.

Pr.: — Did he take out the revolvers?

Acc.: — I don't remember. It seems to me that he showed
a Browning.

Pr.: — Did he say how many bombs and revolvers there
were?

Acc.: — I don't remember.

Pr.: — Didn't you agree as to who would transport them?

Acc.: — Princip asked that the peasants carry the bombs
under their belts (a wide, sash-like belt), three bombs and two
revolvers each. He didn't say explicitly how many there were.
At the same time Princip asked me to write a letter.

Pr.: — You involved your god-relative and his whole family
in the affair. Did they say to whom they were carrying revolvers and bombs?

Acc.: — As soon as we met, before Princip began to threaten,
before he spoke of the assassination, he asked me would I be so
good as to recommend to him a man in Tuzla in case he should
need something. I knew Misko Jovanovic as a very honest man.

Pr.: — Were you sure that Misko would accept them?

Acc.: — No.

Pr.: — Did you know that Misko Jovanovic was somebody in the *Narodna odbrana?*

Acc.: — Yes. When I talked with Bozo Milanovic, he asked me whether I could find a man in Tuzla. I was never an agent of the *Narodna odbrana* and I never worked in that direction. What I said, I said only for the sake of form. I told him I didn't know, but if I could, I would send him word. When I met with Misko Jovanovic I told him that I had said to Bozo Milanovic, "If you wish, you can go there on an important occasion," because I knew that Misko visits his sister in Belgrade, and if he goes that way he could stop off at Milanovic's and talk with him. Later Misko Jovanovic said that he accepted that honor.

Pr.: — Were you confident that he would accept the students?

Acc.: — No.

Pr.: — What did you write him?

Acc.: — I don't remember the words exactly. I said it to help them.

The President shows the defendant the statement of 22 July: "to accept, believe, and to agree with them."

Acc.: — If I said that, I would remember it better. I generally recommended them.

Pr.: — You said before that you took the bombs and revolvers from the saddle-bags.

Acc.: — I didn't take all of them out.

Pr.: — You agreed that they would take the bombs and revolvers. Did Mitar know that Nedjo and Cvijan would transport them?

Acc.: — I don't recall that. Mitar was there.

Pr.: — Did Blagoje know?

Acc.: — They all went in and out. One cannot say when somebody was in.

Pr.: — And Jovo?

Acc.: — I don't know that Jovo was.

Pr.: — At what time of night did they leave?

Acc.: — I don't know. I went home.

Pr.: — Did you say for what purpose they were going to Tuzla?

Acc.: — In Kerovic's house I didn't say.

Pr.: — Did you say outside?

Acc.: — Outside Blagoje asked me. He said, "Brother, it's bad." "What is?" "We've fallen into a great misfortune." "What kind?" "The students are carrying weapons to carry out an assassination of the Heir Ferdinand if he comes to Sarajevo."

Pr.: — Did Nedjo hear that?

Acc.: — Yes, he heard it. I left.

Pr.: — Didn't you worry about that?

Acc.: — No.

Pr.: — Did you ask Kerovic whether the arms were transferred?

Acc.: — I asked Cvijan Stjepanovic; "Did you hand them over?" "Yes." "Did he accept them?" "Yes." We talked about that in the store.

Pr.: — After that did you go to Tuzla?

Acc.: — I was in Tuzla on 20 May by the old calendar.

Pr.: — Thus 2 June.

Acc.: — On the eve of the feast of Emperor Konstantine and Empress Helen (an Orthodox feast) I was with my wife. We went to the doctor. We spent the night at an inn, and we had lunch at Misko Jovanovic's because we were in a friendly and god-relative relationship with him.

Pr.: — Did you both speak about these things?

Acc.: — I asked whether the arms had been transported, and he said that they were not, that he still had them. At lunch he said that a man had come who would take the weapons.

Pr.: — Did you talk with him about the purpose of the weapons?

Acc.: — At the inquiry I told Mr. Filipovic: "I cannot guarantee even to the extent of a word of honor that I said that. It seems to me that I said that." Mr. Secretary was in the office that same day and raised the same question and I said that I intended to tell him, but I cannot confirm whether I really did.

The President shows the defendant the statement of 19 July where it says that he told Misko Jovanovic that an assassination would be carried out on the Heir with those weapons.

Acc.: — That same day I was in the office and I corrected that statement.

The President shows the defendant the statement of 24
July where the defendant talked with Jovanovic about these
bombs on the way to the railroad station, and asked Misko
whether he knew what the students would do with the bombs.
He doesn't recall whether he told the purpose of those bombs,
but "I intended to tell him that they would carry out an
assassination."

Acc.: — I know that I had that intention.

Pr.: — Are you an adherent of the Yugoslav idea?

Acc.: — No.

Pr.: — Are you satisfied with the position of the Serbs in
Bosnia and Hercegovina?

Acc.: — I am not satisfied. In the constitutional view
Bosnia and Hercegovina, I want the autonomy of Bosnia and
Hercegovina under the Hapsburg monarchy. Every administra-
tion is good which is good for the people.

Pr.: — Did you teach your students to be devoted to the
Almighty Dynasty?

Acc.: — I worked according to the instructional plan which
was prescribed for us.

Pr.: — You did not think that Bosnia and Hercegovina had
to be annexed to Serbia?

Acc.: — No.

Pr.: — Did the *Narodna odbrana* have that objective?

Acc.: — I don't know.

Pr.: — Did you receive reports from the *Narodna odbrana*?

Acc.: — No.

The introduction and report of the *Narodna odbrana* are
read.

Pr.: — Here it is admitted that besides its cultural goals, the
Narodna odbrana had also other goals which were not permitted
to be published even in Serbia.

Pr.: — In what year was that book published?

Pros.: — 1909.

Acc.: — I didn't know that book. If Milanovic had de-
scribed the work of the *Narodna odbrana* in those terms, I
would have rejected him. (Reads the report of the inspector of
the Avornik region, Commander of the Drina Division, dated 5
October 1911 in regard to the channel.)

Pr.: — Now you know what the *Narodna odbrana* does.

Acc.: — I didn't know about that work.

Pr.: — Did you help to establish the topographical data in your vicinity and to hand them over to official circles in Serbia?

Acc.: — Yes. All of Serbia was investigated that way.

Pr.: — Are the Serbian lands where Serbs live?

Acc.: — They don't belong to Serbia.

Pr.: — What was the purpose of your work?

Acc.: — There is a constant question, and the most important is the manner of migrations. The greatest importance was assigned to the time when a family migrated.

Pr.: — Was it asked how many rivers, wells, cisterns?

Acc.: — Only in general.

Pr.: — Reads questions from individual pages and shows the defendant a large and a small book of that kind.

Pr.: — Did you work in that direction?

Acc.: — I worked according to the small booklet. I thought it had scientific purposes.

Pr.: — Then you recorded how many Serbs there were, how many springs, how many rivers?

Acc.: — That can be seen on a special map.

Pr.: — You claim that you did not work for the benefit of the *Narodna odbrana* in the sense which you now hear, but only in the cultural field?

Acc.: — I didn't have any kind of connection.

Pr.: — Then what you said before in the protocol of 23 July is not true, that you right away, as soon as you saw the students, knew that the *Narodna odbrana* had sent them. You stated in the inquiry of 11 July that you didn't report because you didn't know about the assassination, that you didn't know that the bombs were for the assassination. You said that the first time you were interrogated. Is that true?

Acc.: — What I said today is exact.

The President further shows the defendant the statement of 7 July.

Acc.: — The statement that I gave today is correct.

The President recessess the court for 5 minutes.

After the recess

Pr.: — Did you receive money from the Serbian Academy and how much?

Acc.: — Yes, 50 crowns.

Pr.: — Did you receive a letter?

Acc.: — Yes, from Dr. Dedijer.[95] He wrote me that I wrote well and that I should work further in that direction.

Pr.: — When the Serbo-Turkish war was on did you collect contributions for the Red Cross?

Acc.: — We all collected and we collected about 200 crowns, and for that we asked the permission of the district authorities.

Pr.: — Did you write an article against Professor Ajzelt of the Tuzla gymnasium and others?[96]

Acc.: — Yes, when I was a youth. That was long ago.

The President shows the defendant letters in which he wrote about the education in the Tuzla gymnasium: "The Truth about Mr. Ajzelt and his Clique."

Pr.: — Why did you need so many brochures from the Belgrade institute, brochures about those questions? Did you give them to others?

Acc.: — I wrote a postcard to the Belgrade institute, and they sent me several copies.

Naumowicz: — You said that to you the entire work of Bozo Milanovic seemed like some Utopia. Why then did you persuade Misko Jovanovic?

Acc.: — Because I promised Bozo Milanovic.

Naum.: — You said that you worked only because of threats. Did you threaten others?

Acc.: — I told Kerovic the kind of impression that the students had made on me. I did not say, "It is bad. You are not allowed to talk."

Naum.: — Did you threaten that you would throw the bombs?

Acc.: — That is a fantasy.

Naum.: — Did you hear that Grabez and Princip threatened?

Acc.: — I can't remember. On one occasion one of the students said, "You must be quiet about that. You are not allowed to talk about that."

Naum.: — Did he tell you that you are not allowed to speak?

Acc.: — He told me that I was not allowed to betray, re-port the matter.

Naum.: — Why was it not dangerous for you when you told others?

Acc.: — I was very friendly with them.

Naum.: — Did you know their political ideas?

Acc.: — They didn't concern themselves with politics, but were very hard-working people, especially in the agricultural *zadruge* (family households).[97]

Hoffman: — Did Princip tell you where the bombs came from?

Acc.: — He didn't, and I didn't ask him.

Hoffm.: — Did he talk about Tankosic and Ciganovic on the way?

Acc.: — No.

Premuzic: — You said that you know Misko Jovanovic. What kind of man is he? What does he do? Does he concern himself with politics?

Acc.: — As a bachelor he lives as a *bon vivant*. He was the center where we youngsters gathered. He was good-hearted, especially with respect to students. When anyone turned to him, he was at their disposition. Later he came to like the *sokol* and worked for it. He is a rather intelligent fellow, and formed himself most in society.

Zistler: — It was said today that the *sokol* was the cover for the tendencies which the *Narodna odbrana* propagated, and you were very active in *sokol* enterprises.

Acc.: — At first in 1910 and 1911 I was very active. After the "exceptional measures" when that association was suspend-ed, it was necessary to apply for a new permit, but I didn't do that.

Zist.: — Do you know the structure of the *sokol*? That *sokol* in Bosnia and Hercegovina, was it isolated or an integral part of a larger net?

Acc.: — As *Sokolsko drustvo* (*Sokol* Association) it fell under an organization *Sokolska zupa bosansko-hercegovacka* (*Sokol* District of Bosnia-Hercegovina). Our district maintained connection with other districts: Slav,[98] Czech, and Croatian.

Zist.: — To which center in the monarchy is the *Spski sokol* subordinated?

Acc.: — To the one in Prague.

Zist.: — Was it connected with the Kragujevac *sokol*?

Acc.: — No.

Pr.: — Did you know that there is a council of all *sokols* in Serbia in Kragujevac?

Acc.: — I only knew the council of *sokols* in Belgrade.

Zist.: — Did you know that recently in Bosnia and Hercegovina there had been work on a fusion of the Croatian and Serbian *sokols*?

Acc.: — Yes.

Pr.: — Did you know that this had been done in some places?

Acc.: — I knew one occasion when they had given an entertainment together.

Zist.: — Didn't you know that in Banja Luka the Croatian *sokol* combined with the Serbian?

Acc.: — I didn't know.

Zist.: — Anyone who wants to disguise himself, who wants to isolate himself, does not get involved. You are an adherent of Kocic's party which seeks autonomy for Bosnia. Is this a conception with respect to the Monarchy?

Acc.: — That Bosnia and Hercegovina should not be annexed to the Monarchy, but that they take a special position within the framework of the Austro-Hungarian Monarchy.

Zist.: — You are married. Did you marry out of love?

Acc.: — Yes.

Zist.: — Did you receive money?

Acc.: — No.

Zist.: — Have you been happy?

Acc.: — Yes.

Zist.: — You said in your defense that everything you did was under suggestion, a certain fear, under Princip's threat. If he threatened you, you would have to decide either for the assassination or not to obey. Thus you were between two evils. You knew that if you did not obey both your family and yourself would suffer.

Pr.: — Please just put questions.

Zist.: — Why did you sacrifice your personal family happiness? You had to know that you would be imprisoned.

Acc.: — I was afraid that my family would be destroyed, my house, which is five hours from the border. Everything could be destroyed in one night.

Zist.: — Do you know that in Serbia there is a revolutionary organization which really does that?

Acc.: — There were such organizations, as long as those regions in Macedonia were not liberated.

Zist.: — How did you know that?

Acc.: — It was known by all that the Bulgarians had such a Central Committee. Those guerrillas committed great atrocities. I was afraid that such a revolutionary organization stood behind Princip. I saw that behind them stood powerful elements. I thought that because one doesn't find bombs on the streets.

Zist.: — Did you know that they took revenge on those who did not submit?

Acc.: — I don't recall the names, but if you take the chronicle of Old Serbia's past, there are hundreds of such cases.

Pr.: — In Old Serbia there was no government with the power to protect its own subjects.

Acc.: — I was more afraid of terror than the law.

Pr.: — Why didn't you defend yourself in that way before?

Acc.: — I didn't dare.

Pr.: — If you testified that they admitted that they planned to carry out an assassination on the late esteemed Heir, then you also could admit it.

Acc.: — In this way I exposed myself, the other way I exposed my family.

Zist.: — How much were you paid as a teacher?

Acc.: — 2470 crowns per year.

Zist.: — Did only you live off that salary, or did you have to support someone?

Acc.: — I helped my brothers, especially Brother Branko who had a stipend of only 10 forints monthly.

Zist.: — Were you compelled to work in the literary field?

Acc.: — I tried to earn money in all possible ways. That was why I wrote for the Serbian Academy, because I thought that I would receive a good payment. However for three months' work I received 50 dinars.

Hoffman: — You said that you were afraid of terror, and to the question as to whether you asked Princip and Grabez where the bombs came from, you answered in the negative.

Acc.: — I wasn't afraid of Princip and Grabez. I was afraid of the students who carried the bombs. I also admired this student, who had the courage to carry bombs across a border which was guarded by gendarmes.

The President shows the defendant bombs and revolvers and asks him whether the weapons he saw were like those.

Acc.: — Yes.

Zist.: — You concerned yourself with politics. Are you an adherent of legal or revolutionary methods?

Acc.: — Legal. I am an opponent of assassination, an opponent of revolution, because the successes of revolution leave behind them bloody traces. I believe in the evolution of the spirit and ideas. I believe in evolution as such.

Perisic: — Stjepanovic, did you say anything about the purpose of the bombs?

Stjepanovic: — No.

Perisic: — Were you present outside the house when he told Kerovic what the students would do?

Stjepanovic: — No.

Premuzic shows the defendant the book: *The History of the Serbian People* by Stevan Kaludjercic for the third class and asks him whether he knows that book.

Acc.: — I know it.

Prem.: — Was it allowed?

Acc.: — Yes.

Prem.: — In this book there are things that don't correspond to the truth.

Acc.: — I did not hold to that book because it was too broad.

Prem.: — Did you notice that there were untruths?

Acc.: — There are.

Prem.: — Did you hold to it?

Acc.: — No.

Prem.: — (Reads the section from the book which tells

how the Serbs after the battle of Slankamen passed into Hungary under Arsenije Crnojevic.) There is no mention of Prince Eugene of Savoy.

Acc.: — One doesn't accept everything which is in this book but only what is written in capital letters.

Prem.: — Did you explain the pictures to them?

Acc.: — Everyone looked on his own.

Prem.: — Did you teach that Tvrtko I was a Serb?

Acc.: — I taught that Tvrtko I was a ruler who worked for the integration of all lands in the south.

Prem.: — How long was that book used in the autonomous Serbian schools?

Acc.: — Twenty years.

Pr.: — Did you tell the students that the Serbs in Bosnia and Hercegovina were brothers with the ones across the border, that they were one people?

Acc.: — We are all one people because we speak one language.

Feldbauer: — You said that Blagoje was curious and that you said to him: "It's bad, the students carry weapons. I think they intend an assassination." According to the statement of Blagoje, you are a terrorist.

Acc.: — I had in mind that we give away the matter.

Feldb.: — Did you have an influence on him and on the Kerovic family?

Acc.: — I had as a teacher.

Feldb.: — You said: "Both of us will lose our heads."

Acc.: — I didn't use those words, but I said something like it was a dangerous thing for both of us, to the effect that we could be destroyed.

Pros.: — Do you have your own property in Priboj?

Acc.: — No.

Pros.: — How is that, while you are getting involved in an assassination you can lose your job. You were afraid for your family. You could have moved.

Acc.: — I have a wife and children. It is difficult.

Pros.: — But you knew you would lose your job since you were involved in an assassination. What tied you to Priboj when you knew that you would be imprisoned?

Acc.: — My wife is a teacher in Priboj.

Pros.: — Did you know that the bombs were from Serbia?

Acc.: — When I learned about the bombs I knew that they were from Serbia.

Pros.: — You said that you were afraid of terrorism. How could the Serbian state, the revolutionary committee, attack you because you confessed?

Acc.: — They would come.

Pr.: — They told you that you were not allowed to talk about it, and you concealed it. Otherwise you would have immediately admitted that they really had the intention of carrying out an assassination.

Acc.: — I didn't consider it necessary to say that.

Pros.: — The threat was a marginal thing; the assassination was the main thing.

Acc.: — I had to admit the assassination and what I knew about it as soon as they put me in jail, because the thing was given away. I thought the threat was a bigger thing than the assassination because of my family. That way my family would be left alone.

Premuzic: — You were present at the St. Sava celebrations.[99] Tell us, how were they arranged?

Acc.: — Usually someone made a speech about the life of St. Sava as a patron of the schools. That would be a priest or teacher. I too would give a lecture. Someone would talk about abstinence. After that they sang songs, hymns, and everything was reported to the district authority.

Prem.: — Was it said that St. Sava was the patron of all Serbs?

Acc.: — Yes. St. Sava strengthened the Orthodox faith and gave it the direction to become national.

Prem.: — Did you do that everywhere?

Acc.: — Wherever there were Serbian schools.

Malek: — Did you say before Obren Milosevic that the Heir was coming?

Acc.: — No.

Malek: — Did the students say so?

Acc.: — Not in front of me.

Premuzic announces that Cabrinovic wants to say something.

Cabrinovic: — Before the assassination itself I read a book, *Underground Russia*, and the newspaper, *Vihor* (the Whirlwind),[100] when I thought about carrying out the assassination, and it influenced me. Even if I hadn't carried out the assassination I wouldn't have remained here from fear of the government. And could we be positively assured that Vojin Tankosic would not come here?

Pros.: — He wouldn't come. He's dead.

THE HEARING OF MIHAILO (MISKO) JOVANOVIC
14 OCTOBER 1914

Call Misko Jovanovic.

Pr.: — Do you consider yourself guilty?

Acc.: — I don't consider myself guilty at all, sir.

Pr.: — Not at all?

Acc.: — No.

Pr.: — You are not guilty?

Acc.: — I am guilty insofar as I accepted the arms.

Pr.: — Isn't that a crime?

Acc.: — To that extent I am guilty.

Pr.: — And nothing else? What school did you finish?

Acc.: — Four grades of the basic school, two classes of the Business School and three classes of the private German *real* school in Tuzla.

Pr.: — You speak German?

Acc.: — Pretty well.

Pr.: — And after that?

Acc.: — I was in business with my father.

Pr.: — Did you receive pay?

Acc.: — No. I was in business up to August of last year when my father built a building for the cinema. I got married and he gave me the building. I acquired the necessary things, began to work, and lived and worked in the cinema.

Pr.: — Did your father give you money for the equipment?

Acc.: — No. The Serbian Bank gave it to me on personal credit.

Pr.: — What other honorary offices did you hold in Tuzla?

Acc.: — I was the first president of the Serbian *sokol*, a member of the *Srpska crkvena opcina* (Serbian Church Community), a member of the *Eparhijski savjet* (Episcopal Council), and a member of the board of the Serbian Bank.

Pr.: — What kind of duties did you have as a member of the Church Community?

Acc.: — To participate in the work.

Pr.: — For example, to participate in the appointment of teachers, the appointment of priests, the determination of their salary?

Acc.: — Yes.

Pr.: — You did know what kind of tasks you had to fulfill?

Acc.: — Yes.

Pr.: — What did you have to do as a member of the Episcopal Council?

Acc.: — I decided on things which came up on the agenda, for example, the proposals of the School Council and the like.

Pr.: — And what did you do as a member of the board of the Serbian Bank?

Acc.: — I audited the books, the accounts.

Pr.: — Were you consulted when someone sought a loan?

Acc.: — No.

Pr.: — Did you have any honorary position in Tuzla?

Acc.: — I was president of the Serbian *sokol*.

Pr.: — What kind of task did the *sokol* have?

Acc.: — To cultivate the physical and spiritual health of its members.

Pr.: — From the political point of view?

Acc.: — Excluded.

Pr.: — In the Tuzla *sokol* too?

Acc.: — Generally in every *sokol*.

Pr.: — Weren't you allowed to concern yourselves with politics?

Acc.: — If anyone began a political discussion I stopped it.

Pr.: — Did you have some other kind of honorary office which was connected with Serbia?

Acc.: — Yes. I was a representative of the *Narodna odbrana*.

Pr.: — What is the *Narodna odbrana*?

Acc.: — I read in the newspapers that it holds lectures, educates the people.

Pr.: — How was it that you became a member of the *Narodna odbrana* and a representative?

Acc.: — That was in 1912. A *sokol* exercise was held in Priboj. At that time Cubrilovic told me that he had been in Sabac, that the president of the *Narodna odbrana* Milanovic had received him and asked me whether I would like to be a representative. I said that I would think it over and left. I thought that I shouldn't accept because I already had enough duties. In March and April of the same year I was in Berlin for a long time. At that time I became acquainted with the association *Deutschland fur's Ausland* (Germany for Foreign Lands). There I saw how much that association worked for their settlers in Bosnia and Hercegovina. While I was in Berlin I subscribed to their organ *Deutsche Stunden* (German Hours). When I came from Priboj to Tuzla, I received that paper and I remembered Cubrilovic's words. I was ashamed that I had turned it down when I read that people thousands of kilometers away worked for their people. That stimulated me to go to Sabac to Bozo Milanovic. I found him and told him that Veljko Cubrilovic urged me to be the representative of the *Narodna odbrana* and that I was willing. Then he told me that the *Narodna odbrana* distributed the books of Zivojin Dacic among the people.

Pr.: — What were those books written about?

Acc.: — On the education of the people, about the economic situation.

Pr.: — And about politics?

Acc.: — They don't deal with it.

Pr.: — You are a representative of the *Narodna odbrana* and you don't know what its aims are?

Acc.: — I don't know.

Pr.: — You know your tasks in all associations except this one?

Acc.: — I knew it from practice.

Pr.: — But as a representative of the *Narodna odbrana* you had to know the goals.

Acc.: — It has educational, cultural goals. This is what I was told.

Pr.: — Did you know that they trained guerrilla bands into armed forces and provided them with arms?

Acc.: — Yes, in time of war.

Pr.: — Is that thought cultural and educational?

Acc.: — That is in time of war. At such times the most humane institutions work in that way.

Pr.: — The Red Cross does not arm soldiers. You were a representative at that time, and you did not receive orders to give contributions for that purpose?

Acc.: — No.

Pr.: — Did you receive other books, brochures from the *Narodna odbrana*?

Acc.: — When I left Bozo Milanovic's he gave me some 20 to 30 brochures about Bosnia which dealt with the people in Bosnia.

Pr.: — Did you distribute them?

Acc.: — Yes. I gave them to the *sokol*, and also to peasants when I saw them.

Pr.: — You said that the *soko* had no political goals, and yet you gave them the kind of books which said that the Moslems, Serbs and Croats were one people and must be unified. You worked in the political field when you distributed those brochures. What are your political ideals?

Acc.: — I never concerned myself with politics.

Pr.: — During the war[101] did you go to Belgrade to participate in the war?

Acc.: — Yes, I went, but I did not participate. I have a sister, Vukosava, married to Mihajlo Sonda, an industrialist. When the war broke out he and his two brothers went to the war. My sister, their two sisters and their old mother stayed at home. I knew that it was hard for my sister when her husband left, perhaps never to return. I have a strongly-developed sense of family and I went to my sister to console her. I was there for eight days. If it had been possible I would have remained at my sister's the whole time.

Pr.: — Were you engaged then?

Acc.: — No. I became engaged on July 1st of last year.

Pr.: — Did you already know your wife at that time. Did you correspond with her?

Acc.: — Yes.

Pr.: — You never had the wish to participate in the war?

Acc.: — I knew that I was not fit for the war.

Pr.: — Did you write anything about that to your fiancee?

Acc.: — I did not write anything.

Pr.: — Did she know that you went to Serbia?

Acc.: — Yes.

At that **The President** shows the accused her letter which was found at the defendant's and reads it.

Acc.: — I never had any other intentions when I went to my sister's. Before I went to Belgrade I learned that Serbia would not accept volunteers because she had 60,000 of them and I wouldn't have been accepted in any case, and I was not a soldier.

Pr.: — And why did she write (Reads): "You don't say what you intend, or whether they will send you back in another way for dear Serbia."

Acc.: — She might have thought about Serbdom.

Pr.: — In that letter it says further that you "work voluntarily, and if not with a rifle on your shoulder, still you expose yourself to danger."

Acc.: — I worked enough for the *sokol* and exposed myself to danger travelling in bad weather. That was what my fiancee had in mind. After that, I was in Srebrenica on one occasion but then the then-director drove me from Srebrenica. I had to return, and that was in February on a stormy night.

Pr.: — Was that danger a sacrifice laid on the altar of freedom?

Acc.: — Spiritual freedom.

Pr.: — She received a final letter from Belgrade and did she answer that letter?

Acc.: — I don't know what I wrote her.

Pr.: — If you did not concern yourself with politics, then why did you say in a circular letter which you wrote to all *sokols*: "Dear Brothers, to us, to whom it is not yet given to pawn our lives for freedom." Was that in the sense of health?

Acc.: — That was written in enthusiasm.

Pr.: — Of course, I know that. You said further: "It is our holy duty to contribute to the help of our brothers, collecting and adding contributions to the Red Cross." That circular letter went to all *sokols*.

Acc.: — I didn't intend to raise revolution with bombs. My only intention was to collect as many contributions as possible for the Red Cross.

Pr.: — What did you mean by: "To us, to whom it is not yet given to pawn our lives for freedom?"

Acc.: — If we are not dying, our duty is to help.

Pr.: — When did you think that the time would come? Perhaps now?

Acc.: — I didn't know.

Pr.: — Then to you that was an empty phrase?

Acc.: — My only objective was to collect as many contributions as possible.

Pr.: — What was your opinion with respect to our Almighty Ruling Dynasty?

Acc.: — Good.

Pr.: — Are you a loyal man?

Acc.: — No one can say that I am not loyal.

Pr.: — How far does your loyalty go, when you prepare revolvers and bombs in Sarajevo for the assassination?

Acc.: — I did not prepare them.

Pr.: — You personally went from Tuzla to Doboj and carried weapons in a box and gave them to Ilic.

Acc.: — I went occasionally to Doboj.

Pr.: — Did you carry the bombs from Tuzla to Doboj?

Acc.: — Yes.

Pr.: — Did you know that Ilic would go to Sarajevo?

Acc.: — Yes.

Pr.: — Then your loyalty went so far as to permit you to bring the means by which the late esteemed Heir Apparent would be killed.

Acc.: — I didn't know that they were for the assassination.

Pr.: — You admitted many times that you knew.

Acc.: — I didn't know directly that they were for the assassination, nor did I say that they were for the assassination or the Heir.

The President shows the defendant his statement in which he said that he did not remember Cubrilovic's words, but from his talk he understood that he intended to carry out an assassination.

Acc.: — From the words "atentat no prestonasljednika" (attempt on the Heir) I did not conclude that he would kill him.[102]

Pr.: — You knew about the assassination, you had weapons, yet you wish to say that you thought that there would be a demonstration and that you were loyal.

Acc.: — I wasn't told that there would be an assassination of the Heir.

Pr.: — Why are you loyal?

Acc.: — Because it is my duty as a citizen.

Pr.: — Earlier in the inquiry you mentioned another reason: because things are good for you under the Austrian administration.

Acc.: — Yes.

Pr.: — Did you telegraph something after the assassination?

Acc.: — No.

Pr.: — Did you give some kind of written note of sympathy?

Acc.: — All of our institutions expressed sympathy, and they also called on me as president to express sympathy before the *sokol*.

Pr.: — On what occasion?

Acc.: — Because an unpleasant accident happened that there was an assassination of the Heir.

Pr.: — What does it mean that there was an *atentat*?

Acc.: — That he was killed.

Pr.: — You gave the weapons; you knew about the *atentat*.

Acc.: — That was from the side of the *sokol*. I had to do it as the president of the *sokol*.

Pr.: — How did it happen that you kept weapons at your place?

Acc.: — One day about seven o'clock in the morning Mara Sainova, a relative of my wife's who was with us as a guest, woke me up and told me that two peasants were calling on me. I got up from the bed, drew on a gown, and went outside. A couple of peasants waited there. After the usual greetings they gave me bombs and revolvers. They delivered a note: "Dear Misko, Keep these things. greetings, your Veljko." The peasants said that students would come later, and I mentioned that I didn't know who those students were. One of those two peasants, that must be Cvijan Stjepanovic, said that the students would come to the reading-room at nine o'clock. At that the peasants left.

Pr.: — Why didn't you throw out the peasants and bombs?

Acc.: — I didn't even think of that.

Pr.: — Just on the basis of the letter from Veljko Cubrilovic you accepted the bombs and revolvers?

Acc.: — I didn't know what purpose they would serve.

Pr.: — Everyone knows for what purpose.

Acc.: — I know that even the most honorable people carry arms.

Pr.: — Not bombs. I never saw that honorable people carry bombs. Maybe in Serbia.

Acc.: — I had to receive the people, and they put the bombs and revolvers on the table and left.

Pr.: — Where did you hear that students were carrying bombs?

Acc. (Is silent): — The Serbian reading-room is in the same building where I live. The reading-room is on the second floor and I am on the third. I went to the reading-room at nine o'clock. Cvijan Stjepanovic was sitting in the reading-room and reading the newspaper. I asked him, "Where are the students?" He answered, "They will come soon." I took the newspaper. In the meantime two young men entered. Then Stjepanovic got up and said, "These are the two students," and left. I went with them into another room and they told me that they were graduates from Belgrade. Then I said, "Those peasants left weapons with me and said to give them to you." They said to me, "Because we are travelling without passports and because stricter controls might be taken because of the arrival of the Archduke Ferdinand, would you be willing to take the weapons there?" I said that I wouldn't. Then they said, "If you will not, then please keep them a few days at your place. I shrugged my shoulders: "Okay." Then I mentioned that I did not know their friend. Then I was told, the one who would bring a sign . .

Pr.: — Why not a letter?

Acc.: — I don't know.

Pr.: — Who figured out that the sign should be a box?

Acc.: — Perhaps I myself said, "A box of *Stefanija* cigarettes," because I always smoke *Stefanija* cigarettes.

Pr.: — According to your words, they told you that they would carry the bombs to Sarajevo and they reminded you that there were exceptional measures, because Leopold Salvator and the Heir Apparent would come to Sarajevo.

Acc.: — Yes.

Pr.: — The others said that you are an intelligent man. Didn't you connect the bombs with the Heir Apparent?

Acc.: — There were stricter measures in general.

Pr.: — As soon as they said that the Heir was coming to Sarajevo, you should have immediately connected this with the students from Serbia who carried weapons.

Acc.: — When I told them that they should bring me as identification a box of Stefanija cigarettes, Princip said, "Don't play around with the idea of betraying us, Sir, because I will destroy you and your entire family." I shrugged my shoulders and left.

Pr.: — You were satisfied, so let it be. Couldn't you have thrown the students out and denounced them, and so freed yourself of danger? Why did you keep the bombs at home?

Acc.: — I had to because they forced me into it.

Pr.: — You did not. You are the president of the *sokol*. You would only have had to call your guards (cete) and they would have protected you from the others. How is it that students arrived from outside and they could force you into this?

Acc.: — I was afraid for my family. I left, and I have no idea when they left and where.

Pr.: — How many days did the bombs stay at your place? Where did you hide them?

Acc.: — When the peasants left the bombs, I put them in the cabinet in the corridor. I remembered at once the kitchen supplies were stored there and that my wife would see it and be frightened. Because I live on the third floor, I took them to the attic. Four tenants live in the same building. Each tenant has one room in the attic. In one room I found an old box and put the things into it. I think it was Sunday morning, between nine and ten o'clock. I was working at home when my wife came into the room and announced that a young man wished to see me.

Pr.: — Was that the same day or before the arrival of Veljko Cubrilovic?

Acc.: — On Saturday evening there was an exercise of the *Serbian sokol.* I left for the exercise and my wife and Mara Sainova went to the cinema. When I returned from the exercise, Veljko and his wife had arrived and stopped at the inn. I wanted to visit them after the performance, and after ten o'clock, when the performance was over, my wife, Mara Sainova, and I went to the inn. There I found Veljko, his wife, and Gasa Gavric and his wife from Priboj. The same evening Stjepan Sain was supposed to come from Mostar to take Mara home. When it was time for the train, we went to the railroad station. Veljko said, "I will go with you," and he went. On the way I told Veljko, "Those students left things with me and said that they would come, but they are not here yet." And he answered, "If they said that, maybe they will come." And he asked me, "Do you know why?" I said, "I don't know," and he said, "Be silent, poor fellow. It's better for you if you don't know."

Pr.: — Veljko, did you say this?

Cubrilovic: — I said, "Better that you don't know."

Pr.: — You did not say that in the inquiry.

Cubr.: — I said it during the confrontation with Misko Jovanovic.

Jovanovic: — Then he said, "Don't you see how he despises us?" It seemed to me that he meant Potiorek. "Just now, when the Heir Apparent is coming . . ." Meanwhile my wife who walked in front of me, came to us and asked whether the train had arrived at the station. I looked at the station and said that it had arrived. There were many people and police and we did not talk any more. Meanwhile Stjepan arrived and we went home, and Veljko left for the inn. The next day Veljko was busy with his business and said that he would go to Zenica. At 12:30 he came back. When we were together at dinner, Scepan, Mara, Veljko and his wife, on one occasion I whispered to Veljko, "Veljko, someone came after those things." He said, "Yes, it's okay." Around 2:30 in the afternoon Veljko left and took two or three books. I went to the cinema at three o'clock because the performances were beginning.

Pr.: — What happened the next day?

Acc.: — When Ilic came, my wife told me that a young man wished to talk to me. I said, "Let him in." He entered and showed me the box of *Stefanija* cigarettes, and I said, "How will you carry it?" because six bombs and four revolvers cannot be carried in the pocket. He said it should be packed in a box. Then I said, "When shall I give it to you?" and he replied, "Please find a man. Let him carry those things to the station, to the first station after Tuzla." I had two servants: Jovan Jovanovic, a poor man, who had an old father and a mother and sister who had already been ill for two years. He had to support the family on 60 crowns. If the police should catch him . . .

Pr.: — You knew that this could bring misery on him.

Acc.: — Then I thought: I have to go to Doboj tomorrow anyway because I had lumber there and had to find people who would make ties of it.

Pr.: — How long did you have this lumber in Doboj?

Acc.: — Four years.

Pr.: — And you had to go there just this very day?

Acc.: — I went several times. The firm Berger from Zagreb wrote me that its clerk . . .

Pr.: — How long before that?

Acc.: — Fifteen or 20 days. I found workers who worked at another place and I thought: when they finish here then they can go to Doboj.

Pr.: — What's the name of this firm?

Acc.: — "Berger-Actiengegesellschaft."

Pr.: — And who was the representative?

Acc.: — It seems to me, Miksic. He had already come to Tuzla once. I wrote to this firm several times.

Pr.: — Had you gone to Doboj before because of the lumber?

Acc.: — Yes. Because earlier I had wanted to arrange for the ties in Bokunje. Then I asked Ilic, "Will there be someone to meet me?" And he answered that he would try to get someone, that there were many of them. However, he did not tell me what he would do and I said good-bye to him. The next day

Mara Sainova and Scepan left. I went with them to Doboj and took the things with me.

Pr.: — Who took the box?

Acc.: — I did.

Pr.: — What were you wearing?

Acc.: — The same as now. Because it was cold, I had a pelerine.

Pr.: — In what kind of box?

Acc.: — In a sugar box.

Pr.: — Was it white or black?

Acc.: — Black.

Pr.: — Was it wrapped in paper?

Acc.: — Yes.

Pr.: — How was it tied?

Acc.: — With a rope.

Pr.: — Did you carry it in your hands?

Acc.: — Yes.

Pr.: — All the way to the station?

Acc.: — Yes.

Pr.: — And who carried the things to your sister-in-law?

Acc.: — The servant of Jovan Jovanovic.

Pr.: — In the inquiry you didn't say you carried the box. You explicitly said that you did not carry it. Your female relative also says the same. But she says that she carried a sugar-box.

Acc.: — Maybe she carried some sort of sweets.

Pr.: — A box of sweets is different. When you started to take it away, she said, "Don't you dare."

The President shows the defendant the statement from the inquiry.

Acc.: — Maybe she carried sugar and sweets. My wife prepared sweets from strawberries. I carried that box to the station and I thought: I will give it to Ilic at the station. A train came. People sat in the cars, and I also sat. I thought that three stations later I would see Ilic, but I didn't see him and I thought perhaps he had fallen asleep. When I came to Doboj I looked to see whether Ilic was there. I didn't find him. Then I went to the station and left that box in the second-class waiting room, threw the robe over it, and went outside. I looked and still there was no Ilic. Afterwards I went into the town.

Pr.: — You left the box with the bombs and revolvers at the station. Couldn't someone have taken them?

Acc.: — I didn't think anyone would take them.

Pr.: — That was very dangerous for you, but you didn't dare give it to the servant to carry from the house to the station?

Acc.: — I didn't because of the servant. I left it there and I thought that I would return immediately. Meanwhile I went into the city with the box and went to Vaso Jovanovic's, and from there to Vuko Jaksic's.[103] He wasn't in his workshop. There was only an apprentice. I left the box with him and hung my coat on a hook. I left them there to stay until I came back. Then I went to the merchant Kosta Marinkovic to ask him to find me people to work. I was with him for one hour.

Pr.: — Did you find people?

Acc.: — He promised me that he would let me know when they all arrived.

Pr.: — How much time did you spend?

Acc.: — Oh, an hour and a half.

Pr.: — And meanwhile the box was in the store. Weren't you afraid someone would see it?

Acc.: — I never thought of that. When I finished, I went to Vuko Jaksic's. That was after ten o'clock. We sat and talked about affairs in Tuzla. When it was time for the train to come I left and said to Vuko, "If you go to lunch before I come back, please don't close the store because a man will come to whom I must give a box."

Pr.: — Was it necessary that you give it to him in the store?

Acc.: — It was not necessary, but at that time I didn't think of that.

Pr.: — And he left the store unlocked more than half a day?

Acc.: — I went to the station. Meanwhile the train arrived and Ilic came. When I came to Vuko's workshop it was not locked, and no one was inside. Then Ilic took the box, and I went to a restaurant for lunch.

Pr.: — Why didn't you hand over the box in the station? That would be much simpler.

Acc.: — I didn't know how to hand it over. It was time for

the train. I went to telegraph my wife, and then to the restaurant. In the afternoon I returned home.

Pr.: — When did you hear about the assassination?

Acc.: — Sunday afternoon at 3 o'clock.

Pr.: — Did you hear who did it?

Acc.: — They said at once. Some students.

Pr.: — What did you think then? Did it occur to you that
you gave arms to those students.

Acc.: — I thought of those weapons.

Pr.: — As you admitted, as a result of your mediation this
assassination was carried out with those weapons which you
hid. Was there some kind of celebration in Tuzla that day?

Acc.: — There was supposed to be one, but it was cancelled.

Pr.: — Wasn't that a student celebration?

Acc.: — No.

Pr.: — You don't know? In the *Trpeza*?[104]

Acc.: — I don't know.

Pr.: — It seems to me that your wife is the president?

Acc.: — She is the secretary of the *Trpeza*, the Women's
Club.

Pr.: — That day an entertainment by the students of the
gymnasium was held in the *Djacka trpeza* (Student *trpeza*) after
which you heard about the assassination.

Acc.: — I didn't know that. When we heard about the
assassination we didn't hold entertainments, rather we cancelled
them. Already about 3 o'clock the cinema was closed and my
wife and I went walking outside the town. We returned home
in the dark. How it was in Tuzla at that time neither my wife
nor I know.

Pr.: — Did you write articles in the newspapers against the
government and against Austria?

Acc.: — I did not write against the government. I wrote
two or three short notes when they expelled me from Srebrenica,
and once I wrote them after we made an excursion in the vicinity of Tuzla and they gave us a fourth-class railroad car although we had bought second-class tickets.

Pr.: — And about propagandizing the *sokol*?

Acc.: — When they expelled me from Srebrenica. There was

considerable public discussion about the *sokol* affair. I took part in that discussion.

Pr.: — Is your *sokol* in Tuzla connected with the same association in Serbia?

Acc.: — No.

Pr.: — Do you know the Kragujevac association *Dusan silni?*105

Acc.: — No.

Pr.: — Did you know that this association arranged a celebration this year at which they made speeches against Austria?

Acc.: — I did not.

Pr.: — Have you received forms which you had to fill out for the *Sokol Dusan Silni* in which the members of all *sokols* in Bosnia and Hercegovina, Dalmatia, and Croatia were listed?

Acc.: — I did not.

Pr.: — Did you receive letters or anything else from the *Narodna odbrana* in Sabac?

Acc.: — No. Only in August of last year I received about ten pamphlets about cholera, and in December ten to twenty pamphlets about tuberculosis. Sometimes I received clippings from newspapers, mainly when they wrote about persecutions of Serbs in Bosnia and Hercegovina.

Pr.: — What did you do with these?

Acc.: — I read them, sometimes in the cafe in company.

Pr.: — What kind of company was it with which you communicated?

Acc.: — Djordje Mihajlovic, Petrovic,106 the merchant Kelber. I have many friends. I cannot remember exactly.

Pr.: — If you have many friends, then you should easily remember. Were there lawyers, physicians, pharmacists, merchants?

Acc.: — I am acquainted with lawyers, but they did not read it.

Pr.: — Did you give the clippings to the members of the *sokol?*

Acc.: — No.

Pr.: — Why did you conceal everything at the beginning?

Acc.: — I didn't conceal it.

Pr.: — You did. You concealed that you are a member of

the *Narodna odbrana*. You stated explicitly that you did not know Bozo Milanovic. You concealed those things.

Acc.: − I said in the inquiry that after the assassination I read in the Viennese newspaper *Arbeiter Zeitung* that the *Narodna odbrana* had sent weapons, so I was afraid and did not want to tell.

Pr.: − What were you afraid of?

Acc.: − Because they wrote.

Pr.: − Do you know that the *Narodna odbrana* had the task of spying on all fortresses and conditions in Tuzla?

Acc.: − They didn't tell me.

Pr.: − Didn't you work for that?

Acc.: − No.

Pr.: − Did you find anyone?

Acc.: − I did not find anyone.

Pr.: − Did you communicate in writing with Bozo Milanovic? By mail, or did you send the letters through peasants?

Acc.: − I never wrote to him. In July or August of one year, when there was a celebration of *Prosveta*[107] in Sarajevo, Bozo Milanovic said that he would come, and I had to arrange with him so that he would come to Tuzla. However, he did not come.

After that **The President** showed the defendant the bombs and revolvers. The defendant admits that they were of that kind.

The President recesses the hearing until three o'clock in the afternoon.

Ends at 12 o'clock

**CONTINUATION OF THE MAIN HEARING
OCTOBER 14, 1914.
In the afternoon
CONTINUATION OF THE HEARING OF MISKO
JOVANOVIC AND PARTIAL HEARING OF GRABEZ**

Pr.: − Grabez, you told us yesterday or the day before that, after Cabrinovic had thrown the bomb you stood on the bridge.

Grabez: — Yes.

Pr.: — On the Emperor's Bridge? For the purpose of carrying out the assassination of the Heir Apparent should he return to the palace? Is this the truth?

Acc.: — Yes.

Pr.: — It is not, because the policemen Silvester Kruzih, Peter Kammerer, Aleksander Szilagy, Mile Ljustine, Muharem Hero will confirm that not a single person was allowed to wait on the Emperor's Bridge.

Acc.: — I stood on the Emperor's Bridge. If you are interested in defending me, that's all right. I defend myself as best as I can.

Pr.: — Call those policemen who have been picked for this on the basis of article 266 of the penal code for Tuesday morning.

Pr.: — Misko Jovanovic, tell me once more, did you wish that Bosnia and Hercegovina be united with Serbia?

M. Jovanovic: — I was not concerned with this.

Pr.: — Was it your wish that Bosnia and Hercegovina be annexed to Serbia?

Acc.: — I don't know.

Pr.: — Answer yes or no.

Acc. (Silent): — I don't know.

Pr.: — Was that your wish before you were president of Serbian *sokol*?

Acc.: — I didn't work on that.

Pr.: — But what was your wish?

Acc.: — I didn't work at that. I didn't want that. In the end I wouldn't even be able to do it.

Hoffman: — How many rooms did the Serbian reading-room in Tuzla have?

Acc.: — Six.

Hoffman: — In which room did you await Princip and Grabez?

Acc.: — In the middle one.

Hoffman: — Where did you carry the bombs?

Acc.: — I didn't carry them from above.

Hoffm.: — Then you called Princip to another room. Then you talked with him to one side. What did he say to you about the bombs?

Acc.: — He did not tell me from where he brought them.

Hoffm.: — Didn't you ask him?

Acc.: — No.

Hoffm.: — Did you know that he came from Belgrade?

Acc.: — They said that they were Belgrade graduates.

Hoffm.: — So you did not ask him?

Acc.: — I didn't ask him. I was with him four or five minutes in order to ask him when he would take the bombs away, to get rid of them.

Hoffm.: — A clever man would have asked: "Where did you get the bombs. Who gave them to you?"

Acc.: — I did not ask him.

Pros.: — Do you know Dr. Pilar[108] in Tuzla?

Acc.: — Yes.

Pros.: — He was also president of the Croatian *sokol* in Tuzla.

Acc.: — Yes. Earlier he was. Probably he is still.

Pros.: — Had he ever told you that he had gotten the report of the Kregujevac *sokol* and the forms?

Acc.: — No.

Pros.: — Probably he didn't tell you that those were not for the Croatian *sokol*, but for you?

Acc.: — No.

Pros.: — Why did the Serbs celebrate St. Vitus' Day?

Acc.: — He is a national saint from the time of the fall of the Serbian empire.

Pros.: — Why do you celebrate the fall?

Acc.: — Memories of the misfortune.

Pros.: — Is there any sort of wish expressed thereby?

Acc.: — That is a commemoration. Just as we have other saints, we took this one for the national saint.

Pros.: — And no kind of wish is expressed?

Acc.: — I didn't declare him a saint. I don't know. All Serbs celebrated him, and I with them.

Pros.: — I don't ask personally, but in general. Thus St. Vitus' Day is the day when one commemorates the fall of the Serbian empire?

Acc.: — Yes, nothing else. At least I don't know.

Pros.: — When one celebrates the fall, then probably one is expressing the wish that things be better?

Premuzic: — If you had known that those weapons were for the assassination, would you have prevented it?

Acc.: — I don't know whether I would have been in a position to prevent it, but at least I would have told them, "People, what are you doing?"

Prem.: — Why could you not have prevented it?

Acc.: — I will give you an example where I sacrificed myself for someone else. There is a landowner named Sahinagic. His son once was swimming in the river Sprec and began to drown. There were about twenty of us on the bank and all of them began to laugh, and I jumped into the water to save him. He grabbed me around the neck so that I almost choked and drowned. Now, gentlemen, I have a wife and child which she carried for seven months under the heart, and why should my family suffer. Then I thought that those two peasants also had families, and Veljko is my god-relative, and I absolutely could not do that, I could not prevent it. Maybe I could have said, "Don't do it, man. Think about what you're doing!" I was under the influence of newspaper articles about the demonstrations in Mostar[109] and about the expulsion of students from the theater. Twenty-five academic citizens came to look for entertainment. I had no idea about the conspiracy. They didn't say that they wanted to kill the Heir. Had I known, I would have said, "Wait, man. Think it over." If I had not been able to divert them, at least I would have told them that, but I didn't know what they were doing. I was in a difficult position. I could not. I did not have reason to make so many people unhappy.

Prem.: — Don't you see that this is a greater misfortune yet?

Acc.: — I didn't set the scene, nor did I give the means. I just fell into such a position. If you were in my position, what would you have done?

Hoffm.: — Yesterday you said that you knew that something evil was planned. If you had wanted to prevent it, you could have.

Acc.: — I didn't know what kind of evil they would do.

Hoffm.: — One doesn't play with bombs.

Acc.: — It didn't have to come to a bad end. How many times do people shoot, and of thousands, maybe one hits.

Hoffm.: — Did you try the bombs?

Acc.: — I hadn't seen one in ages. They can be thrown in a place where they won't do harm.

Pr.: — Have you seen a bomb? (Shows him.)

Acc.: — Until now I have never seen one.

Pr.: — When this explodes, it has to kill.

Acc.: — If one wants to, it can be thrown in such a place that it won't kill. A revolver also kills, and at the time of the demonstrations because of the assassination of the Heir, the demonstrators in Tuzla fired revolvers many times and did not kill anybody, and still a revolver also kills. And now here is an example that the bomb did not kill, but the revolver.

Prem.: — You remember your child, the wife of Cubrilovic, etc. That's all very well, but one should also remember that the late Archduke also had children. Didn't you think of that? It is certainly difficult to believe your defense. Therefore as your defense counsel I admonish you, if you knew what was involved, it would be better for you if you would humbly repent before everybody. Maybe then everything will be completely different.

Acc.: — Gentlemen, I said that I didn't know. I recalled the children, because I have a child. I did not know that an assassination of the Heir was at stake.

Prem.: — If you had known, would you have agreed?

Pr.: — Those possibilities have no objective. Does anyone else have further questions? (There are none.) Call Lazar Djukic if he has come. (He has not come.) I recess the hearing until he comes.

After the recess

THE HEARING OF LAZAR DJUKIC
14 OCTOBER 1914

Pr. (to Lazar Djukic): — Are you guilty?

Acc.: — I don't know.

Pr.: — How old are you?

Acc.: — Eighteen.

Pr.: — Tell me what school you attended?

Acc.: — I was a student in the second class of the Teacher's School.

Pr.: — And before?

Acc.: — I was in the fifth class of the gymnasium, and I left the fifth class three months before the end.

Pr.: — Why did you leave?

Acc.: — I failed in mathematics and then I went the next year to the Teacher's School.

Pr.: — Here in Sarajevo?

Acc.: — Yes.

Pr.: — Did you have any kind of student association?

Acc.: — Yes, we did.

Pr.: — What was it called?

Acc.: — *Srpsko-hrvatska nacionalisticka omladina* (The Serbo-Croatian Nationalistic Youth).

Pr.: — What were the objectives of that association?

Acc.: — The unity of Serbs, Croats and Slovenes.

Pr.: — What kind of unity?

Acc.: — Cultural.

Pr.: —And as concerns political unity?

Acc.: — We never talked about that.

Pr.: — Nor that you wished that it be realized?

Acc.: — No, only cultural.

Pr.: — Some of your colleagues who were also in that association say completely differently.

Acc.: — I was in the kind of an organization as I said. I don't know anything else.

Pr.: — Did you think that the cultural unification would be realized inside the framework of the Austro-Hungarian Monarchy, or outside?

Acc.: — I never talked about that.

Pr.: — Did you know Princip?

Acc.: — I knew him. He was with me in the gymnasium.

Pr.: — Did you know his ideas and objectives?

Acc.: — While he was in school we did not concern ourselves with those questions.

Pr.: — Here on the ninth of July you stated in the inquiry:
"With regard to the Yugoslavs, by 'unity' we understood that it
be realized within the framework of the Austro-Hungarian Monarchy." Is what is written here true?

Acc.: — Cultural unity is understood.   That all Serbs,
Croats, and Slovenes be one nation.

Pr.: — That doesn't make sense as you stated it here.
Apparently you thought of political unity?

Acc.: — The honorable investigation judge asked me whether I thought of unification with Serbia, and I said that I only
speak about the Monarchy.

Pr.: — Then you didn't have any kind of intentions that
Bosnia and Hercegovina be separated from Austria and annexed
to Serbia?

Acc.: — I never talked about that.

Pr.: — How are you disposed toward the Almighty Ruling
Dynasty?

Acc.: — I have nothing against it.

Pr.: — Did you learn anything to the effect that some sort
of assassination was in preparation?

Acc.: — Yes.

Pr.: — How was that?

Acc.: — I learned it from Ilic. He met me one day and in
the conversation he said to me that they would carry out an
assassination on the Archduke, and he talked as if I too had to
perform the assassination. I said that I wouldn't. Then he told
me to ask some other student whether he would. I parted from
him and left, but he met me several times and asked me whether
I had asked someone who would perform the assassination. He
did that several times, but I didn't name anybody. On one
occasion I talked with Cubrilovic before the *real* school, and I
remembered on that occasion the visit of His Highness and how
we paraded before him, and then we talked about that[110] and I
told it to Vaso. And I mentioned the talk someone had with
me about the assassination of the Heir, and that I would not
agree. Then he said that he was ready, so I introduced him to
Ilic.

Pr.: — On what occasion?

Acc.: — On the quay.

Pr.: — How did that happen?

Acc.: — When Cubrilovic told me that he was ready, I told Ilic that there was a man who would be willing. Ilic said that it was not necessary to introduce him to that man, rather that I should be the mediator. I said that I wouldn't be the mediator, rather that I would introduce him and so I did on the quay.

Pr.: — Did you have anything against the Heir?

Acc.: — No.

Pr.: — You say that you are a loyal Austrian subject and that you are loyal to the Almighty Ruling Dynasty and that you didn't have anything against the Heir. You learned about the assassination. You did not want to participate, but you found a person who would carry out the assassination. You informed the one who gave you the order to find that person. That is obviously participation. How does this agree with your statement?

Acc.: — I did not know Ilic well. I didn't believe him. I thought that he wanted to test me.

Pr.: — Later you told Cubrilovic about the assassination and you told Ilic that you had found a young fellow. When you were on the quay you introduced them. That is participation.

Acc.: — I did not believe that there would be an assassination. I thought Ilic wanted to test me.

Pr.: — Was he also in your student association?

Acc.: — No.

Pr.: — What right does he have to test persons?

Acc.: — I didn't know him. If I had known him, I would have believed sooner that there would be an assassination.

Pr.: — After that, did you talk about the assassination with Ilic or Cubrilovic?

Acc.: — I did not talk with Ilic, and I couldn't believe Cubrilovic. When I talked with him, he said that it would be harmful to our idea.

Pr.: — Had you been in Serbia before that?

Acc.: — Two years ago I was there for about ten days.[111]

Pr.: — What did you do there?

Acc.: — When I left the gymnasium I intended to take the examination there, but I only visited later.

Pr.: — Did you communicate with political persons?

Acc.: — No.

Pr.: — What happened on the eve of the assassination on the quay with Perin and Cubrilovic?

Acc.: — I was at home on the eve of the assassination. That was before. We stood on the quay, and everything was like a joke. There were Cubrilovic, Perin and I. Perin in jest said, "If he isn't lying, he is getting ready to do something," and he pointed at Cubrilovic. I was silent. Later I asked Cubrilovic, "Did Perin tell you that you would carry out the assassination?", and he told me that he had.

Pr.: — Who said: "This one is getting ready for an assassination?"

Acc.: — Perin said it.

Pr.: — Did Forkapic say anything?

Acc.: — I don't really remember how it was with him.

Pr.: — Was he there then, because earlier you explicitly said that he was?

Acc.: — I don't remember whether he was at that time, or whether he came later. He was there that day.

Pr.: — What did he say?

Acc.: — There was no money and then we discussed how to get money. Then Forkapic, said, "How would it be if we accused someone of the assassination so that we could get money?" I met Cubrilovic accidentally.

Pr.: — What did Cubrilovic say?

Acc.: — I don't remember.

Pr.: — At that time you said that Cubrilovic said: "Be free to announce it, but take the responsibility on yourself."

Acc.: — I really don't remember.

Pr.: — Did you know that Forkapic knew about the assassination?

Acc.: — No.

Pr.: — And Perin?

Acc.: — Cubrilovic told me that he told him.

Pr.: — And Kalember?

Acc.: — He didn't know anything.

Hoffm.: — You said that you knew Ilic only slightly. How

come you didn't know that man? He asked you to find people
for the assassination, and you immediately agreed?

Acc.: — I didn't look for someone immediately. I did not
know him.

Hoffm.: — But agreed immediately.

Acc.: — I did not agree immediately.

Hoffm.: — But?

Acc.: — He met me later several times.

Hoffm.: — Why just you? Were you in communication?

Acc.: — I was not in communication with him. I knew
him only in that I knew that he had finished the Teacher's
School.

Hoffm.: — You said that you were loyal to the Monarchy,
and he tells you: "Find people," and you immediately agree.

Pr.: — Vaso Cubrilovic presented this differently. He says
that when he talked with you, you said one should welcome
him, if there were people for that, or to assassinate him.

Acc.: — I did not say that.

Pr. (to Cubrilovic): — He says that is not true.

Cubrilovic: — I said that one had to lie in wait for him, and
he only said, "If there were people." I said that one had to lie
in wait for him and he said that there were people.

Pr.: — Djukic, did you say that "there are people?"

Acc.: — I don't remember. I remember well that I said
that a man told me that it is necessary to carry out the assassination, and I said that I wouldn't.

Malek: — Did Ilic tell you for what reasons an assassination
of the Heir had to be carried out?

Acc.: — He spoke in general of nationalism, in order to en-
hance the militant spirit among the youth.

Pr.: — Then what did Ilic say?

Acc.: — That the youth would be invigorated if there were
an assassination. I don't know what he meant by that.

Pr.: — Why did you say that it would benefit nationalism?

Acc.: — He said that it would benefit nationalism.

Pr.: — What is that nationalism?

Acc.: — The idea of the unity of Serbs and Croats.

Pr.: — Was it necessary to kill the Heir because of that?

Acc.: — I said that I wouldn't. Ilic said that to me. He conceived that as revolutionary.

Pr.: — In what sense? That political union is necessary?

Acc.: — I think that he thought so.

Malek: — Did Ilic mention to you what particular role he had in the assassination?

Acc.: — He told me.

Malek: — Did you discuss anything with Cubrilovic in that direction?

Acc.: — No.

Malek: — Did you tell Cubrilovic what was sought in the assassination?

Acc.: — No. I told him that a man spoke to me and he accepted.

Malek: — Thus only in generalities?

Acc.: — Yes.

Pr.: — Where were you on the very day of the assassination?

Acc.: — In Kljuc.

Feldb.: — Now you say that there was no money and of Forkapic that he said jokingly: "What about informing the police?" Why didn't you say so before the investigating judge?

Acc.: — I don't know that I said anything else.

Feldb.: — I request that the statement be shown to him.

Acc.: — He didn't talk about an assassin but he accidentally ran into Cubrilovic.

Pr. (Reads.): — "It seems to me that those same words were also said by Forkapic" . . . (Reads further.)

Feldb.: — In the record after Forkapic he (Djukic?) was confronted. He said that he didn't remember. We heard from someone that it was because of the defacing of the firms' signs. Was that charge involved?

Acc.: — I don't remember about that.

Zist.: — Why did you just turn to Cubrilovic?

Acc.: — I happened to be in front of the *real* school when I remembered that we learned to parade when His Highness came, and I wondered why we were not learning it now.

Zist.: — How long did you know Vaso Cubrilovic?

Acc.: — From Sarajevo.

Zist.: — What connection does parading have to participation in the assassination?

Acc.: — We met accidentally while I was recalling the parading and I told him that a man told me that there would be an assassination of the Heir.

Zist.: — So naive?

Acc.: — That's not naive.

Zist.: — What kind of fellow is Vaso? Does he accept everything?[112]

Acc.: — I didn't know him.

Zist.: — Did you associate with him?

Acc.: — I associated, but I didn't know him well enough to be sure that he would do the assassination.

Prem.: — You mentioned a little earlier that in your association you spoke of the cultural unification of Croats and Serbs. Were there Croats in your association?

Acc.: — Yes.

Prem.: — Why did you speak only about cultural, and not about political unification?

Acc.: — We were not allowed to talk about political unification.

Prem.: — Did you try?

Acc.: — No.

Prem.: — In your association did you sometimes quarrel?

Acc.: — No.

Prem.: — All were in agreement?

Acc.: — Yes.

Prem.: — Were you in the council?

Acc.: — Yes.

Prem.: — What kind of decisions did you make?

Acc.: — There were no kind of decisions.

Pr.: — Who was the president of the association?

Acc.: — We didn't have one.

Pr.: — Was there a council?

Acc.: — Yes.

Pr.: — Who was on the council?

Acc.: — The council consisted of five persons.

Pr.: — Were all members of the council in communication? Was that a Central Council?

Acc.: — Yes.

Pr.: — Were you in the Central Council?

Acc.: — Yes.

Pr.: — How was it that there was only unification in the cultural field, when we know that the council worked to raise a spirit for political annexation within the nationalistic youth?

Acc.: — We never spoke about that.

Zist.: — How many of you were there in the organization?

Acc.: — I don't know how many there were. Each organization was on its own.

Zist.: — Were there more organizations?

Acc.: — Certainly there were more.

Prem.: — Were there women in these organizations?

Acc.: — No.

Pros.: — Do you know the program of the *Narodna Ujedinjenje* (National Unification)?

Acc.: — I heard about it.

Pros.: — Wasn't that your program?

Acc.: — No.

Pros.: — Yes, it was. Yes. (Shakes head in denial.) You are on trial just because of that.

Pr.: — Did you read that program?

Acc.: — My defense counsel showed it to me, but it was not just like that.

Pr.: — Was there talk about the political unification of all (South) Slavs?

Acc.: — Yes.

Pr.: — Why do you say that it was only cultural unification? That is not so. Rather this was your true program. The association was founded on this program.

Acc.: — It was not founded on this program.

Pr.: — How did that association come about? Who was the first founder?

Acc.: — A student. He came from abroad, from Ljubljana.[113] I don't know his name. He spoke to us about organizations of Serbs, Croats, and Slovenes. He said that we had to found such an organization among us in Sarajevo.

Pr.: — For what purpose?

Acc.: — That Serbs, Croats and Slovenes draw together.

Pr.: — Did he give you some kind of letter and tell you how it should be composed?

Acc.: — Not at all. He talked about the idea of the unity of the Serbs, Croats and Slovenes.

Pr.: — Only in the cultural field?

Acc.: — Yes, always in the cultural field.

Prem.: — What is that cultural field?

Acc.: — That Serbs, Croats and Slovenes be one people.

Prem.: — And the borders?

Acc.: — We did not speak about it.

Prem.: — Who would arrange that?

Acc.: — Nobody would. If the Germans became one nation, why not we?

Perisic: — That is territorial unity. Culturally it is completely different.

Acc.: — They should get one language, one literature, etc.

Prem.: — Did you hear about the Young Croats?

Acc.: — Yes.

Prem.: — Who are they?

Acc.: — They are a special kind of Croats.

Prem.: — Do they want unity?

Acc.: — They say: "If the Serbs want it, we do too."

Pr.: — Under what conditions?

Acc.: — I don't know.

Pr. (to Cabrinovic): — Cabrinovic, how long did you stay in Belgrade?

Cabrinovic: — The last time for seven months.

Pr.: — Did you know one Vladimir Peganovic?[114]

Acc.: — No. Maybe I knew him, but I didn't know his name.

Pr.: — Did you know one Stefan Vecerinac?[115]

Acc.: — No.

Pr.: — Princip, did you know that pair?

Princip: — Neither of them.

Pr.: — And you, Grabez?

Grabez: — Neither one.

Cubrilovic: — What Djukic said about Forkapic, the letter did not only say about me, but also about Djukic: "We should denounce you for the assassination." I know that for sure.

Pr.: — Djukic, was that so?
Djukic: — I don't know.

THE HEARING OF IVO KRANJCEVIC
14 OCTOBER 1914

Pr.: — Has Kranjcevic come? (Yes.) What is your name?
Acc.: — Ivan Kranjcevic.
Pr.: — Father's name.
Acc.: — Djuro.
Pr.: — How old are you?
Acc.: — Nineteen.
Pr.: — What do you study?
Acc.: — I was in the second class of the Business School in Sarajevo.
Pr.: — Are you guilty?
Acc.: — Yes.
Pr.: — Of what are you guilty?
Acc.: — I did not report that there would be a killing.
Pr.: — Why was that? You studied at the Business School, did you have any kind of student association? (Yes.) Were you a member of that association?
Acc.: — I was a member for one month. I attended only one meeting.
Pr.: — What is the name of that association?
Acc.: — Yugoslav-nationalistic.
Pr.: — What were its objectives.
Acc.: — I didn't know the objectives at all because I was only at one meeting.
Pr.: — What happened?
Acc.: — At the meeting a council was elected and it was decided to hold a meeting once a week.
Pr.: — Were you in the council?
Acc.: — Yes.
Pr.: — What are your opinions about politics?
Acc.: — In politics I was a progressive.
Pr.: — What does that mean?
Acc.: — A friend of the union of Serbs and Croats.

Pr.: — Are you also a nationalist?

Acc.: — No. I only wanted to become acquainted with that idea.

Pr.: — What kind of nationalistic objectives are they?

Acc.: — The objectives are: the union of Serbs and Croats.

Pr.: — And as a progressive, do you have the same objectives? (Nods in agreement.) But what do you understand by the word, union?

Acc.: — Joint work of Serbs and Croats.

Pr.: — In what field?

Acc.: — In the political. If the Serbs and Croats don't do anything, German trade advances and ours declines. The seashore went into Hungarian hands.

Pr.: — Which shore?

Acc.: — The seashore expropriation.[116]

Pr.: — Did you know the objectives of the Serb nationalists? What did they want to achieve?

Acc.: — I heard that they wanted to create a large state which would separate Bosnia from Austria.

Pr.: — Did the students say that?

Acc.: — Not the students. I heard that from a certain student.

Pr.: — Was that here in Bosnia?

Acc.: — No, but the *Narodna odbrana*.

Pr.: — Did you hear from your student colleagues that Bosnia and Hercegovina be separated by force from Austria and that it be annexed to Serbia?

Acc.: — Yes.

Pr.: — Were you in agreement with that?

Acc.: — No. Maybe Vaso Cubrilovic can confirm that I told him that I would never agree to that.

Pr.: — How does he know that? Did you talk with him? How else can he confirm it?

Acc.: — I didn't talk with him specifically about that. We went to a meeting and on the way we talked about Serbia, Croatia, Germany and Austria, and on this occasion Vaso said how free it was in Serbia, how King Petar was friendly with the people and how much better it was than with us where everything is held back. And he told how King Petar went to war together with his people before he became king, and how he talked intimately with them.[117] He told how he remembered the fountain in Tuzla at which they rested. This meant to me that he believed King Petar thinks of Bosnia and Hercegovina as one. I said that in no way would I allow King Petar to come to Bosnia.

Pr.: — What did Vaso Cubrilovic tell you about the late Heir? How come you are involved in this affair?

Acc.: — First Popovic told me that he would plan an assassination, and then later Vaso Cubrilovic told me the same thing.

Pr.: — How was it with Popovic?

Acc.: — I was strolling one evening along Cekalusa. Popovic came by and we talked. He said, "I intend to carry out an assassination on the Heir."

Pr.: — How many days before the assassination?

Acc.: — Ten to twelve days before.

Pr.: — Did you ask him why?

Acc.: — I said, "I wouldn't do that because the thing is dangerous." Then, "Would we gain anything by that?"

Pr.: — What do you mean by "we"?

Acc.: — I had in mind the Slavs in general.

Pr.: — What did he say to that?

Acc.: — Nothing. He shrugged his shoulders and we changed the subject.

Pr.: — Then, how was it with Cubrilovic?

Acc.: — Several days later Cubrilovic told me, "Ivo, I too think of doing the same thing." I told him the same thing I said to Popovic, "It's stupid to do that when you don't know what the consequences will be." Then several days later Cubrilovic told me that he intended to go home from Sarajevo and asked whether I would go. I advised him to go. I went with him to get the permit, but he did not leave.

Pr.: — You did not previously talk about the bombs?

Acc.: — I had asked him where Cubrilovic would get the weapons. He said that he did not know exactly, but he thought that some kind of guerrillas might have them, because one has no way of knowing whether they kept them. They always get them from there. Then he asked me whether I would keep the

weapons, and I said no in this sense: if they were not used for
the assassination, then I would.

Pr.: — Did he say that he would leave them before or after
the assassination?

Acc.: — He said, "After the assassination."

Pr.: — According to his statement it seemed that he said
that he would leave them before the assassination.

Acc.: — Yes, but I said that I would not accept them if
they were for the assassination. Then on the eve of the assassination he asked me whether I would wait for him on Skenderija
street so that he could give them to me, and I told him I would.
When I saw that the assassination had taken place, I did not
want to wait for him, but then he came and was trembling all
over.

Pr.: — What did you do with the weapons?

Acc.: — I took them to Momcinovic's house.

Pr.: — Whom did you find there?

Acc.: — I found a little sick girl.

Pr.: — What did you say?

Acc.: — That I brought two old revolvers that wouldn't
fire and that my father wanted to give them to the museum,
and that I wanted to hide them so that he could not give them
to the museum.

Pr.: — What did you do with the bomb?

Acc.: — I wrapped it up and then put it in a trunk.

Pr.: — Which room was the trunk in?

Acc.: — In the one where the old man sleeps.[118]

Pr.: — Was the trunk open?

Acc.: — Yes, it was open.

Pr.: — Then was did you do?

Acc.: — Then I went home.

Pr.: — Were you in that house on the day before the
assassination?

Acc.: — Yes.

Pr.: — What did you do there?

Acc.: — I wanted to see who was in the house.

Pr.: — What did you say?

Acc.: — Nothing, because there was no one at home but
that little sick girl.

Pr.: — What did you want?

Acc.: — I waited for a friend.

Pr.: — What friend?

Acc.: — I waited for a friend and drank a glass of water.

Pr.: — Before the assassination did you tell anyone in that house that you would bring some things to keep?

Acc.: — No.

Pr.: — Earlier you said otherwise. Here it says (He reads.): "I told Ivan Momcinovic several days earlier that I would bring weapons."

Acc.: — Not several days, but long before.

Pr.: — You also stated here that Popovic first told you about the assassination, and earlier, on July 6th, you said (Reads.): "I admit that I am guilty and that I did not talk with Cvjetko Popovic."

Acc.: — I admitted that later.

Pr.: — Why did you earlier say otherwise? Why didn't you tell the truth at once?

Acc.: — I wanted to lie. I told only about Cubrilovic, and about Popovic, I . . .

Pr.: — Why did you want to hide the things at Ivan Momcinovic's, and not at home?

Acc.: — If I had gone home I would have had to carry them a long way and someone might have caught me, and then I thought: Those people are not educated. They are plain folks, and they will believe me that these are old pistols.

Pr.: — You had talked about the two revolvers before that.

Acc.: — Then I thought that they would believe me because they had known me from childhood.

Pr.: — Why didn't you denounce the whole thing? Not only did you not denounce it, but you concealed it. You knew that an assassination was carried out. You knew that this was a conspiracy.

Acc.: — I did not know.

Pr.: — If you didn't know, you might have guessed it because of the connection with Popovic and Cubrilovic.

Acc.: — I took them because Cubrilovic didn't do anything. I felt sorry for him. When I found him, he was trembling all over.

Pr.: — Did you make an agreement before the assassination?

Acc.: — I wouldn't have taken them if he had not found me.

Pr.: — Had you promised?

Acc.: — I couldn't say anything else when he asked me.

Pr.: — Why didn't you denounce the whole thing? Don't you see what tremendous harm you've done to the whole world?

Acc.: — I didn't denounce it because I thought that it was necessary to protest against the German influence which destroys us.

Pr.: — In what way? In what sense is the German influence in Bosnia and Hercegovina destructive?

Acc.: — Not only in Bosnia and Hercegovina. Austria is a Slavic state, but Germany is not a Slavic state, and that's what Germany wants. All persecutions of Slavs come from Germany.

Pr.: — Where are those persecutions?

Acc.: — The high treason trial is in Sarajevo, Zagreb and in the Ukraine. A *sokol* jamboree in Vienna was promised, and later was forbidden because the Germans insisted.

Pr.: — You wanted to join in the protest?

Acc.: — In order to free ourselves from German influence.

Pr.: — What does it mean? Did you think that you would be liberated when the Heir was killed?

Acc.: — That would be a warning to leading circles in Vienna who do whatever Berlin wants.

Pr.: — Do those ideas represent the common opinion, or merely your own?

Acc.: — There are plenty of us who think the same. Popovic also thought likewise, as I learned from the conversation with him.

Pr.: — So, a warning was necessary.

Acc.: — Yes.

Pr.: — Now you see that it turned out otherwise because of this deed. How could you believe that the assassination would turn out in such a way that there would be no persecution? You are not a child. You should have thought and known that such an assassination would have other consequences.

Acc.: — I did not anticipate that. As Popovic and Cubrilovic said, that's the way it was; and for the others, I had no idea that it would turn out in such a way.

Pr.: — Earlier you gave as a motive for not reporting this: "I did not betray it because if I had, none of my friends would have spoken to me."

Acc.: — Yes.

Pr.: — So, today you gave the true cause?

Acc.: — I did.

Pr.: — Then you were in agreement with the assassination?

Acc.: — Yes.

Pr.: — Completely in agreement?

Acc.: — Yes.

Pr.: — Do you approve of the assassination?

Acc.: — I did not approve of the assassination of the Heir because he is not guilty. The leading circles are responsible. I said that it was foolish to kill just the Heir.

Pr.: — If you thought it was foolish, why didn't you denounce it? Not only did you not denounce it, but you even participated in the sense that you helped. In the inquiry of July 10th you said that you did not put the package in the trunk, but rather on the divan.

Acc.: — I put it in the trunk.

Pr.: — But here you stated that you put it on the divan?

Acc.: — It was on the divan. I expected someone to come. When he didn't, I put it in the trunk.

Pr.: — After the assassination, did Franjo Sadilo tell you anything about it? (Nods yes.) How many days afterward?

Acc.: — He came the same day to ask me what I had brought him. And I said, "Two old revolvers." Then he said, "Take them away! If they aren't safe for you, they aren't safe for me either. Why should I stick my neck out?"

Pr.: — Why should they be dangerous to him?

Acc.: — He asked me what I brought and I answered, "Two old revolvers."

Pr.: — And when he said, "Take them."?

Acc.: — I said that I would take them away, but I didn't; instead I asked my mother to bring them, and she did.

Pr.: — What is Ivan Momcinovic to you?

Acc.: — We are god-relatives.

Pr.: — Why did you have to bring such misfortune to him?

Acc.: — I thought that he wouldn't even look to see what it was, that he wouldn't know what it was, and that it would stay that way.

Pr.: — What did your mother say to you when she found out about it?

Acc.: — She asked me whether I didn't have something better and smarter to do, whether I was out of my mind to ruin myself and them.

Pr.: — What was the purpose of the assassination? Did Vaso Cubrilovic and Cvjetko Popovic tell you?

Acc.: — As I said: to free ourselves of German influence.

Pr.: — They told you that?

Acc.: — Yes.

Pr.: — Did you talk about that with other students? with Kalember?

Acc.: — Not with anybody. I didn't know Kalember.

Pros.: — Why did Sadilo say: "Take them away so that you don't ruin me?"

Acc.: — If they were dangerous to me, then they were dangerous to him, too.

Pros.: — Why, two old revolvers? What kind of danger is that?

Acc.: — They couldn't stay at my place and I took them and asked him to take care of them. I said that those were two old revolvers that my father wanted to give to the museum, and I didn't want him to.

Pr. (Shows him the revolvers.): — Were they like these?

Acc.: — No. I don't know what they looked like. I saw them for only a moment.

Pr.: — You didn't see the revolver?

Acc.: — I did not.

Naumowicz: — Today you said that Sadilo said: "If they aren't safe for you, they aren't safe for me." Why safe? Was he talking about the old revolvers?

Acc.: — He didn't say that to me, but he told me to take them. After the assassination he was afraid. I brought him something that he didn't know what it was and felt uneasy about.

Naum.: — You used the expression: "It is not safe with me."

Acc.: — That's what I said now. He didn't say it to me.

Pr.: — You said earlier that Sadilo said: "That I should take the things, because he wouldn't keep them in the house, that he wouldn't be guilty."

Acc.: — He was afraid of the two old revolvers, that if they were found with him after the assassination he would be under suspicion.

Pros.: — Who told you about the *Narodna odbrana*?

Acc.: — Popovic.

Pros.: — What did he say? What is the *Narodna odbrana*?

Acc.: — He said that it gathers guerrilla bands and arms them; and Cubrilovic told me how they fight with the Turks in Serbia.

Pros.: — What role does the *Narodna odbrana* play in Bosnia?

Acc.: — None whatever.

Pros.: — How did you come to mention the guerrillas? Was that a political conversation between you?

Acc.: — He talked about the Balkan wars and then he talked about the guerrilla bands.

Pros.: — But as you said, a great state would have to be based on unity. What would it be called? Did you discuss how it should be named?

Acc.: — Great Yugoslavia.

Pros.: — Which dynasty should rule in it?

Acc.: — The same as in Serbia.

Pros.: — Thus a Serbian. And which one is that?

Acc.: — King Petar Karadjeordjevic.

Pros.: — Thus King Petar should rule in this Yugoslavia. And did he say anything about the Heir?

Acc.: — No.

Zist.: — Did you approve of the assassination in general? You have talked about the German oppression in the Monarchy. Did you approve of the assassination as a means of protest against the oppression, or did you agree only with the assassination of the Heir in order to protest?

Acc.: — I did not favor any kind of assassination. When

Popovic said that he would carry out an assassination on the Heir, I said, "If you think it will do any good, go ahead."

Pr.: — He said explicitly that he did not denounce it because he agreed with the assassination as a sign of protest.

Zist.: — At the same time he altered his statement and said that he did not think of the Heir, that he was not in the governing circles. I would like to clarify this contradiction in the statement.

Pr.: — When I asked why you did not denounce it, you said that you approved of it as a sign of protest against the German hegemony here. Then later I asked: Did you have anything against the Heir? You said that you did not agree and that you had told Cubrilovic that it was foolish. How does that go together?

Acc.: — I have nothing against the Heir.

Pr.: — So you did not approve of the assassination?

Acc.: — I don't understand what you are asking.

Zist.: — What did you think in general of the attitude of the Heir toward the Croats?

Acc.: — He was a friend of the Croats.

Zist.: — From what do you infer this?

Acc.: — In general he was a friend of the Slavs, because when he went to Pest to open the Parliament, he never stayed longer than half an hour, or however long the opening took, and then he left right away. In general he interceded on behalf of the Slavs.

Zist.: — Did you concern yourself with politics?

Acc.: — Yes.

Zist.: — With literature, or with politics? With which did you concern yourself with the most?

Acc.: — With literature. I concerned myself with politics insofar as I talked with my colleagues.

Zist.: — Did you follow politics in the Banovina?[119]

Acc.: — Yes.

Zist.: — Did you belong to any political party?

Acc.: — Yes, to the Coalition.[120]

Zist.: — Do you know the political program of the Coalition?

Acc.: — The unity of the Serbs and Croats.

Zist.: — What is the Coalition?

Acc.: — Croats and Serbs. The unity of Serbs and Croats.

Zist.: — Do you know the fundamentals of the politics of the Coalition? Do you know any other political party besides the Coalition?

Acc.: — I know the Rightists.[121]

Zist.: — What are the differences between the Rightists and the Coalition?

Acc.: — I was once a Rightist.

Zist.: — Why did you change to the Coalition?

Acc.: — Because I saw that while the Serbs and Croats quarrel, the Hungarians do as they please. They open schools in Croatia and they got the seacoast.

Zist.: — Do you know what the *Nagodba* (Compromise) is?[122]

Acc.: — Yes. That is the Hungaro-Croatian Compromise.

Zist.: — What is the attitude of the Coalition toward that Compromise? Is that the basis of the structure of the Austro-Hungarian Monarchy?

Acc.: — It does not reject the Compromise.

Per.: — It accepts the Compromise?

Pr.: — He does not understand the whole matter. Did you know for sure that the Heir was a friend of the Slavs, especially the Croats?

Acc.: — Yes.

Pr.: — Why did you allow this friend of the Croats to be killed as a means of protest against Germanization, that a friend of the Croats be killed?

Acc.: — His Highness[123] is not our enemy, but the Slavs are persecuted anyway.

Pr.: — Then, God help us, you would approve also an assassination of His Highness?

Acc.: — That's not so. I wanted the assassination of a leader. I approved of the assassination of a minister, but not of the Archduke. If someone wanted to risk his head for the sake of protest, then I agreed.

Pr.: — Although you knew he was a friend of the Slavs?

Acc.: — Yes.

Pr.: — And that he would arrange things differently?

Acc.: — He couldn't arrange things differently.

Pr.: — I call for a recess of five minutes.

After the recess

Perisic: — I would like to clear up something about Kranj-cevic and his relations with Sadilo. Tell me, Kranjcevic, did Sadilo say to you: "If the thing is not safe for you, it isn't for me either."

Acc.: — That is my conclusion. He didn't say that to me.

Per.: — Tell me, did you ever say to him before or after the assassination that there were bombs?

Acc.: — I said that those were two old revolvers which my father wanted to give to the museum, and I didn't want him to and so wanted to leave them with him.

Per.: — How do you make that agree with the fact that as a Croat you approved of the assassination of the Heir? Do you approve of the assassination of the Heir?

Acc.: — I don't approve. He is a friend of the Slavs.

Pr.: — Why didn't you denounce the assassination?

Acc.: — I didn't know about all that.

Pr.: — You said (Reads.): "Austria is a Slavic state, but persecutes the Slavs."

Acc.: — I don't even know what I said.

Zist.: — Are you nervous? Let's determine that.

Pr.: — Does that correspond to your opinion?

Acc.: — Please read it once more.

Court clerk (Reads.): — "Austria is a Slavic state" . . . etc.

Pr.: — That is the reply when I asked you, why you didn't denounce the assassination? I told you that you had previously said in the inquiry that you were afraid that the students wouldn't speak to you.

Per.: — I ask you once more: Do you approve of the assassination which was carried out against the Heir?

Pr.: — Why didn't you denounce it?

Per.: — He is responsible for this. I ask him whether he approves?

Acc.: — I don't approve.

Pr.: — Did you approve before the assassination?

Per.: — Did you ever approve?

Acc.: — I never did.

Pr.: — Why did you say earlier that you did? Did it correspond to your opinion?

Acc.: — No. I don't know myself what I answered.

Zist.: — He talked with me during the recess, and asked me: "What did I say?" I pointed out to him the contradictions but he still did not understand. He doesn't understand now either.

Pr. (To the Court clerk): — Please write down the words which the gentleman just said, that he called the accused and that the accused did not understand what he said. (To the defense counsel): What did you tell him?

Zist.: — I pointed out to him the two contradictory statements, and he straightened it out by saying that he never approved of the assassination.

Pr.: — Are there any more questions? (There are none.) Then call Branko Zagorac.

THE HEARING OF BRANKO ZAGORAC
14 OCTOBER 1914

(The accused enters.)

Pr.: — Are you Branko Zagorac?

Acc.: — Yes.

Pr.: — You are eighteen?

Acc.: — Yes.

Pr.: — What did you study?

Acc.: — I finished the first class of the Business School.

Pr.: — Were you a member of any kind of association in the Business School?

Acc.: — I was a member of the *Pobratimstvo* Brotherhood.[124] That was a school association, but I didn't belong to any others.

Pr.: — Weren't you a member of a nationalistic association?

Acc.: — I was a nationalist, but I was not a member of an association.

Pr.: — What does "nationalist" mean?

Acc.: — As I consider it: the unification of the Serbs and Croats.

Pr.: — How did the others consider it?

Acc.: — As I read it in the indictment, they considered it the unification of all South Slavs, and I only of the Serbs and Croats.

Pr.: — Tell me, how did you conceive of this unification?

Acc.: — In the cultural field.

Pr.: — What is that?

Acc.: — I thought that the Serbs and Croats, if they were joined together in the cultural world, would be distinguished in literature and other things.

Pr.: — In what other matters?

Acc.: — If the Serbs and Croats in Bosnia and Hercegovina were united, it would be easier to work in the Parliament.

Pr.: — You did not think about the Serbs in the kingdom of Serbia?

Acc.: — No.

Pr.: — Nor of the Croatians who are in Croatia?

Acc.: — I did think of the Croatians. No one explained that to me. I was a nationalist merely because the greater part of the students were.

Pr.: — Was it not your wish that all lands in which South Slavs lived be united?

Acc.: — I never thought about that.

Pr.: — Did you ever hear that other students were thinking about it?

Acc.: — No.

Pr.: — Did you know Lazar Djukic and Vaso Cubrilovic?

Acc.: — Yes.

Pr.: — What were their opinions?

Acc.: — They were nationalists. I talked with them because we were friends, and I knew Djukic because he lived on the same street. Ten days before the assassination Cubrilovic told me that there would be one.

Pr.: Where was that?

Acc.: — On a street in Sarajevo, I don't know the name. He said that there would be an assassination and that he would carry it out, but he didn't tell me with whom he was associated nor what kind of weapons would be used. Later I asked him with what he would do it, and he said, "That's easy, there are weapons."

Pr.: — What did you reply to that?

Acc.: — I was silent.

Pr.: — But that's hard to understand.

acc.: — I didn't think he would do it because he didn't reveal any emotion.

Pr.: — Did you tell him that?

Acc.: — No, I kept quiet and on June 25th I went home.

Pr.: — Did he tell you that once or many times?

Acc.: — The first time he told me that there would be an assassination, and later he told me that he would do it.

Pr.: — The second time did he also tell you that he had weapons?

Acc.: — Once when I asked him whether he had weapons he said, "That's easy to arrange." The second time he said that the weapons had arrived.

Pr.: — Didn't you try to dissuade him?

Acc.: — No. I didn't believe him. I thought that it was a simple joke, because he showed no emotion.

Pr.: — Why didn't you denounce it?

Acc.: — I didn't believe him.

Pr.: — Now you believe that he was serious?

Acc.: — Of course I believe it now.

Pr.: — Did you talk about that with Lazar Djukic too?

Acc.: — Never.

Pr.: — Do you approve of the assassination?

Acc.: — I have never thought about that. I didn't know the Heir as a political person.

Pr.: — Or as a friend of the Slavs?

Acc.: — No.

Pr.: — Then you are not sorry about the assassination?

Acc.: — I don't know.

Pr.: — And for the victims? For the late duchess?

Acc.: — I don't feel sorry for her.

Pr.: — And for him?

Acc.: — I don't know exactly. I didn't know him as a political person, as a person one would have to kill.

Pr.: — Then one has to know how a person thinks politically in order to know whether one should kill him?

Acc.: — I did not know whether one would have to kill this man.

Pr.: — Do you believe that there are cases in which it is permissible that a man be killed?

Acc.: — Of course there are no such cases.

Pr.: — How can that agree? Does one have to know a man's political opinions in order to know whether it is good to kill him?

Acc.: — One has to know the man in order to know whether he has to be killed.

Pr.: — Does that presuppose that you think that there are cases in which an assassination is necessary?

Acc.: — There are such cases.

Pr.: — Then in what cases?

Acc.: — If the man is a tyrant.

Pr.: — Then anyone is allowed to kill him?

Acc.: — Not anyone, but whoever wants to.

Pr.: — That is anyone.

Acc.: — Not anyone, only whoever wants to.

Pr.: — It is.

Acc.: — Whoever is convinced.

Pr.: — In the jail you changed. At first you said explicitly that you did not approve of the assassination of the Heir as a political person and as an important man.

Acc.: — I said that I did not know him as a political person and an important man and I had no reason to approve of the assassination. (The statement of July 9th is shown to him in which he answered the question: "Do you approve of the assassination of the Heir as an important man and a political person?" "I do not approve because I knew it would stir up a great sensation . . .").

Pr.: — Did you know that Cubrilovic told still others about it?

Acc.: — Kalember and Marko Perin.

Pr.: — Did you know that he told Forkapic?

Acc.: — I didn't know.

Pr.: — And Popovic too?

Acc.: — No.

Pr.: — Did you know Perin and Kalember?

Acc.: — Yes.

Pr.: — Did you talk about the assassination?

Acc.: — No.

Naumowicz: — You did not talk with Djukic about the assassination?

Acc.: — No.

Pr.: — What did Cubrilovic on one occasion tell you about Lazar Djukic?

Acc.: — When I asked him, "What kind of a fellow is he?" he said that he was a coward.

Pr.: — Why did you talk about him?

Acc.: — As about a friend. He was my friend and I asked what kind of a fellow he was, what he thought of him, because I was friendly with him.

Pr.: — Did you know whether Lazar Djukic told him anything about the assassination?

Acc.: — I don't know. He didn't talk about it at all.

Hoffm.: — When Cubrilovic told you that an anarchistic party was established, did you tell him that you wanted to join it?

Acc.: — I did, as a joke.

Hoffm.: — Did you tell him for what purpose?

Acc.: — No.

Pr.: — Did Cubrilovic try to get you to take part in the assassination also?

Acc.: — No.

Pr.: — You said in the inquiry that you really talked about the assassination with Djukic and that he evaded your questions?

Acc.: — I said at the inquiry that Djukic and Cubrilovic never said anything about the assassination in my presence.

Pr.: — Did you think it wasn't serious, especially when Djukic evaded your questions?

Acc.: — I didn't ask Djukic.

Pros.: — Did you know that Djukic travelled through Bosnia to organize students into nationalistic associations?

Acc.: — No.

Pr.: — Why didn't you denounce the assassination?

Acc.: — I didn't think it was serious and if I had denounced it that would have created a sensation and innocent persons could have been jailed.

Premuzic: — If you had thought it was serious, would you have denounced it?

Acc.: — Of course I would have denounced it if I had taken it seriously.

Prem.: — To whom would you have denounced it?

Acc.: — To the court, to any court.

Feldb.: — Do you know Forkapic?

Acc.: — Yes.

Feld.: — Were you on friendly terms with him?

Acc.: — Yes.

Feldb.: — Do you know anything about the defacing of the signs of firms in Sarajevo?

Acc.: — No.

Pr.: — Are there any further questions? (There are none.) Call Marko Perin. (He enters.)

THE HEARING OF MARKO PERIN
14 OCTOBER 1914

Pr.: — Marko Perin, where did you study most recently?

Acc.: — In Sarajevo. The sixth class of the gymnasium.

Pr.: — What are your political opinions?

Acc.: — Nationalist, Yugoslav.

Pr.: — What does that mean?

Acc.: — First of all it signifies the cultural unification of all South Slavs, and then the political.

Pr.: — How did you imagine that the political unification of all South Slavs could be achieved thereby? In what way?

Acc.: — I had not completely thought that through. I was a nationalist because it seemed to me that idea was the most in accord with the times.

Pr.: — What did the other students think about it?

Acc.: — There were advocates and opponents.

Pr.: — Did you have in mind political unification under Austria or outside of it?

Acc.: — That depends on how it could be done.

Pr.: — Then it didn't matter to you how the unification was achieved, so long as it was done?

Acc.: — As long as there was unification, so that the foreigners could not oppress us.

Pr.: — Were you a member of any kind of political association among students?

Acc.: — The association existed only on paper.

Pr.: — What was on paper? Was there some sort of program?

Acc.: — We in the gymnasium didn't even create a program. We didn't even meet.

Pr.: — Who was a member of that association in your class?

Acc.: — Maric, Vaso Cubrilovic, Dragan Kalember, Djuro Banjac and I were supposed to be members.

Pr.: — And were there also members in the seventh and eighth classes, or did each class have its own association?

Acc.: — The entire upper gymnasium had only one association.

Pr.: — Thus there were still more students?

Acc.: — Yes, from the fifth and seventh, but there were none from the eighth.

Pr.: — Who was its founder?

Acc.: — Viktor Rupcic and Lazar Djukic. They called us to a cafe for a meeting. It happened that I was late. I was being tutored, and I don't know what they had been talking about. Milan Prica told me.

Pr.: — When did you first learn that they intended to carry out an assassination?

Acc.: — Cubrilovic told me at the beginning of June, I think it was in Kosevo. I don't know how it came up. He had already bragged before that he was a kind of hero, and now all of a sudden he had the idea that he would kill the Heir.

Pr.: — What did you say?

Acc.: — I didn't say anything. At first I was amused.

Pr.: — Did you talk about it at other times?

Acc.: — Yes. He offered me a bomb and revolver to hide, and I refused.

Pr.: — Why?

Acc.: — What would I do with them?

Pr.: — Did he show you the bomb and revolver just on the eve of the assassination?

Acc.: — He didn't show them to me, but he offered to show them. He only drew my attention to the revolver and asked me to touch it; but I didn't handle it, nor did I see it, nor did I say those words.

Pr.: — How was that? You met once with Cubrilovic, and Lazar Djukic was also present. Did you say anything to Cubrilovic?

Acc.: — I said something as a joke.

Pr.: — What?

Acc.: — I don't remember that.

Pr.: — Did you say: "Here's the one who thinks he's going to assassinate the Heir!"?

Acc.: — I don't know whether I mentioned the Heir exactly, but I do know that I spoke jokingly. Forkapic was there too, and later Cubrilovic came too and threatened to kill me. Not he himself, but rather that I would not know from what direction the bullet would come, if I should give it away. I thought that this was a musing of an idealist, and there was nothing behind it, but when I heard the threat I became uneasy.

Pr.: — Was Kalember present when you talked?

Acc.: — No.

Pr.: — What happened after that joke?

Acc.: — Perhaps Forkapic added something like, "This pair is rather suspicious. It would be good to denounce them to the police. Maybe we would get several hundred crowns."

Pr.: — What did Cubrilovic say?

Acc.: — I don't know. I don't remember.

Pr.: — Did he say you should denounce it if you dare?

Acc.: — I don't remember.

Pr.: — Did Cubrilovic mention anything about the Tuzla students?

Acc.: — Yes, how they are hard-working, how they work among the people and how some took part in the war, how some of them were in the guerrilla bands.

Pr.: — The instructions for a general staff map were found at your place?

Acc.: — Yes.

Pr.: — What was it doing there?

Acc.: — I got it from Professor Mandic[125] because of tourism. We received all of them from the corps headquarters.

Pr.: — Why didn't you denounce the assassination?

Acc.: — First of all I wasn't allowed, and I couldn't do it as a colleague.[126]

Pr.: — Why weren't you allowed?

Acc.: — He threatened me that the first bullet would hit me, that I wouldn't know where it came from.

Pr.: — Why as a colleague?

Acc.: — From a feeling of comradeship.

Pr.: — Did you approve of the assassination?

Acc.: — No.

Pr.: — For what reason?

Acc.: — I didn't think about that. When I thought about my own head,[127] I joked that it didn't interest me.

Pr.: — Earlier you said otherwise: that you did not approve of the assassination because . . .

Acc.: — Maybe I said so. I don't know.

Pr.: — You said: "Assassination is not a good and peaceful way, rather it's simply killing." Do you think the same way now?

Acc.: — Yes.

Pr.: — And that the South Slavs will never achieve anything that way?

Acc.: — In general, nationalism cannot be helped in any way by assassination. There are many examples in history.

Naum.: — You learned from Cubrilovic that he wanted to kill the Heir?

Acc.: — Yes.

Naum.: — Did he say for what reasons?

Acc.: — I don't remember.

Naum.: — Did you ask him?

Acc.: — It didn't interest me. I didn't ask him, because I didn't believe that he would do it. I didn't believe that Cubrilovic could do it.

Hoffm.: — Why were you afraid?

Acc.: — I was not afraid of Cubrilovic. But he said, "There are still other people."

Feldb.: — You said: "Perhaps Forkapic added that it would be a good idea to denounce it to the police." Are you positive of this?

Acc.: — Yes, he added that.

Feldb.: — Where did he hear that?

Acc.: — He didn't talk about the assassination, but in general. As the police bought suspicious persons, maybe one could also denounce those persons and maybe get something out of it. And he spoke about Djukic and Cubrilovic.

Pr.: — Did you in some way influence Cubrilovic to carry out the assassination?

Acc.: — No.

Pr.: — Didn't you incite him toward the assassination and support in him the inclination toward the assassination?

Acc.: — I didn't say anything at all to him about the assassination, nor did he hear anything from me to the effect that I would approve of his doing it.

Naum.: — Is it true that when you touched the revolver, you said that you were acquainted with that kind of weapon?

Acc.: — I never touched it. Cubrilovic stated that I said that, but Kalember said that he did not hear it.

Naum.: — Did you say it, or didn't you?

Acc.: — I didn't say it. How could I say it when I had never held a Browning in my hands?

Pr.: — I will question Branko Zagorac once again. (He comes.) Did you in any way sustain Cubrilovic in the mood for the assassination? Did you approve of the assassination in his presence?

Zagorac: — I never said anything to him about that.

Pr.: — You never supported him in his intentions?

Zag.: — No.

THE HEARING OF NIKOLA FORKAPIC
14 OCTOBER 1914

Pr.: — Call Nikola Forkapic. (He comes.) Are you Nikola Forkapic?

Acc.: — Yes.

Pr.: — Are you 19 years old?

Acc.: — Yes.

Pr.: — Where did you study?

Acc.: — The Teacher's School.

Pr.: — Which class?

Acc.: — I finished the fourth class.

Pr.: — Were you a member of any kind of student association at the Teacher's School?

Acc.: — No.

Pr.: — Of any other?

Acc.: — I never joined a student association. The only thing I did was to help in preparing a party which we held for the benefit of Croatian schools.

Pr.: — Are you an adherent of the nationalistic party?

Acc.: — No.

Pr.: — What then?

Acc.: — Of the radical, purely Serbian party.

Pr.: — You don't want the unification of the Serbs and Croats?

Acc.: — Politically not at all.

Pr.: — Do you consider Bosnia and Hercegovina to be Serbian lands?

Acc.: — Well, Serbs live in them, but I consider them to be Austrian countries.

Pr.: — Do you want Bosnia and Hercegovina to be joined to Serbia?

Acc.: — I don't want that.

Pr.: — Were you aware that the nationalists prepared some kind of an assassination of the Heir?

Acc.: — No.

Pr.: — Did anyone tell you about that?

Acc.: — I never talked about it with anyone, nor could I have thought of it.

Pr.: — Did you know Cubrilovic?

Acc.: — I got to know him on the occasion of the party.

Pr.: — Did he tell you anything?

Acc.: — Never, merely about the work for the party.

Pr.: — You met once with Perin, Djukic and Cubrilovic. Was there talk then about an assassination?

Acc.: — If anything was said, it was about the party, because I was on friendly terms with them only while we worked on the party and until we handed over the money I never talked with anyone about the assassination.

Pr.: — Still, Djukic heard that you said something about money?

Acc.: — If we talked, it was in connection with the party, otherwise what could he have said?

Pr.: — That you talked, that you might get two to three hundred crowns if you denounced them for the assassination.

Acc.: — How could I denounce an assassination when I didn't know anything about it?

Pr.: — Or could it be concerning the signs?[128]

Acc.: — I don't know whether I discussed them with him. There was talk about it among the students because it was announced in the newspapers that there would be a reward for those who denounced the perpetrators. There was no talk about an assassination.

Pr.: — Do you approve of the assassination?

Acc.: — No.

Pr.: — Why not?

Acc.: — I do not approve of the assassination of my ruler. That does not agree with my ideas.

Pr.: — If you had known of the assassination, would you have denounced it?

Acc.: — I would have, whoever he might have been.

Pr.: — What do you think of the assassins?

Acc.: — I don't know myself how to say it. That didn't make any kind of sense, like a flood, without any kind of system.

Pr.: — Are there any further questions? (There are none.) Has Dragan Kalember arrived? (No.) I call for a recess until he comes.

After the recess

Pr.: — Perin, tell me, after the assassination did Cubrilovic say anything to you about the assassination?

Perin: — He told me that he fired two shots when Cabrinovic threw the bomb.

Pr.: — At whom?

Acc.: — At the Heir.

Pr.: — Did you believe him?

Acc.: — No. Where would he run and how would he run?

THE HEARING OF DRAGAN KALEMBER
14 OCTOBER 1914

Pr.: — Call Dragan Kalember. (He comes.) How old are you?

Acc.: — Sixteen.

Pr.: — In what class are you?

Acc.: — I finished the sixth.

Pr.: — Are you a member of any association?

Acc.: — I am, of a progressive one.

Pr.: — Is there also a student association in your class?

Acc.: — Not in ours.

Pr.: — Didn't Perin invite you?

Acc.: — Yes, he said, "Become a nationalist."

Pr.: — What does that signify?

Acc.: — Progressive.

Pr.: — What does "progressive" mean?

Acc.: — To me, it means only "forward!"

Pr.: — What is your opinion of the South Slavs? What do you think should be done?

Acc.: — I don't know anything about it.

Pr.: — You knew before, maybe you have forgotten?

Acc.: — Perin told me once: "Become a nationalist," and I said, "Okay." What it means, I don't know.

Pr.: — You said here: "I am a nationalist. Our goal is the cultural unification of all South Slavs, and I worked on it by educating myself." Is that true?

Acc.: — Yes. That is progressive.

Pr.: — Do you know the political objective?

Acc.: — I never concerned myself with politics because I am too young, and besides my father also forbade it.

Pr.: — Did you read any books about nationalism?

Acc.: — Yes, for nationalistic culture like *Vihor* (The Storm) which was published in Zagreb. Perin gave me *Srpsko-Hrvatski nacionalizam* (Serbo-Croatian Nationalism) by Dr. Jovan Skerlic to read.

Pr.: — Did you know what the objectives were when you read it? What did you think of it?

Acc.: — I wanted only harmony between Serbs and Croats, at most a cultural unity, because that is very necessary for us.

Pr.: — Were you an adherent of terrorism?

Acc.: — I don't know anything about that. I am not.

Pr.: — Did you ever think about political union?

Acc.: — Never. I never went into politics.

Pr.: — Before the assassination did you ever talk about the assassination?

Acc.: — Yes, with Vaso Cubrilovic.

Pr.: — What did he say?

Acc.: — One time when we strolled along the quay he came up to me and said, "Because we saw in the newspapers that the Heir is coming, I will assassinate him. I have a bomb and revolver for that."

Pr.: — What did you say?

Acc.: — I laughed at him. I simply didn't believe him.

Pr.: — Did Cubrilovic add anything to that?

Acc.: — Not at that time. Only that.

Pr.: — Did he tell you that you could talk about it freely?

Acc.: — He didn't say that I shouldn't tell anybody.

Pr.: — Earlier you said otherwise: "He threatened me not to tell anybody."

Acc.: — He didn't threaten me.

Pr.: — But why did you say that before?

Acc.: — We were confronted, but I didn't remember that he threatened me. He didn't say that to me, didn't threaten me. Mr. Pffefer confronted him with me. And then, I don't remember, I would surely remember if he had told me. I would never have believed that Vaso Cubrilovic would do such a thing.

Pr.: — Very well, you are right. He didn't threaten you. What did he tell you afterwards? Did you meet before the assassination, on the eve of the assassination, on Saturday?

Acc.: — On Friday 27 June we received our diplomas. I spent the whole week in Reljevo, and on Friday morning I returned for my diploma, mine and my brother's. I met with Cubrilovic and he told me, "I can't do it because a detective is following me, and I am being hustled[129] out of Sarajevo within 24 hours. If I do not leave, my sister will be held responsible." With that he retracted what he had said before, that he would carry out an assassination and that he had a bomb and revolver.

Pr.: — What happened on Saturday?

Acc.: — On Saturday we met again. Perin and I were strolling and we met him at the Cathedral. We dropped into the pastry shop in the old Turkish marketplace and there he said that he had a bomb and revolver with him. We had already eaten our ice cream and began to pay, and he asked, "Do you want me to show them?" I said it wasn't necessary, I believed him, because he had vindicated himself on Friday, and I thought that he had nothing. Then when we began to pay, he asked, "Do you want to handle it?" I didn't touch it, and as for Perin I don't know.

Pr.: — Who left first?

Acc.: — I don't know. It seems to me that I was first. Then we went on together, Perin, he, and I, and we didn't talk any more about the assassination.

Pr.: — When Cubrilovic had left, did you talk with Perin about the assassination?

Acc.: — No.

Pr.: — On the day you were interrogated you said: "Perin and I laughed at those words, and when Cubrilovic later left us, Perin tried to convince me, saying, "You will see. Tomorrow there will be an assassination," and at that I said, "There cannot be. I don't believe it." Is that true?

Acc.: — I don't know whether it's true.

Pr.: — Why did you lie? You did not tell the truth before the investigating judge.

Acc.: — This is certainly the truth. I was sick of the jail, so I had to say something more.

Pr. (to Perin): — Perin, did he say that?

Perin: — I don't know. I don't remember.

Pr.: — Did you say to him: "By God, you will see that tomorrow there will be an assassination?"

Perin: — I did not.

Pr. (to Kalember): — Did you meet with Cubrilovic after the assassination?

Kal.: — Yes.

Pr.: — What did he say?

Acc.: — After the demonstrations[130] Franicevic and I looked over the ruins of the houses and we went to the Cathedral so Franicevic could buy the *Knjizevne novosti* (Literary News) and then Cubrilovic came, and the former looked him over from head to feet and he left, namely Franicevic. Then Cubrilovic said, "Let's go see," and we went to look at the ruins after the demonstrations. We didn't talk about the assassination.

Pr.: — He didn't comment on it at all?

Acc.: — Yes, it seems to me that he said jokingly, "I fired one shot."

Pr.: — Then he said that he fired one shot?

Acc.: — Yes, one shot. He told me as in jest.

Pr.: — Did you believe it?

Acc.: — If he had shot, he would have been arrested.

Pr.: — Did he say before the assassination, "Don't go on the quay."?

Acc.: — Yes.

Pr.: — Why?

Acc.: — He said jokingly, "Don't go on the quay if you want to remain alive."

Pr.: — Was that a joke?

Acc.: — I came to the quay and walked there, and I thought that he had gone home. On Sunday I walked everywhere. It was St. Vitus' Day and I went to church and walked along the quay and along Franz Josef[131] Street and there I saw my father.

Pr.: — Did you in any way approve of his intentions, did you encourage him in the decision to kill the Heir?

Acc.: — I didn't even know that he would do it.

Pr.: — Why didn't you denounce it? You knew. He warned you not to go to the quay.

Acc.: — I could not know that. I became suspicious on

Saturday when we ate ice cream, because while we were sitting there he told me that he had a bomb and revolver. When we got up and began to pay, he said, "Do you want me to show them to you?" And when we left the sweetshop there were no people outside. So, why didn't he show them then if he had them?

Pr.: — Do you approve of the assassination?

Acc.: — No.

Pr.: — For what reasons?

Acc.: — How can I approve of it when I see what the consequences are?

Pr.: — But as for the act itself?

Acc.: — How can I approve of it. I never approve of such things. I could feel as sorry only for my parents and brother.

Hoffman: — Did you tell your father at home?

Acc.: — No.

Hoffm.: — Why not?

Acc.: — When the assassination took place my father was beside me. I turned pale and at once I asked, "Is it Cubrilovic?" That is the best proof that I did not believe. If I had known about the assassination I would not have been astounded. My father asked me, "What is it?" and I replied, "Was it Cubrilovic who did the assassination?" When they said Cubrilovic, I was frightened. Only later, when I heard that Cabrinovic did it, I calmed down. Even then I didn't know about Cubrilovic because I hadn't seen him on Sunday.

Pr.: — Are there any further questions? (There are none.) I recess the hearing until tomorrow at 7:45.

The Fourth Day

CONTINUATION OF THE MAIN HEARING
15 OCTOBER 1914
Beginning at 8:15

PARTIAL HEARING OF MISKO JOVANOVIC
AND DRAGAN KALEMBER

Pr.: — Misko Jovanovic, do you know Ciganovic?

Acc.: — No.

Pr.: — Why did he refer the students to you?

Acc.: — I have no idea.

Pr.: — Your father and his brothers are very wealthy?

Acc.: — Yes.

Pr.: — How did you acquire this fortune?

Acc.: — In business.

Pr.: — Not by selling army supplies?

Acc.: — Not as far as I know, he didn't.

Pr..: — Were you a supplier to the army?

Acc.: — No.

Pros.: — Do you know Heinrich Schultz?

Acc.: — No.

Naum.: — Kalember, you were on an excursion to Tuzla. Did anyone there talk about the assassination?

Acc.: — No.

Naum.: — Was Vaso Cubrilovic there?

Acc.: — Yes.

Naum.: — Did he tell you about his communications and connections in Serbia?

Acc.: — Yes. He said that, with the help of some people, he could pass anyone he wanted into Serbia at any time.

Naum.: — Vaso Cubrilovic, what kind of connections were those?

Acc.: — I never said that I could get just anyone into Serbia.

Pr.: — Kalember, did he really say it as you told it, or did you add something?

Kalember: — I didn't add anything.

Vaso Cubrilovic: — I didn't say I could get people through.

THE HEARING OF MICO MICIC
15 OCTOBER 1914

Pr.: — Call the defendant Mico Micic. Are you Mico Micic?

Acc.: — Yes.

Pr.: — What is your occupation?

Acc.: — I am a baker.

Pr.: — You don't work at your trade any more?[132]

Acc.: — No. I live from my land. I have 30 *donums*, my sister's and mother's. I work as a farm laborer.

Pr.: — Where do you live?

Acc.: — In Janja.

Pr.: — How far is it from Janja to the Drina?

Acc.: — Two kilometers.

Pr.: — And to Isakovic's Island?

Acc.: — Isakovic's Island is right there.

Pr.: — Did you go to that island?

Acc.: — Yes.

Pr.: — Since when?

Acc.: — About one year.

Pr.: — When did you hand over your bakery?

Acc.: — One year ago.

Pr.: — Then from the time you handed over your bakery to someone else, you went to Isakovic's Island? For how much did you give up the bakery to someone else?

Acc.: — For nine forints monthly.

Pr.: — What were you doing on the island?

Acc.: — I went there for brandy. The sergeant let me. I also went to Ljesnica to dance and have fun with the girls.

Pr.: — You are not married?

Acc.: — No.

Pr.: — Is it customary for strange revenue officers and guards to let people pass?

Acc.: — Many people pass, especially Moslems. On

Isakovic's Island I drank with Milan Cule. On Isakovic's Island brandy is sold for three *seksers*[133] per measure.

Pr.: — Our revenue officers and guards must have been there.

Acc.: — Nevertheless one could pass.

Pr.: — How was that possible? Wasn't there anybody?

Acc.: — Nobody. Most smuggling goes on there.

Pr.: — Nevertheless it's dangerous to go, because if a gendarme or revenue officer caught you without a pass, you would be punished.

Acc.: — Up to 14 days in jail.

Pr.: — It's hard to believe that for the sake of a few glasses of brandy you would take the risk of 14 days in jail.

Acc.: — I used to go there to Ljesnica and have a good time. There they dance the *kolo*.[134]

Pr.: — Don't they dance it on our side?

Acc.: — They dance it. But that's just my trouble.

Pr.: — What kind of trouble?

Pros.: — There are gendarmes in Janja, and before you cross from Janja to the island, there is the Drina.

Acc.: — There is, but from this side the water isn't up to your knees. There are dry spots, so it's easy to jump over.

Premuzic: — The Drina changes its course there, so one can pass over to the island in no time. It's true that the water isn't even up to one's knees.

Pr.: — Since one can go so easily from our side into Serbian lands, I should think that they watch there more carefully. Have you ever been in Serbia?

Acc.: — In Ljesnica.

Pr.: — Did you stay there for a longer time several years ago?

Acc.: — I did, in 1907, and then I was sentenced to 14 days in jail.

Pr.: — Still you went there just for brandy. Tell me, did you see soldiers in Janja last year when war was brewing, at the time of the Serbo-Bulgarian war?

Acc.: — I don't know anything about that.

Pr.: — Were there armed forces from the other side?

Acc.: — I don't know.

Pr.: — Did you get orders to do some kind of scouting?

Acc.: — Nobody gave me any orders.

Pr.: — Perhaps somebody else? A soldier or an officer?

Acc.: — I only know Milan Cule and two of his friends.

Pr.: — In Ljesnica you didn't correspond with some soldier?

Acc.: — No.

Pr.: — How did you forward your letters to the girls?

Acc.: — By mail.

Pr.: — What are their names?

Acc.: — Milica Radovanovic and Ljeposava Cvitanovic.

Pr.: — Did you correspond with both of them at the same time?

Acc.: — Yes.

Pr.: — What happened after St. George's Day on the island?

Acc.: — I went to Isakovic's Island and I found two young men there.

Pr.: — For what purpose did you go?

Acc.: — For brandy.

Pr.: — At what time of day?

Acc.: — Before noon. There I found Sergeant-Major Grbic and two young men.

Pr.: — How old is Grbic?

Acc.: — I don't know.

Pr.: — Has he been there all the time since you began going over to the island?

Acc.: — Yes.

Pr.: — Where is his watchtower?

Acc.: — Right across from Isakovic's Island, on the other side of the Drina.

Pr.: — What were the young men doing?

Acc.: — They were sitting. The sergeant told them to sit.

Pr.: — Was the owner of the cottage, Milan Cule, present?

Acc.: — He was in the kitchen. I went into the kitchen and I said to Milan, "Pour the brandy," because Milan was hiding the sale of the brandy from the sergeant. I tood a swig at the brandy behind my hand, and went into the room, and Grbic said to me, "Here are two students. They are from Sarajevo. They want to go to Tuzla and then to Sarajevo."

Pr.: — Did he tell you their intentions?

Acc.: — Yes, he said they were going somewhat secretly. They didn't have passports.

Pr.: — Did he say anything else about Sarajevo?

Acc.: — I don't remember. I don't think he said anything else.

Pr.: — You said earlier in your statement that they went secretly, and that they wanted to do something in Sarajevo.

Acc.: — He didn't say "to do something."

At that **The President** shows the accused his statement at the inquiry, and his signature, and asked him whether that is his signature, which the accused confirms.

Pr.: — Was this read to you?

Acc.: — Yes. The sergeant told me: "in order to do something."

Pr.: — Did he tell you not to say anything?

Acc.: — He said that later. He asked me, "Do you know Jakov Milovic? Go and tell him to come here. But don't talk about that or you could lose your head."

Pr.: — How was it possible that Sergeant-Major Grbic from another country could order you to bring your friend, threaten you with your head, and you obey right away? Did he have the power to kill you from across the border if you had stayed home in Janja and not come?

Acc.: — No.

Pr.: — Then why did you obey?

Acc.: — The devil made me do it. That's my bad luck.

Pr.: — You immediately obeyed and went to Janja?

Acc.: — I went and found Jakov in the marketplace.

Pr.: — What was he doing?

Acc.: — I found him on the street.

Pr.: — He's a farm laborer. Surely he doesn't just stroll around the streets?

Acc.: — He comes to the marketplace a lot.

Pr.: — Was it Sunday?

Acc.: — I don't know what day it was. I said to him, "Sergeant-Major Grbic wants you to come to Isakovic's Island."

Pr.: — Had you seen Jakov Milovic before together with Grbic?

Acc.: — I hadn't seen them on Isakovic's Island.

Pr.: — How come he immediately listened to Grbic?

Acc.: — I don't know. I said to him, "Go," and he said right away, "I'll go." Then I returned to Isakovic's Island.

Pr.: — Before you left for Janja, did you see what the students had with them?

Acc.: — I didn't see because it all happened quickly.

Pr.: — When you went into the house, didn't you see anything on the table?

Acc.: — No.

At that **The President** shows the accused his statement that on the table in the house of the cottage Milan Cule had seen a box and revolvers, and that they were firing with them through the windows.

Acc.: — I saw them later. Here are the students. Let them tell it.

Pr.: — Earlier you were in error before the investigating judge?

Acc.: — I don't know what I said.

Pr.: — Earlier you said that before you went for Jakov you had already seen them.

Acc.: — I said that I had seen the box on the table and the revolver. I said that later. When I talked to the secretary I was lost. When I came to Isakovic's Island, I said to the sergeant, "Jakov will come."

Pr.: — Why did you return?

Acc.: — The sergeant told me to come back and tell him whether Jakov would come or not.

Pr.: — How long does it take to go from the island to Janja and back?

Acc.: — Two kilometers one way.

Pr.: — Even though he threatened your life, you still listened to him?

Acc.: — I went back because there was some brandy left.

Pr.: — But isn't there any brandy in Janja? You are rich. You can buy it and you didn't have to return when you saw that there was dirty business afoot. Why did you go back?

Acc.: — I don't know myself. Then the sergeant-major said to me, "Did you call him?" "Yes." "Sit down." Then I saw that at the table a student was unwrapping something from a rag and put it on the floor. The sergeant-major said, "It will blow up and then we will all be gone."

Pr.: — Was it this kind of a box? (He shows him the bomb.)

Acc.: — Yes.

Pr.: — Didn't you know what this was?

Acc.: — No.

Pr.: — Did you hear that they had bombs?

Acc.: — I didn't until the sergeant told me.

Pr.: — You knew that there were bombs?

Acc.: — The sergeant said, "These are bombs." Then he put them under the same rag. Then we sat and talked.

Pr.: — And the revolver?

Acc.: — One student fired the revolver through the window. After that Jakov came. We went to Zivan's house.[135] I wanted to go home, but the sergeant said to me, "Don't go now, it will be dark soon, and you can go with them."

Pr.: — When did Jakov Milovic arrive?

Acc.: — At three o'clock.

Pr.: — Before he arrived did you fire the revolver and walk on the island?

Acc.: — No.

Pr.: —Did you know that they shot the revolver on the island?

Acc.: — I didn't see them.

Pr.: — At what time did all of you leave Isakovic's Island?

Acc.: — Before dark.

Pr.: — How did you pass to this country without being seen by the revenue officers and the guards?

Acc.: — There wasn't anybody around.

Pr.: — How did you decide who went first?

Acc.: — Jakov first, I after him, and the students behind us.

Pr.: — How far apart were you?

Acc.: — About twenty paces.

Pr.: — Did you agree that you would give a signal if you saw a suspicious person?

Acc.: — We took it easy.

Pr.: — Where did you cross the water?

Acc.: — We crossed two branches of the stream. I don't know what they are called.

Pr.: — Where did you separate?

Acc.: — They went on through the alleys and I took the main road home.

Pr.: — Did you ever return to the island for the same purpose?

Acc.: — Yes, once.

Pr.: — How many days afterward?

Acc.: — I don't know how many days. The sergeant was just ready to leave. The sergeant said, "Did they leave?", and I said, "They did." He asked, "Why didn't you come back a little sooner so we could sit a little?" I answered, "I had to go to Ljesnica. I had some business there."

Pr.: — Did you learn afterwards that the Heir had been killed?

Acc.: — Yes.

Pr.: — When did you learn about it?

Acc.: — The same day he was killed. St. Vitus' Day.

Pr.: — Did you hear who killed him?

Acc.: — I heard that they were students.

Pr.: — Did you think that those were the students who did it?

Acc.: — No.

Pr.: — How come that at the beginning you didn't want to admit anything, neither that you knew Grbic, nor that you saw the students?

Acc.: — I remembered that those students did it when the secretary showed them to me.

Pr.: — Who told you to admit it?

Acc.: — No one. I admitted it myself.

Pr.: — Didn't you meet in the jail with the others and they told you to admit it?

Acc.: — Jakov and I were jailed and Bjeljina.

Pr.: — What did Jakov tell you?

Acc.: — "It would be better to admit that they did it." I said, "They didn't do it."

Pr.: — Did you write letters to Grbic at the island, or did you observe how strong the military forces in Tuzla were and notify him?

Acc.: — I never notified anybody of anything.

Pr.: — Do you know the teacher Jakovljevic in Mali Zvornik?

Acc.: — No. I have never been further than Ljesnica.

Pr.: — At the teacher Jakovljevic's in Mali Zvornik this letter was found (He reads the letter: "Call the baker Micic from Janja and tell him to come personally to Pavlovic the day after tomorrow."), which positively proves that you were connected with the teacher.

Acc.: — I was not, nor did I ever see the teacher.

Pr.: — Is there another baker Micic in Janja?

Acc.: — No. I knew the sergeant-major and two cottagers.

Pr.: — It wasn't your job to ask, but to get in touch with Jovo Pavlovic. He was supposed to tell you everything, and you were to inform Grbic.

Acc.: — Maybe he told the teacher some lies.

Pr.: — This was found among the teacher's letters in Mali Zvornik, and no one knew that we would occupy that place.

Acc.: — The sergeant-major cost me money, because I lent him some.

Pr.: — Didn't you have income from these things?

Acc.: — I don't know.

Pr.: — How could you live on nine forints monthly?

Acc.: — I spent my inheritance. Within two or three years I sold half of the land and I spent my property. Last year I sold a piece of land.

Pr.: — And last year when you began to visit the island?

Acc.: — I would spend and draw money from the bank. I mortgaged my land and spent the money.

Pr.: — Do you know the *Narodna odbrana*?

Acc.: — I have heard of it.

Pr.: — Is that an association, a business enterprise, or a house?

Acc.: — I don't know. I heard where people are talking about the *Narodna odbrana*. I read about it in the indictment.

Pr.: — If you read about it, then you know what purpose it serves.

Acc.: — I have forgotten.

Pr.: — Do you know the kingdom of Serbia?

Acc.: — Yes.

Pr.: — Do you know which circles there want Bosnia and Hercegovina to be separated from Austria and annexed to Serbia?

Acc.: — I read about it in the indictment.

Pr.: — Then you did not hear about it before?

Acc.: — I don't know whether I heard.

Pr.: — If there were an annexation, would there have to be a war between Serbia and Austria?

Acc.: — So I heard.

Pr.: — Why should there be a war?

Acc.: — I don't know why.

Pr.: — When was this war supposed to be?

Acc.: — 1908.

Pr.: — Did the annexation take place in 1908?

Acc.: — Yes.

Pr.: — What did that annexation signify?

Acc.: — War.

Pr.: — You are not as stupid as you would like to pretend.

Naum.: — Did you fire on the island when the students were there?

Acc.: — I did not.

Naum.: — You said earlier that you took the gun from the sergeant-major and fired?

Acc.: — Yes.

Naum.: — How come the sergeant gave his military weapon to a civilian stranger who came from across the border? He must have had great confidence in you.

Pr.: — Apparently they don't have to account for the cartridges.

Hoffm.: — Why did you give up the bakery?

Acc.: — Business was bad.

Hoffm.: — Didn't Grbic pay you to work for him?

Acc.: — Ljesnica cost me a lot of money, by God!

Hoffm.: — You knew that the students were carrying bombs and revolvers. Did they tell you where they were going?

Acc.: — Nobody said anything.

Hoffm.: — What did you talk about on the way?

Acc.: — Jakov and I went ahead and we were silent.

Hoffm.: — You saw the students were carrying bombs and

heard that there had been an assassination. How could you say that those students didn't do it?

Acc.: — I saw one bomb and one revolver.

Hoffm.: — Didn't you know before what the students planned?

Acc.: — No.

THE HEARING OF JAKOV MILOVIC
15 OCTOBER 1914

Jakov Milovic is brought before the court.

Pr.: — Are you Jakov Milovic?

Acc.: — Yes.

Pr.: — You are a farm laborer?

Acc.: — Yes.

Pr.: — Do you own property?

Acc.: — Yes.

Pr.: — Do you have land from the lord (aga)?[136]

Acc.: — No.

Pr.: — Do you support your children on your labor?

Acc.: — Yes.

Pr.: — Are you guilty?

Acc.: — The law and you know.

Pr.: — You must have your own feelings.

Acc.: — I am guilty, of course.

Pr.: — Of what are you guilty?

Acc.: — That I led them across the border.

Pr.: — How did it happen?

Acc.: — On that day it rained for half a day. I couldn't work. I went to Janja.

Pr.: — Where is your house?

Acc.: — In Obrijezje, in the district of Bijeljina.

Pr.: — How far is it from Obrijezje to Janja?

Acc.: — One hour and a half. When it is muddy, two and a half. It was raining at dawn and I went to Janja and found Micic.

Pr.: — Where did you find him?

Acc.: — In the marketplace after *icindija*.[137]

Pr.: — Did you know him before?

Acc.: — I did. "There are two young men," he said, "who want to pass over to Bosnia. Will you lead them?" "I can't do it now." It was *icindija* then. "Maybe later I can." When I walked around the corn field, I found two young men there.

Pr.: — Did he tell you that someone was calling you?

Acc.: — He didn't say so, but I went by myself.

Pr.: — Is it a usual thing that you help students?

Acc.: — No. Smuggling has cost me 1100 crowns.

Pr.: — And where did you get the money?

Acc.: — I earned it.

Pr.: — You have five children? Did he promise you something?

Acc.: — He didn't promise me anything.

Pr.: — Did you know Sergeant-Major Grbic?

Acc.: — Yes.

Pr.: — Did he come to the island?

Acc.: — Rarely. Once or twice. I came. The teamsters took me over to Milan's cottage because the ground was dry.

Pr.: — How could Grbic give orders for them to call you?

Acc.: — I don't know anything about Grbic. I don't know whether Grbic gave the order, rather Micic told me, "The cottager Milan calls you."

The President shows the accused his statement at the inquiry from which it is evident that Micic told him that Sergeant-Major Grbic summoned him.

Acc.: — Not he, but Milan Cule said that Grbic called me. Something else was written down.

Pr.: — And he didn't mention that there were students?

Acc.: — He said, "Milan is calling you. They have two students." He didn't say anything about Grbic.

Pr.: — Micic, did you tell him that the students were waiting on the island?

Acc. Micic: — I said that Sergeant Grbic was calling him.

Acc. Milovic: — He told me that Milan was calling me, that they had two students. I'm telling you, that's the truth.[138] Even if you cut me into pieces, I can't say anything different. Then after *icindija* I had no watch. I left. When I came to the island I found at Milan's: Grbic, those two and we two.

Pr.: — When did Grbic leave?

Acc.: — He said, "If you can, bring them over." He left. So I stayed, and as soon as it grew dark we crossed the island.

Pr.: — What did the students say?

Acc.: — "We are Bosnians. We have the right to live in Bosnia. We have fathers there. We have families. We have mothers." That deceived me. Otherwise I wouldn't have taken it on myself.

Pr.: — Did they tell you to take them to somebody?

Acc.: — "Take us halfway and find somebody to take us to Tuzla."

The President shows the accused the statement, from which it becomes evident that he had said that he would take them to Veljko Cubrilovic.

Acc.: — The students didn't say that. Maybe that was written. I was confused then.

Pr.: — Did you see that they had weapons?

Acc.: — I didn't see that they had two revolvers until we got to Priboj. In Priboj they bound them around themselves with ropes.

Pr.: — And did you see the revolvers on the island?

Acc.: — While I was there they did not fire.

Pr.: — In what order did you walk?

Acc.: — We all went together in a group through the corn fields.

Pr.: — Was the road wide?

Acc.: — The corn was low. We went all the way to the road.

Pr.: — Isn't it dangerous because of the gendarmes?

Acc.: — It is a field. There are no woods.

Pr.: — How could one pass over?

Acc.: — Everybody crosses just like that.

Pr.: — Is it forbidden to cross the border?

Acc.: — God, it is strictly forbidden. Our people cross, carrying firewood. Half of Janja is heated with wood from that island. Then we came by way of Cengic to Trnovo. One could see as if it were day. Then suddenly it began to rain. We couldn't go on and stayed overnight in a stall. When we went on, we came to Obren's village and there they asked for oatcakes.

Pr.: — Was Obren at home?

Acc.: — No. Half an hour later Obren came. I said, "I don't know how to go any further. Just go to Veljko. It's halfway to Tuzla."

Pr.: — How did you remember that you should take them to Veljko?

Acc.: — I know the man there. He would rent a cart.

Pr.: — Did you know Veljko before?

Acc.: — For about a year. I am in the *sokol* association, and I got acquainted with him there.

Pr.: — What did Veljko tell you then?

Acc.: — He didn't say anything.

Pr.: — Did you do Veljko any kind of favors?

Acc.: — Never in my life.

Pr.: — Did you carry letters?

Acc.: — Never.

Pr.: — It seems to me that your memory isn't worth much.

Acc.: — Now I tell it as if my life depends on it! Do what you like!

Pr.: — Veljko never sent you with a letter?

Acc.: — I came last year and visited him. Just at the Catholic Christmas.

At that **The President** shows the defendant the statement in which he says that last year Veljko Cubrilovic sent a letter every time, "and I went to Isakovic's Island."

Acc.: — Maybe I was confused. Last year I got two letters from my brother-in-law.

Pr.: — Why did you want to flee?

Acc.: — If I had had the occasion, I could have run away a thousand times, not just one time. Serbia is right next door.

Pr.: — What happened at Obren Milosevic's?

Acc.: — We didn't find Obren at home. They sent a child for him and he came. Then they asked for bags and he gave them a bag. I don't know where he got it.

Pr.: — What did they put in the bag?

Acc.: — The revolver and the boxes.

Pr.: — Did he show the bombs?

Acc.: — I don't know what they look like.

Pr. (Shows him a bomb.): — Did he say what this is?

Acc.: — They say it's a bomb, but I never saw one before.

Pr.: — Had you heard that there are bombs in Serbia?

Acc.: — I heard that, but I never saw them.[139]

Pr.: — What did they do?

Acc.: — They wrapped the things in the rag and put them into the sack.

Pr.: — Were all the bombs together, or mixed?

Acc.: — Mixed.   I don't know how they put them in. They packed them.

Pr.: — Did you see how they packed them?

Acc.: — Yes, I saw.

Pr.: — Who took the bags?

Acc.: — They carried them on further.

Pr.: — Obren Milosevic says that you carried them.

Acc.: — Neither Obren nor I carried them; rather they did.

Pr.: — How many of those boxes were there?

Acc.: — My God, I don't know: four, three, five. As to the bombs, I don't know for sure how many there were.

Pr.: — And the revolvers?

Acc.: — Four.

Pr.: — How many hours is it from Obren's cottage to Veljko's house?

Acc.: — Almost four. Then we went together: Obren, I behind Obren, and then they behind us until we came to Priboj. Then we accidently met Veljko and the priest. Veljko asked, "Where are you going?" and we said, "Two students for Tuzla." "What's going on?" "I don't know." Then Veljko gave me five crowns. We returned, and they stayed.

Pr.: — Did they say why they carried weapons?

Acc.: — No.

Pr.: — Did they tell you not to say anything about it?

Acc.: — They didn't say anything to me.

Pr.: — They didn't threaten you?

Acc.: — No.

Pr.: — Did you ever go to Sabac?

Acc.: — I did. Five years ago when I was a smuggler.

Pr.: — Did you know anyone in Sabac . . .?

Acc.: — Not a single merchant.

Pr.: — I request that it be recorded that he answered

before I completed the question. Do you know the merchant where you buy bread, meat?

Acc.: — I am in Sabac for two or three hours. I come in the morning when the black marketing takes place.

Pr.: — Do you know any merchants to whom you sold?

Acc.: — We only bought livestock. I didn't know anybody, because I didn't work with any merchant.

Pr.: — You don't know a single merchant?

Acc.: — No.

Pr.: — Not even Bozo Milanovic?

Acc.: — Not even Bozo Milanovic. God forbid.

Pr.: — How come you know when you have to say, "God forbid!"?

Acc.: — I didn't know. I didn't know. How could I say something that I didn't? Did I lie? I said how it was. I told everything. I told everything.

Pr.: — Veljko Cubrilovic, do you know this man?

Cubrilovic: — Yes.

Pr.: — What did he say when he presented himself after the conversation with Bozo Milanovic?

Cubr.: — It was about as he said. He let me know that if we should need something from Serbia, that he would bring it over.

Pr.: — Did he introduce himself as Bozo Milanovic?

Acc.: — He didn't remember the name of Bozo Milanovic. I understood that the man about whom he spoke was Bozo Milanovic.

Pr.: — Is it true that he said it?

Milovic: — Please, I did not. I would say if I had, but I didn't.

Cubrilovic: — I don't remember that he mentioned the name of Bozo Milanovic.

Pr.: — Princip, did you carry those bags?

Princip: — No, those two carried them. I said it is as it was. That is irrelevant for the case.

Milovic: — They dropped one revolver in the crib and looked for it.

Princip: — Tell the truth, that it lay in the stall.

Pr.: — Grabez, did you carry the weapons?

Grabez: — Princip and I carried them to Trnovo. We didn't carry them away from Obren Milosevic's. The peasants carried them. Just Jakov.

Pr.: — Grabez, did you threaten him?

Grabez: — No.

Princip: — I did. I said that they had better not tell anyone, because otherwise we would kill them.

Milovic: — I don't recall. I have forgotten. He certainly said it.

Pr.: — Before he left, did Veljko Cubrilovic say, "Let one go up by the high road and the other down by the low road"?

Acc. (Milovic): — No. I jumped onto the other bank, then onto the bridge, and from there I left.

Naum.: — You said that you were a smuggler. It seems that you know the vicinity well.

Acc.: — Bijeljina, Janja, Zvornik, beyond that I didn't know the roads.

Naum.: — Did Obren ask what the students wanted?

Acc.: — He didn't ask anything. I said, "The students want to travel." Then I said, "I can't take them to Tuzla."

Naum.: — Did you agree with the students how much they were to pay?

Acc.: — They told them to pay and they paid five crowns.

Naum.: — You had never seen those people and you believed them at once and went with them the whole night?

Acc.: — We didn't go the whole night. One hour only. Then it began to rain and we took shelter until dawn.

Naum.: — How much did you lose until you returned home?

Acc.: — The next day I couldn't work.

Naum.: — Did Obren agree at once?

Acc.: — I called him. If he hadn't I couldn't have told him. One couldn't find work. Things were different.

Naum.: — Did you have money with you?

Acc.: — Not a single penny.

Naum.: — Did you show money to Obren?

Acc.: — I did not.

Naum.: — Did you pay Obren?

Acc.: — No.

Naum.: — When Obren Milosevic told you that he could not go, did you give him money to hire someone?

Acc.: — No. I said something like, "Look, a heavy rain is falling in the early morning. If the weather were good, Obren, I would pay a laborer to work. But because you can't work anyway . . ."

Naum.: — Why would you pay a laborer for strangers?

Acc.: — The people would pay us.

Naum.: — Obren explicitly stated that he gave you a forint so that you could hire a laborer.

Acc.: — He said that he could not go, but the weather was not good, so he could not work.

Pr.: — You did not agree as to how much they would pay you?

Acc.: — No.

Pr.: — Did you know that they had money? They could have deceived you.

Acc.: — It would be bad if they had deceived us, but they paid five crowns.

Hoffm.: — Did you take the saddlebags from the horse and give them to Veljko Cubrilovic?

Acc.: — We handed them over and put them to one side.

Hoffm.: — Did you talk with Veljko?

Acc.: — Yes.

Hoffm.: — Did you see what they put inside?

Acc.: — No, we didn't.

Naum.: — When you met Veljko, who spoke first?

Acc.: — The priest went first, and Veljko after him. Both were riding horses. The priest had a white horse, and Veljko a bay. I took off my cap and greeted them, "There are two students for Tuzla. They want to go to Sarajevo. They have families there." And Veljko turned back a little and we returned. There we said good-bye. They gave us five crowns and we left.

Pr.: — When you first saw Veljko, did he say to the priest, "I won't go on with you"?

Acc.: — The water was deep. The priest could hardly cross it, and Veljko said, "I won't do it. I can't wear out the horse."

Malek: — Grabez wants to say something.

Grabez: — The indictment says that we got things from

the *Narodna odbrana* and it appears that Ciganovic as a member of the *Narodna odbrana* gave them to us. From my personal acquaintance with Ciganovic, it is possible that he was a Freemason. It's possible that Major Tankosic was also. Thus why should a cultural association be blamed because one of its members gave bombs and revolvers for the assassination of Ferdinand?

Pr.: — You are the accused here, not the *Narodna odbrana*.

Acc.: — I am accused because of the *Narodna odbrana*.

Pr.: — Do you have facts to cite?

Acc.: — Yes. The *Narodna odbrana* is an association that has political tendencies. Yesterday there was a whole booklet in which it said that the *Narodna odbrana* for certain reasons cannot . . .

Pr.: — Those are your conclusions. Sit down. Later you will have the floor, and you can speak.

The accused Obren Milosevic is called.

THE HEARING OF OBREN MILOSEVIC
15 OCTOBER 1914

Pr.: — Are you Obren Milosevic?

Acc.: — Yes.

Pr.: — Are you guilty?

Acc.: — I am not, God willing.

Pr.: — Then how come you are sitting here?

Acc.: — I hired a Turk to do plowing for me. And he and his son plowed that day. Then they went home. I stayed with the oxen. It was midnight. It began to rain and I took shelter. Then I grazed the oxen until noon. After grazing them, I tied the oxen and went home and found Jakov Milovic.

Pr.: — Was he alone?

Acc.: — My wife was making coffee. I said, "Make the coffee and look after the oxen!" There were also two students. After we drank the coffee, I was again with the oxen. They told me to show them the road.

Pr.: — Who told you to show them the road?

Acc.: — I cannot say who.

Naum.: — Did the students?

Acc.: — One student. They said, "Show us the road. You have to show us."

Pr.: — Did you know them before?

Acc.: — Never.

Pr.: — How could they threaten you?

Acc.: — They just did. They demanded that I have to show them the road.

Pr.: — Did you see whether they had weapons?

Acc.: — Because I said, "I can't show you the road," they showed me the revolvers. Then Jakov winked at me to keep quiet and to take bacon and bread sprinkled with salt and go with them. "Do you have some rags?" "What do you want?"

Pr.: — Who said that?

Acc.: — They. "Do you have bags?" "No," I said. "And what's that?" I said, "Those are saddle-bags on the hook." They took out *djumle* . . .[140]

Pr.: — What are *djumle*?

Acc.: — What you use for weighing on the scale.

The President shows a bomb to the accused.

Acc.: — Yes, it looked like that. When they wrapped it up, they loaded us with it, and Jakov carried the revolvers.

Pr.: — Did you see the revolvers? (He shows them to the accused.) Were they like these?

Acc.: — They were.

Pr.: — Who carried these things?

Acc.: — I carried the *djumlets*.

Pr.: — Were they heavy?

Acc.: — Yes.

Pr.: — And Jakov?

Acc.: — The revolvers to Priboj.

Pr.: — Did they tell you where you had to take them?

Acc.: — They didn't say, "Show us the road to Tuzla." When we came to Priboj, the sun came out again. I thought about the oxen and wanted to go home. They asked me, "Do you know the teacher Veljko?" We reached the top of the hill and we said, "Do we have to go further?" Then we met the priest and the teacher. Jakov talked with them about something. I didn't hear what he talked about with the teacher.

Pr.: — Jakov, when you were together in the cottage, did the students demand that you take them to some person?

Milovic: — No.

Pr.: — They did not say it immediately?

Milovic: — I said that I would take them to Veljko.

Milosevic: — I don't know how he said it.

Pr.: — In the inquiry you stated: "The students told me to take them to Veljko," and he said it the same way.

Jakov Milovic: — Sir, they didn't.

Milosevic: — Yes, they said it. When I said that I couldn't go further. "Do you know anybody here?" they asked. "I don't know." "Do you know the teacher Veljko?" I said, "I know him."

Pr.: — Did the students say it?

Acc.: — Yes. "Let's go to the teacher." And so it was. Then we went up the hill. We didn't want to go further. They said, "Tell the teacher we are here, and you get yourselves on home." Then we crossed the water and met the teacher and priest. Jakov talked with that teacher.

Pr.: — What did he say?

Acc.: — I don't know. Then they returned and the teacher gentleman[141] met them.

Pr.: — How come you immediately obeyed those students who had weapons and revolvers?

Acc.: — Oh, if I only knew!

Pr.: — Did they threaten you?

Acc.: — They never threatened me. They only said, "You have to show the road."

Pr.: — What did they do when they said that?

Acc.: — They showed the revolvers.

Pr.: — What did they intend to say by that?

Acc.: — I don't know.

Pr.: — Was that a threat that you had to do it?

Acc.: — We had to show the road. The oxen were not mine. A man left them. I had to look after them.

Pr.: — Did they pay you?

Acc.: — Yes, one forint. And before that they gave three crowns.

Pr.: — And how much are the saddlebags worth?

Acc.: — One forint. They are not worth more.

Pr.: — Did you get them back?

Acc.: — No.

Pr.: — Who kept them?

Acc.: — They did and took them with them.

Pr.: — Did you agree before the departure?

Acc.: — Not at all. I didn't dare to ask.

Pr.: — Why didn't you dare?

Acc.: — Why, there were officials. If I had known they were students, things would have been different.

Pr.: — You said: "When at the door two students appeared."

Acc.: — Did I say, "There were two students."? I said, "Two young men appeared."

Pr.: — Where did they put the weapons when they took them from the bag?

Acc.: — On the bedspread.

Pr.: — How many pieces did you see?

Acc.: — Six.

Pr.: — Of what?

Acc.: — Revolvers.

Pr.: — And bombs?

Acc.: — I don't know how many there were.

Pr.: — You said: "I saw them on the mat in the room before the students," so you knew that they were students?

Acc.: — I didn't know. Later Jakov told me that they were students, but I didn't know that they were students.

Pr.: — When you arrived there in Priboj, in the village of Tobut, did the students wait openly in the road or did they hide?

Acc.: — In the field near the town.

Pr.: — Did you say anything to the teacher?

Acc.: — No, but when we met, he said to one of them, "You go down that way, and let him go up that way."

Pr.: — Why?

Acc.: — I don't know. I left earlier, and Jakov later. I went down by the low road, and he went up by the high road. Later on we met, said "Good-bye, good-bye" and we parted.

Pr.: — Jakov, did the teacher say, "Let one go down, and the other up."?

Milovic: — That's not true. Rather: "Good-bye," and we said good-bye to each other.

Pr.: — Veljko, did you say it?

Veljko Cubrilovic: — I did not say that. It is impossible. I will prove it.

Naum.: — Did you receive the five crowns all at once?

Acc.: — No, at first three.

Naum.: — From whom?

Acc.: — I don't know.

Naum.: — And when you parted?

Acc.: — Two to Jakov, and two to me.

Naum.: — And when at home you said that you had to work, that you had a hired hand, did anyone promise you money?

Acc.: — No sir. Nobody did.

Naum.: — At the inquiry you said: "In the house I found Jakov Milovic who was sitting before the fire, and at the door two students. Jakov says, 'Do you want to go to Priboj?' I said, 'I can't,' and Jakov, offering me a forint, said to find a hired hand for the oxen."

Acc.: — No, by God!

Naum.: — That's what you stated before the judge.

Acc.: — I don't know that I said it that way. Maybe I did say it.

Naum.: — You said in the inquiry that he offered you a forint.

Acc.: — He gave me one forint when we parted.

Naum.: — Did Jakov offer you a forint at home?

Acc.: — I don't remember.

Naum.: — Why did you make false statements?

Acc.: — I don't know. Maybe he said it to me.

Naum.: — What did they do with the bags?

Acc.: — They shoved them into the saddlebags.

Naum.: — Who shoved them?

Acc.: — They.

Naum.: — When the teacher told you, "You go up," did you see that the teacher took the bags from the students and put them in the saddlebags on his horse?

Acc.: — That's how it was.

Naum.: — Did you see that the teacher put the bags into the saddlebags, or did the students do it?

Acc.: — The students had them. Then the teacher took them and shoved them into the leather saddlebags.

Naum.: — Did you then talk with Jakov about what had happened?

Acc.: — I asked, "What's this all about, Jakov?"

Naum.: — And what did he say?

Acc.: — "Bombs." I asked, "What do they want?" "They want to go to Misko in Tuzla." That's what Jakov said.

Naum.: — Do you know Misko?

Acc.: — No.

Naum.: — Did you ask Jakov what the students were doing with bombs and revolvers?

Acc.: — I never thought of that.

Naum.: — The students hide bombs, revolvers, and bags at your place. They hide themselves in the field. You must have thought that there was something wrong.

Acc.: — What can I think when intelligent people do it?

Naum.: — Are those intelligent people who carry bombs?

Acc.: — Everyone who wears city clothes is an official.

Naum.: — Did you hear later that there was an assassination?

Acc.: — I heard about it when we were at the monastery. A gentlemen, an officer, came and said that our kind was killed.

Naum.: — And did you doubt it?

Acc.: — No, I didn't doubt it.

Naum.: — Did you learn later that Veljko Cubrilovic was arrested?

Acc.: — Yes.

Naum.: — Were you afraid?

Acc.: — Why should I be afraid?

Naum.: — And when were you arrested?

Acc.: — Later, sometime before Assumption.[142]   About 15 days later.

Naum.: — Didn't you ever think that you might be arrested?

Acc.: — I never thought of it.

Naum.: — You said later that you heard from one Marko that the gendarmes took Veljko Cubrilovic and Mitar Kerovic away and after that that you were afraid that you would be arrested and expected the gendarmes every moment.

Acc.: — I don't know that I said it.

Naum.: — And were you worried about yourself?

Acc.: — No.

Naum.: — Did you expect the gendarmes?

Acc.: — I never expected them.

Naum.: — Didn't you ever think that what you had done wasn't good: to conduct students secretly?

Acc.: — When Marko told me that, it was in Zvornik. Thus Kerovic and the teacher gentleman were arrested because of those who had crossed over the border. About Jakov I wasn't sure. I thought for sure they would arrest me too.

Pr.: — Did you know that those students did it?

Acc.: — Marko told me so later. That those students from Serbia did it.

Naum.: — How did he know?

Acc.: — He is from their village.

Naum.: — From whose village?

Acc.: — Where the teacher gentleman is from. Thus he heard it.

Naum.: — Did you know Jakov before?

Acc.: — I knew him for about one year.

Naum.: — Did he pass your house several times?

Acc.: — I don't know. I didn't see him.

Naum.: — Do you know whether he went to Priboj before?

Acc.: — I don't know.

Naum.: — When you met the teacher who spoke first: you or he?

Acc.: — I don't know. I only saw the teacher gentleman twice. When we met, we saw that the priest came first, then the teacher after him. So we met and Jakov greeted them.

Naum.: — Whom did he greet?

Acc.: — The teacher. We said, "Keep God," and Jakov greeted them.

Naum.: — What did Jakov say?

Acc.: — I didn't hear, by God!

Naum.: — Didn't he speak about the students?

Acc.: — I didn't hear anything that he said.

Naum.: — Earlier you stated differently: "As soon as the teacher noticed us, he informed the priest."

Acc.: — I believe that I said it.

Naum.: — When you went back, where were the students?

Acc.: — The teacher gentleman was on his horse, and I followed him.

Naum.: — Did he talk then too?

Acc.: — I didn't see or hear anything.

Naum.: — Earlier you said you did.

Acc.: — They spoke when they met, and the teacher gentleman said, "One can't go now."

Naum.: — When he met with the students, did he speak with them, and then discuss you, or did he dismiss you first, and only then talk with them?

Acc.: — They took the bombs and shoved them onto the horse and said, "Good-bye, good-bye!"

Naum.: — Didn't the teacher talk with the students before he shoved the bags into the saddlebags?

Acc.: — They said good-bye and left.

Naum.: — In the inquiry you stated very exactly: "After that the teacher did not say a single word to the students, rather he said to me, 'You go down that way, and Jakov, - you go up that way.' " He dismissed you before he talked with the students.

Acc.: — They had hardly met when he said that.

Naum.: — He said it immediately, before he talked with the students?

Acc.: — Yes.

Pr.: — Jakov, he said that you carried the bags?

Acc. Jakov Milovic: — They carried the revolvers.

Milosevic: — I carried the bombs, and Jakov the revolvers.

Naum.: — Veljko Cubrilovic, this one says that when you met with the students you did not say anything?

Veljko Cubrilovic: — His statement is incorrect.

Pr.: — Did you leave together?

Milosevic: — Yes.

Pr.: — Did you say: "You go up, and you go down."?

Veljko Cubrilovic: — Absolutely impossible.

Malek: — Since when did you know the teacher Cubrilovic?

Obren Milosevic: — Last year I came from Tuzla. My horse ran away and I went after him and came to a village. There I sat down for a drink, met the teacher and got acquainted with him.

Malek: — Weren't you in the *sokol* celebration?

Acc.: — No.

Malek: — Have you ever been in Serbia?

Acc.: — No.

Malek: — On Isakovic's Island?

Acc.: — No.

Malek: — Did you know that others go there?

Acc.: — No.

Malek: — Have you ever heard that there are people who observe how many soldiers there are, how many cannons, and so on?

Acc.: — Never.

Malek: — Didn't you carry letters from the teacher Veljko or other persons into Serbia or from Serbia?

Acc.: — No.

Malek: — Did you know that some people in Serbia want to take Bosnia and Hercegovina away from Austria?

Acc.: — No.

Naum.: — Are you a member of the *sokol*?

Acc.: — I don't know what that is.

Naum.: — Do you know the association *Pobratimstvo* (Brotherhood)?

Acc.: — No.

Naum.: — Do you drink?

Acc.: — Yes.

Premuzic: — Have you heard of Misko Jovanovic?

Acc.: — Not until then. I thought he was a Hungarian.

Malek: — Were you a soldier?

Acc.: — Yes, for two years.

Malek: — If someone had said to you that those students were going to Sarajevo to kill the Heir, what would you have done as a soldier?

Acc.: — I don't know what I would have done.

Mitar Kerovic is called.

DATE DUE